# Dorothy Wordsworth
## *The Grasmere Journals*

**Pamela Woof** is Lecturer in Literature at the Centre for
Continuing Education, University of Newcastle upon Tyne.

# Dorothy Wordsworth

# *The Grasmere Journals*

Edited by
PAMELA WOOF

Oxford   New York
OXFORD UNIVERSITY PRESS
1993

*Oxford University Press, Walton Street, Oxford* OX2 6DP

*Oxford New York Toronto*
*Delhi Bombay Calcutta Madras Karachi*
*Kuala Lumpur Singapore Hong Kong Tokyo*
*Nairobi Dar es Salaam Cape Town*
*Melbourne Auckland Madrid*

*and associated companies in*
*Berlin Ibadan*

*Oxford is a trade mark of Oxford University Press*

© *Pamela Woof 1991*

*First published 1991*
*First issued as an Oxford University Press paperback 1993*

*All rights reserved. No part of this publication may be reproduced,*
*stored in a retrieval system, or transmitted, in any form or by any means,*
*without the prior permission in writing of Oxford University Press.*
*Within the UK, exceptions are allowed in respect of any fair dealing for the*
*purpose of research or private study, or criticism or review, as permitted*
*under the Copyright, Designs and Patents Act, 1988, or in the case of*
*reprographic reproduction in accordance with the terms of the licences*
*issued by the Copyright Licensing Agency. Enquiries concerning*
*reproduction outside these terms and in other countries should be*
*sent to the Rights Department, Oxford University Press,*
*at the address above*

*This book is sold subject to the condition that it shall not, by way*
*of trade or otherwise, be lent, re-sold, hired out or otherwise circulated*
*without the publisher's prior consent in any form of binding or cover*
*other than that in which it is published and without a similar condition*
*including this condition being imposed on the subsequent purchaser*

*British Library Cataloguing in Publication Data*

*Data available*

*Library of Congress Cataloging in Publication Data*
*Wordsworth, Dorothy, 1771-1855.*
*The Grasmere journals / Dorothy Wordsworth; edited by Pamela Woof.*
*Includes bibliographical references and index.*
*1. Wordsworth, Dorothy, 1771-1855—Diaries.   2. Authors,*
*English—19th century—Diaries.   3. Lake District (England)—Social*
*life and customs.   I. Woof, Pamela.   II. Title.*
*PR5849.A8   1991*
*828'.703—dc20 [B]   90-40539*
*ISBN 0-19-283130-5*

3 5 7 9 10 8 6 4 2

*Printed in Great Britain by*
*Biddles Ltd*
*Guildford and King's Lynn*

# ACKNOWLEDGEMENTS

People have been very kind when I have asked them specific questions, and I would like to thank particularly: Susan Dench of the Cumbria Record Office, Carlisle, Jim Grisenthwaite of the Kendal Office, Naomi Evetts of the Liverpool Office, Malcolm Thomas of the Library of Friends House, Mrs Needham, the Old Manor House, Helmsley, John Murdoch of the Victoria and Albert Museum, and Peter West of Ponteland, Northumberland. Jeff Cowton at the Wordsworth Library, Grasmere, has been entirely helpful in my frequent and awkward need to have the manuscripts of the Journals out of the Museum where they are exhibited, and in the Library. To George Kirkby, Head Guide of Dove Cottage, I am grateful for those conversations that move about the house and garden with such love and knowledge of the places that I have invariably come away richer, and closer to the Wordsworths in their time there.

I am grateful to my fellow Trustees of the Wordsworth Trust for allowing me access to the manuscripts and for permission to publish.

My debt to Sally Woodhead at Grasmere is immense: she has coped promptly, often, and accurately with my handwriting, voice, and a word processor.

I have been encouraged by Stephen Gill and by Jonathan Wordsworth. Indeed the whole project began with Jonathan Wordsworth's suggestion that I prepare a commentary on the Grasmere Journals; this grew into an edition, and he has encouraged me in the larger project. Kim Scott-Walwyn and Frances Whistler of the Oxford University Press have been helpful in suggestions, patient with problems, and enthusiastic for Dorothy Wordsworth.

To Robert Woof I am of course most indebted. Marriage to a scholar of such wide and deep learning in so many aspects of the Romantic period has, I hope, not failed to confer on me something of his scholarship. He has responded to all my questions, looked at the manuscripts with me when I have not agreed with the readings of previous editors, suggested directions to me, and prevented me from many a fall into error.

P.S.W.

*University of Newcastle upon Tyne*

# CONTENTS

# Introduction

## I

There is simply nothing like it anywhere else. This Journal calls out to us directly across almost two hundred years, and its writer and her world come alive. It sometimes moves in little rushes when days can be noted with a staccato speed; it sometimes slows down to linger on a single figure: a beggar woman, a leech-gatherer, a child catching hailstones at a cottage door, a bow-bent postman with his little wooden box at his back, an old seaman with a beard like grey plush; it sometimes slows to linger on a whole scene: a funeral, or children with their mother by a fire, or a lakeshore on a windy day with daffodils, or a man with carts going up a hill and a little girl putting stones behind the wheels. It sometimes almost stops as the ear catches a ticking watch, a page being turned over, and the breathing of the silent reader by the fire; and then it starts off again at a great pace with the planting and mending and baking and washing and reading and writing and walking and talking, all the weather and the work crammed into a little space of words. Dorothy Wordsworth had her times for noticing, remembering, and writing, and her times for doing. There are no rules and structures for diary writers, as there are not for living: we take the fast and slow of it as it comes.

And Dorothy lived in a more spacious freedom than most of us. There were few external constraints on her life during those three years of the Grasmere Journal. She had no job outside the house, and no strict routine; if she was tired she could stay in bed or get 'a Drench of sleep' in the day; she and Wordsworth could wait to walk until it was fine, or not walk at all, or be out of doors all day. The Journal conveys directly the unpremeditated rhythms; they seem comfortable with Dorothy's nature;

they reflect her wholehearted acceptance of the experience of living.

The experience Grasmere gave her was that of living with a favourite elder brother in her own home, her first real home since she was 6. On the death of her mother there began for Dorothy a long separation from her brothers. Certainly she was happy enough in Halifax, looked after by her mother's cousin, Elizabeth Threlkeld, and with her bosom friend Jane Pollard across the way; she was less happy in Penrith at her grandmother's house between the ages of 15 and almost 17, for her grandmother was often 'in a very bad humour' and Dorothy would 'sit for whole hours without saying anything excepting that I have an old shirt to mend, then, my Grandmr and I have to set our heads together and contrive the most notable way of doing it'; she was happier again at Forncett Rectory, Norfolk, where her mother's brother, her uncle William Cookson, took her, on his own marriage in October 1788, from the narrow life at Penrith to his new living near Norwich. Here Dorothy, at least until the several children came, lived a proper young lady's life—prayers at nine (in winter), then reading, writing, and, 'I am to improve myself in French till twelve o'clock, when we are to walk or visit our sick and poor neighbours till three'. Dorothy was with her uncle and his young family until the winter of 1793/4. After that she stayed in various places: in Halifax with Elizabeth Threlkeld, now Mrs Rawson; in Newcastle with other cousins of her mother, the Miss Griffiths; at Sockburn with the Hutchinson family, friends from Penrith days; at Rampside, Furness, for a few weeks probably, with cousins on her father's side; at Armathwaite to visit the Spedding family; at Newbiggin to stay with her other maternal uncle, Christopher; but best of all at Windy Brow, Keswick, a house belonging to William Calvert, to live for a few weeks in spring 1794 with her brother William. This was managed again, at Racedown, Dorset, in a house lent to Wordsworth by the Pinney brothers from late September 1795. From here, in July 1797, Dorothy and Wordsworth went to Alfoxden to be nearer Coleridge. From there all three went to Germany, Wordsworth and Dorothy living in lodgings in Goslar, and Coleridge for the most part in the University city of Göttingen. On their return, from May 1799, Dorothy stayed with the Hutchinsons at Sockburn until, on 20 December, when she was almost 29, she and Wordsworth moved into the 'small house at Grasmere empty' and to rent.

Until she was 23 she saw little of her own brothers after early childhood: there were the boys' holidays from Hawkshead school during her months at Penrith, and later Wordsworth visited at Forncett, and was at Newcastle for some of Dorothy's time there. But her sense of deprivation was strong; the family home in Cockermouth was lost to her long before it was lost to her brothers: 'for six years', she wrote in December 1805 to Lady Beaumont, '(the interval between my Mother's Death and his) I was never once at home, never was for a single moment under my Father's Roof after her Death, which I cannot think of without regret for many causes, and particularly, that I have been thereby put out of the way of many recollections in common with my Brothers'. Dorothy seems not to have returned to Cockermouth even for her father's funeral, which took place when she was just twelve. Any one of us with this background would have found the coming to Grasmere an intense delight. This was not a lent house or a furnished house. It was to be the creation of her own family, of herself and her brothers William and John, to furnish as they wished, to make the garden how they wanted it. Dorothy writes passionately of the place and seems to live every day in the spirit of Wordsworth's petition,

> Embrace me then, ye Hills, and close me in;
> Now in the clear and open day I feel
> Your guardianship; I take it to my heart
>
> (*Home at Grasmere*, ll. 129–31)

We can understand this passion to find a home. Dorothy had had it for years. Writing when she was 21 to Jane Pollard, and looking at the 'smiling prospect' of fields and woods on a fine summer's evening at Forncett in July 1793, Dorothy—not for the first time—expressed her yearning,

I am *alone*; why are not you seated with me? and my dear William why is not he here also? I could almost fancy that I see you both near me. I have chosen a bank where I have room to spare for a resting-place for each of you. I hear *you* point out a spot where, if we could erect a little cottage and call it *our own* we should be the happiest of human beings. I see my Brother fired with the idea of leading his sister to such a retreat as Fancy ever ready at our call hastens to assist us in painting; our parlour is in a moment furnished; our garden is adorned by magic; the roses and honeysuckles spring at our command, the wood behind the house lifts at once its head and furnishes us with a winter's shelter and a summer's noonday shade.

It is youthful and self-conscious but the intensity is there. Both her brother and her friend responded to it: in the same letter to Jane Dorothy quoted for her Wordsworth's own words of joy at the thought that he and Dorothy might be together for a little time at Windy Brow,

Oh my dear, dear sister with what transport shall I again meet you, with what rapture shall I again wear out the day in your sight. I assure you so eager is my desire to see you that all obstacles vanish. I see you in a moment running or rather flying to my arms.

And Dorothy, looking forward to seeing Jane again, told her that she would 'palpitate with rapture when I once more throw myself into your arms'.

Dorothy had matured by seven years when she wrote the Grasmere Journal, but all the time the characteristic that everyone first noticed and valued was intensity of feeling. Coleridge, shortly after he met her in 1797, recognized her absolute and uncomplicated strength of feeling and saw it as a kind of innocence. In a letter of July he described her manners as 'simple, ardent, impressive' and he quoted his own lines on St Joan,

> In every motion her most innocent soul
> Outbeams so brightly, that who saw would say,
> Guilt was a thing impossible in her

Wordsworth, a year later, July 1798, recorded in 'Tintern Abbey' his similar sense of Dorothy's impassioned youth and singleness of feeling. His own responses—through political despair at the French Revolution, through personal trouble at the dilemma about Annette—had become complex, chastened, and subdued, and he saw and wanted to preserve in

Dorothy the strong straightforward response that had once been his:

> in thy voice I catch
> The language of my former heart, and read
> My former pleasures in the shooting lights
> Of thy wild eyes. Oh! yet a little while
> May I behold in thee what I was once

Once, 'the sounding cataract haunted' Wordsworth 'like a passion'; and so it still was with Dorothy.

Her background meant that the coming to Grasmere was a dream made real; her nature was such that she responded fully to every experience, and Grasmere in the summer, that first summer of 1800, was new. She and Wordsworth were young, and altogether it is not surprising that the language of the Journal reflects moments of almost overwhelming feeling. 'We lay upon the sloping Turf. Earth & sky were so lovely that they melted our very hearts . . . It made my heart almost feel like a vision to me' (20 June 1802). The sentence before this, incidentally, records their sweet talking 'about the disposal of our riches' (money owed to their long-dead father and finally to be paid): and Dorothy was assuredly innocent of making any connection between the loveliness of earth and sky and the personal hopes of herself and her brothers. 'Melting the heart', or leaving Wordsworth 'feasting upon silence' or being hardly able to find it in her heart to throw away a bitten apple when Wordsworth had gone away for a few days—none of this seems extravagant in the context of Dorothy. Her emotional language is absolute: 'I was oppressed & sick at heart for he wearied himself to death.' This reaction was to no more (and no less) than Wordsworth's difficulties in writing 'The Leech-gatherer' in his own house in Grasmere on a fine May morning. That total succumbing to feeling on the wedding day was inevitable, and Dorothy knew it. She wrote in late September 1802, a few days before the marriage, to Jane Pollard (now Jane Marshall),

I have long loved Mary Hutchinson as a Sister, and she is equally attached to me this being so, you will guess that I look forward with perfect happiness to this Connection between us, but, happy as I am,

I half dread that concentration of all tender feelings, past, present, and future which will come upon me on the wedding morning. There never lived on earth a better woman than Mary H. and I have not a doubt but that she is in every respect formed to make an excellent wife to my Brother, and I seem to myself to have scarcely any thing left to wish for but that the wedding was over, and we had reached our home once again.

She came through the intensity and they did reach their home once again, with Mary now to help with the 'copying out Italian poems for Stuart', to read Chaucer aloud, to attend to the baking of cakes, and to share the simple living, 'I am going to take Tapioca for my supper, & Mary an Egg, William some cold mutton, his poor Chest is tired.'

## II

Dorothy evoked things and people, and let them be. One of our pleasures in the Journal stems from our belief that things were as she says they were; that Thomas Ashburner went to fetch their ninth cart of coals, that they would walk in an evening 'first to the top of White Moss, then round by the White Bridge & up again beyond Mr Olliff's', that one night in the middle of May there was, according to Molly, thick ice on a jug at the door, that Wordsworth ate his broth last thing that morning when they left to go to see Mary before the journey to France and the October wedding, that Dorothy broiled a mutton chop one night and Coleridge ate it in bed, that a mother could trip with a light heart past the graves of her four dead children. We believe in Molly Fisher and Peggy Ashburner and Aggie because Dorothy catches their language, 'Aye Mistress', says Molly to her one day, 'them 'at's Low laid would have been a proud creature could they but have [seen] where I is now fra what they thought mud be my Doom.' The chance travellers on the roads speak their own words and have immediate credible life. We believe in the whole valley. It undoubtedly was for the troubled Wordsworth and the homeless Dorothy a golden world in 1800, but still they both saw that for those people who had been born into the tiny estates of the village and the hill farms, it offered no easy life, and we believe the hard economic facts because they affected people Dorothy knew. Thomas Ashburner had already sold his land; John Fisher feared that others would be 'forced to sell'; Betty Towers, with whom Dorothy had tea in June 1802, said that 'she & her husband were so tender in their health that they must be obliged to sell their land'; old Jim Jackson and his wife, albeit an extravagant woman 'who would make tea 4 or 5 times in a day', were simply getting through 'a clear estate' in 'eating & drinking'. Harsh changes came about in the landscape: 'sad ravages in the woods', 'slashing away in Benson's wood'; and there were harsh changes among the people: Tommy's father died, Goan's child, Mary Watson's son, Mrs Olliff's child, Leonard Holme who had a young family; there was a funeral of a pauper, and a funeral procession of a woman who drowned herself. This was nothing special. Death makes its casual appearance in the Journal— and is the more believable for that. The Boy's answer to John Fisher is the appropriate one, 'Hallo! has aught particular happened?' 'Nay naught at aw nobbut auld Willy's dead' (19 June 1802). Auld Willy had had a little estate, had sunk into being an ostler at Hawkshead, and died a casual pauper's death.

## III

Dorothy was not writing for strangers to read; she was writing for Wordsworth only, to 'give Wm Pleasure by it'; even Coleridge seems not to be thought of as a reader of the diary. This is not as it had been in the Alfoxden time when the three were daily together, observing and writing in constantly shared experience. Nor was Dorothy constructing a fictional world, and so there was no need to explain or to place local people in their context. Here of course is the difference between the Grasmere and the 1803 Scottish Journal, and the later Continental Tours. There, Dorothy was on holiday and had to explain everything to herself as well as to her numerous readers (the manuscripts were passed about among friends). Dorothy, for her one possible reader in Grasmere, could assume a familiarity with the place, and simply because this knowledge was totally assumed, we seem to have it too, and justified or not, whether we know or do not know the valley, the names as they are repeated become well known; the roads to Rydal and Ambleside, to Clappersgate and Keswick, become roads we seem to know; the garden grows, as its plants are put in, almost under our eyes. The different weathers, the various lights of day and night and seasons, the movements of cloud and water, of birds in flight, these are glimpses of a world we recognize; it is almost as though we too saw in passing the meadows 'heaving like sand' or that 'terrible kind of threatening brightness at sunset'; these are our recognitions and they anchor the scenes and people of Dorothy's Journal in a basic familiarity.

We are privileged, by reading this private diary, to know something of the daily life of a poet, though not from his own point of view and not with a central light focused upon him. The diary was for him, and thus is not primarily about him. Dorothy was not a Boswell recording a hero. When she stopped to recollect details, to write an extended and careful description, to re-read and improve her prose, this must partly be because she was offering for Wordsworth's consideration selected items of their common world. He might have forgotten, had not Dorothy's prose taught him to see again, the leech-gatherer or the shore of daffodils. Wordsworth has paid tribute to Dorothy's power to make him see and hear, 'She gave me eyes, she gave me ears.' The gift perhaps was mutual. It may be that Dorothy saw the beggar woman, the old seaman, the leech-gatherer and all those solitaries of the road, because Wordsworth had first noticed and written about the Discharged Soldier and the Old Cumberland Beggar. Dorothy's way of seeing, when she purposively set out to produce a 'character', was to capture first of all the detail of appearance; Wordsworth rarely made use of the fustian or grey cloth of breeches, the patches of darker blue where buttons had been, the paler cloth where seams had been let out; he did not need ultimately the specific misfortunes, so carefully listed, of the leech-gatherer, but used or not, and in whatever way such elements lay behind and 'kindled' Wordsworth's imagination, the derelicts who walk the pages of the Journal have their separate existence. At their most fragmented and mysterious they have life because Dorothy saw them, and becomes herself a figure in their scene; here she is a woman looking through a window on a winter's night:

The snow still lies upon the ground. Just at the closing in of the Day I heard a cart pass the door, & at the same time the dismal sound of a crying Infant. I went to the window & had light enough to see that a man was driving a cart which seemed not to be very full, & that a woman with an infant in her arms was following close behind & a dog close to her. It was a wild & melancholy sight. (12 Feb. 1802)

Dorothy's silent distance, behind the glass, and yet her sympathy, combine to produce for us an image of human solitude and struggle as haunting as any in Hardy.

If her intention was to record possible subjects for poetry for her brother, she ended by giving both her people and her places life. And she clearly discovered, in frequently having the challenge of extended description, the artist's pleasure in creating. Her many revisions are evidence of this. Where the same experience informs both Journal and poem there is for us the fascination of coming closer to the imagination at work; yet finally we can only be glad that we have both, both Dorothy's daffodils alive in wind and dance, with some, like tired children, resting their heads upon the mossy stones 'as on a pillow for weariness'; and Wordsworth's re-creation, not of the detail, but of the whole scene and its continued and permanent life in the mind.

## IV

Dorothy's care was for William. One evening, having left him on the fell by Mr Olliff's, Dorothy came home and wrote out poems: 'I grew alarmed & went to seek him.' The alarm was not for herself. Her concern was totally for him: at the stress, illness almost, that composing and altering poems gave him, at his neglect of meals in order to write, above all at his sleeplessness—'William has not slept all night. It wants only 10 minutes of 10 & he is in bed yet.' Again, with forethought

she threw a cloak out of the window one mild and sweet night
so that he might sit 'a few minutes in the orchard'. When he
'came in sleepy & hurried to bed' Dorothy carried his bread
and butter to him there. This kind of care is a mother's care;
the early loss of their own mother must be an element here.
Dorothy unstintingly looked after her brother. And certainly
Wordsworth understood such feeling. In 1804, with his own
first child still under 1, but having been with Dorothy when
little Basil Montagu, aged 5, was with her in the West Country
in 1796–7 and having himself experienced her care for him,
Wordsworth was able to catch so surely, in a very different
context, the pull of loving protective feeling:

> Earth fills her lap with pleasures of her own;
> Yearnings she hath in her own natural kind,
> And, even with something of a Mother's mind

('Immortality Ode', 77–9)

Somewhere in the complex of Dorothy's feeling there was
'something of a Mother's mind', and at Dove Cottage, first
with Wordsworth and then with him, Mary, and the children
of his marriage, there were demands enough upon such
yearnings. The Journal tells the story of the settling of the
house and garden, of the composition of poetry, of the
marriage and the return, and it can be left to speak this for
itself. It ends in early 1803 with the completion of a notebook,
but at a point too which is a natural end of one phase of life.
Wordsworth did not remain so singly the focus of Dorothy's
care; the 'forward-looking thoughts' that children bring and
their sheer practical needs supplant the writing.

## V

The writing, even during these early years of comparative
space, had to be fitted into corners of the day. Nor did Dorothy
write every day. Sometimes a few days, sometimes two and
three weeks at a time could be recollected; such summary
could be cursory or could give leisure for more formal
concentration on a single figure, like the tall beggar woman,
the leech-gatherer, or Peggy Ashburner as she talked about

the Queen of Patterdale. When Wordsworth was away, and often when he was asleep—'I have been writing this journal while Wm has had a nice little sleep.' (11 Feb. 1802)—entries were more sustained, and sentences longer. The Journal can be brought up to date before our eyes: 'A dull morning. I have employed myself in writing this journal . . . we are going to walk, & I am ready & waiting by the kitchen fire for Wm. We set forward . . .' (26 Jan. 1802). On the morning of their leaving Grasmere in July 1802, the Journal's short breathless sentences about the moment of leaving were written down during those same moments. Dorothy seems almost to be talking to her diary, running through her farewells: '—O beautiful place!—Dear Mary William—. . .—The Swallows I must leave them the well the garden the Roses all—Dear creatures!!' And within all this is the everyday sturdy observation, 'William is eating his Broth—' Thus Dorothy could hurry down both feeling and fact; her most common punctuation mark is the dash. After this July departure much of the Journal is recollected narrative. Sentences, even images, are more elaborate. The writing is not hurried, and many tiny alterations are witness to careful composition. But this may have had to wait until the last week in October when Dorothy, the drama over, was back in Grasmere, and had been 'confined upstairs' for a week 'in the tooth ache'.

But though Dorothy's writing was not accorded any importance in the movement of the days, and though no reader beyond Wordsworth was envisaged, we are given from the Journal the Wordsworth story, both in the larger outline of those years and in the day-by-day activities of Coleridge's coming or Mary's coming, or what books were read or letters written, which poems composed. We get the small stories of the valley people; we get to know the hills and waterfalls; we get to know Dorothy. Our abiding interest in the Journal includes all these things, but it is more. It must have something to do with Dorothy's ability to make us see bits of the world with fresh eyes; and those bits of the world are surprisingly lively. They are not special, but part of an everyday world that gives equal place to reading a little of Chaucer, preparing the goose for dinner, and walking out. In walking that particular morning of November 1801, the Wordsworths saw their 'favorite Birch tree', which, Dorothy wrote, with the sun upon it, 'glanced in the wind like a flying sunshiny shower'; momentarily the tree seems to escape its wooden fixity and it becomes 'like a Spirit of water'. This is a thoroughly cheerful seeing 'into the life of things', to use Wordsworth's phrase from 'Tintern Abbey'. The tree's transformation did not last; when the sun went in it 'resumed its purplish appearance'; Dorothy recorded this too because that is how it was. Similarly, her eye on that same day took in the big arching rainbow that spanned the lake from the island to the foot of Bainriggs and in the next few words noted the detail of catkins coming out, the alder with its 'plumb coloured buds', and the solitary butter flower. These are fractions, not whole compositions. The eye darts from fragment to fragment, and the extended descriptions in the Journal are surrounded by the tiny swift impressions: young bullfinches bustling about among the blossoms and poising themselves like 'Wire dancers or tumblers'; ravens high in the sky with the sun still on 'their bellys & their wings long after there was none of his light to be seen but a little space on the top of Loughrigg Fell'; the ash leaves that lay across the road after a rainy night; the moonlight that lay on hills like snow, or moonshine like herrings in the water. Every reader finds these fragments amidst the domestic daily business of the Journal; they stay as images of the mind.

## VI

The text has been re-read from the manuscripts and a good number of different readings and first-time readings will be noticed. Some, not all, are pointed out in the notes. Dates have been left as Dorothy wrote them; she often recorded the day only and no date, and often in her recollections she was wrong about dates; editorial square brackets will make them clear. A punctuation much closer to that which Dorothy used has been restored, i.e. fewer capital letters at the beginning of sentences, fewer apostrophes and full stops, more dashes, and almost everywhere the hasty ampersand. Dorothy is not consistent with punctuation, and something of the immediacy is lost from her writing if we tidy it overmuch.

She made many small, even minute revisions, some occurring to her even as she was writing: 'the stirring trees & gleaming lake' became, before she had gone any further, 'the stirring trees & gleaming bright chearful lake' with the original 'lake' crossed out (23 Aug. 1800); 'all objects', disappearing in twilight became straightaway 'all distant objects' (9 Dec. 1801); 'Wm read' became 'Wm began to read Peter Bell' (22 Feb. 1802). The Journal is peppered with single words crossed out to be rewritten immediately but with more accuracy. Sometimes the small correction is inserted on re-reading: 'the Rock on each side is very high' becomes, as the sentence is read over, 'the Rock on one side is very high' (23 Apr. 1802). Often nothing is crossed out and words or phrases are added, inserted between the lines or at the end of an entry: these insertions can be explanatory: 'one light in the vale' becomes 'one cottage light . . .' (26 May 1800); when Dorothy looked over Sara's Gate with Mary, now Wordsworth's new wife, 'the Sun shone on Hill & vale, the Birch trees looked like large golden Flowers'; then realizing that only far off trees can look like large golden flowers she inserted the word 'distant'—'the distant Birch trees.' The insertion can be emphatic: in her dismay at the ruined nest of the swallows which Dorothy had watched 'early in the morning, in the day many & many a time & in the evenings when it was almost dark I had seen them sitting together side by side in their unfinished nest' Dorothy's insertion at this point, 'both morning & night', can be only rhetorical (25 June 1802). Often something of the day's events is remembered in an insertion. William's bad head and Dorothy's sympathetic 'I petted him on the carpet' was the final statement before the line concluding the entry was drawn, but it was not after all the final moment of the day: Dorothy squeezed in, '& began a letter to Sara' (31 Jan. 1802). Emendations and insertions are pointed out in the notes, and it is good to have them because they accumulate into a demonstration of Dorothy's scrupulous, almost overscrupulous, care, most often for accuracy, but sometimes for effect, and for the sound of her sentences.

## VII

Although it is true that the Journal's clarities and power make themselves felt without any explanatory notes at all, there are still local points that remain a puzzle if we can bring no familiarity of place or people or poetry to Dorothy's account. We can never come near the knowledge of the Journal's first reader but there are some explanations that can be helpful. Many people can be identified and their relation with Dorothy and Wordsworth understood; some still have not yielded their history. Several authors that Dorothy read are now largely forgotten, and it is interesting to see how the reading of Wordsworth and Dorothy fed their thinking and made its contribution to Wordsworth's writing. Dorothy did not live alone: she lived intensely within a relationship and it has seemed enriching to her Journal to suggest some connections with her brother's poetry. Where else in literature, with the exception of Wordsworth and Coleridge, are there two such minds so closely involved with creative writing. It is hoped that the notes will provide a significant context for both the prose and the poetry of these brilliant short years in the lives of two great writers.

# The Grasmere Journals
## 1800–1803

### I. *14 May to 22 December 1800*

*May 14 1800* [*Wednesday*]. Wm & John set off into Yorkshire after dinner at ½ past 2 o'clock—cold pork in their pockets. I left them at the turning of the Low-wood bay under the trees. My heart was so full that I could hardly speak to W when I gave him a farewell kiss. I sate a long time upon a stone at the margin of the lake, & after a flood of tears my heart was easier. The lake looked to me I knew not why dull and melancholy, the weltering on the shores seemed a heavy sound. I walked as long as I could amongst the stones of the shore. The wood rich in flowers. A beautiful yellow, palish yellow flower, that looked thick round & double, & smelt very sweet—I supposed it was a ranunculus—Crowfoot, the grassy-leaved Rabbit-toothed white flower, strawberries, Geranium—scentless violet, anemones two kinds, orchises, primroses. The heckberry very beautiful as a low shrub. The crab coming out. Met a blind man driving a very large beautiful Bull & a cow—he walked with two sticks. Came home by Clappersgate. The valley very green, many sweet views up to Rydale head when I could juggle away the fine houses, but they disturbed me even more than when I have been happier—one beautiful view of the Bridge, without Sir Michaels. Sate down very often, tho' it was cold. I resolved to write a journal of the time till W & J return, & I set about keeping my resolve because I will not quarrel with myself, & because I shall give Wm Pleasure by it when he comes home again. At Rydale a woman of the village, stout & well-dressed, begged a halfpenny—she had never she said done it before—but these hard times!—Arrived at home with a bad head-ach, set some slips of privett. The evening cold had a fire—my face now flame-coloured. It is nine o'clock, I shall soon go to bed. A young woman begged at the door—she had come from Manchester on Sunday morn with two shillings & a slip of paper which she supposed a Bank note—it was a cheat. She had buried her husband & three children within a year & a half—All in one grave—burying very dear—paupers all put in one place—20 shillings paid for as much ground as will bury a man—a grave stone to be put over it or the right will be lost—11/6 each time the ground is opened. Oh! that I had a letter from William!

*May 15 Thursday*. A coldish dull morning—hoed the first row of peas, weeded &c &c—sat hard to mending till evening. The rain which had threatened all day came on just when I was going to walk—

*Friday morning* [*16th*]. Warm & mild after a fine night of rain. Transplanted raddishes after breakfast. Walked to Mr Gells with the Books—gathered mosses & plants. The woods extremely beautiful with all autumnal variety & softness—I carried a basket for mosses, & gathered some wild plants— Oh! that we had a book of botany—all flowers now are gay & deliciously sweet. The primrose still pre-eminent among the later flowers of the spring. Foxgloves very tall—with their heads budding. I went forward round the lake at the foot of Loughrigg fell—I was much amused with the business of a pair of stone chats. Their restless voices as they skimmed along the water following each other their shadows under them, & their returning back to the stones on the shore, chirping with the same unwearied voice. Could not cross the water so I went round by the stepping stones. The morning clear but cloudy, that is the hills were not overhung by mists. After dinner Aggy weeded onions & carrots—I helped for a little—wrote to Mary Hutchinson—washed my head— worked. After tea went to Ambleside—a pleasant cool but not cold evening. Rydale was very beautiful with spear-shaped streaks of polished steel. No letters!—only one newspaper. I returned by Clappersgate. Grasmere was very solemn in the last glimpse of twilight it calls home the heart to quietness. I had been very melancholy in my walk back. I had many of my saddest thoughts & I could not keep the tears within me. But when I came to Grasmere I felt that it did me good. I finished my letter to MH.—ate hasty pudding, & went to bed. As I was going out in the morning I met a half crazy old man. He shewed me a pincushion, & begged a pin, afterwards a halfpenny. He began in a kind of indistinct voice in this manner 'Matthew Jobson's lost a cow. Tom Nichol has two good horses strained—Jim Jones's cow's brokken her horn, &c &c— —'He went into Aggys & persuaded her to give him some whey & let him boil some porridge. She declares he ate two quarts.

*Saturday* [*17th*]. Incessant rain from morning till night. T. Ashburner brought us coals. Worked hard & Read Midsummer night's dream, Ballads—sauntered a little in the garden. The Skobby sate quietly in its nest rocked by the winds & beaten by the rain.

*Sunday 19th* [*18th*]. Went to church, slight showers, a cold air. The mountains from this window look much greener & I think the valley is more green than ever. The corn begins to shew itself. The ashes are still bare. Went part of the way home with Miss Simpson . . .—A little girl from Coniston came to beg. She had lain out all night—her step-mother had turn'd her out of doors. Her father could not stay at home 'She flights so'. Walked to Ambleside in the evening round the lake. The prospect exceeding beautiful from loughrigg fell. It was so green, that no eye could be weary of reposing upon it. The most beautiful situation for a house in the field next to Mr Benson's. It threatened rain all the evening but was mild & pleasant. I was overtaken by 2 Cumberland people on the other side of Rydale who complimented me upon my walking. They were going to sell cloth, & odd things which they make themselves in Hawkshead & the neighbourhood. The post was not arrived so I walked thro the town, past Mrs Taylors, & met him. Letters from Coleridge & Cottle—John Fisher overtook me on the other side of Rydale—he talked much about the alteration in the times, & observed that in a short time there would be only two ranks of people, the very rich & the very poor, for those who have small estates says he are forced to sell, & all the land goes into one hand. Did not reach home till 10 o clock.

*Monday* [*19th*]. Sauntered a good deal in the garden, bound carpets, mended old clothes. Read Timon of Athens. Dried linen—Molly weeded the turnips, John stuck the peas. We had not much sunshine or wind but no rain till about 7 o'clock when we had a slight shower just after I had set out upon my walk. I did not return but walked up into the Black quarter. I sauntered a long time among the rocks above the church. The most delightful situation possible for a cottage commanding two distinct views of the vale & of the lake, is among those rocks—I strolled on, gathered mosses, &c. The quietness & still seclusion of the valley affected me even to producing the deepest melancholy—I forced myself from it. The wind rose before I went to bed. No rain—Dodwell & Wilkinson called in my absence.

*Tuesday Morning* [*20th*]. A fine mild rain—after Breakfast the sky cleared & before the clouds passed from the hill, I went to Ambleside—It was a sweet morning—Everything green & overflowing with life, & the streams making a perpetual song with the thrushes & all little birds, not forgetting the Stone chats. The post was not come in—I walked as far as Windermere & met him there. No letters! no papers. Came home by Clappersgate—I was sadly tired, ate a hasty dinner & had a bad head-ach, went to bed & slept at least 2 hours. Rain came on in the Evening—Molly washing.

*Wednesday* [*21st*]. Went often to spread the linen which was bleaching—a rainy day & very wet night.

*Thursday* [*22nd*] A very fine day with showers—dried the linen & starched Drank tea at Mr Simpsons. Brought down Batchelors Buttons (Rock Ranunculus) & other plants—went part of the way back. A showery, mild evening—all the peas up.

*Friday 23rd*. Ironing till tea time. So heavy a rain that I could not go for letters—put by the linen, mended stockings &c.

*Saturday May 24th*. Walked in the morning to Ambleside. I found a letter from Wm & from Mary Hutchinson & Douglass. Returned on the other side of the lakes—wrote to William after dinner—nailed up the beds worked in the garden—Sate in the evening under the trees. I went to bed soon with a bad head-ache—a fine day.

*Sunday* [*25th*]. A very fine warm day—had no fire. Read

Macbeth in the morning—sate under the trees after dinner. Miss Simpson came just as I was going out & she sate with me. I wrote to my Brother Christopher, & sent John Fisher to Ambleside after tea. Miss Simpson & I walked to the foot of the lake—her Brother met us. I went with them nearly home & on my return found a letter from Coleridge & from Charles Lloyd & three papers.

*Monday May 26.* A very fine morning, worked in the garden till after 10 when old Mr Simpson came & talked to me till after 12. Molly weeding. Wrote letters to J H, Coleridge, C Ll. & W. I walked towards Rydale & turned aside at my favorite field. The air & the lake were still—one cottage light in the vale, had so much of day left that I could distinguish objects, the woods; trees & houses. Two or three different kinds of Birds sang at intervals on the opposite shore. I sate till I could hardly drag myself away I grew so sad. 'When pleasant thoughts &c—'

*Tuesday 27th.* I walked to Ambleside with letters—met the post before I reached Mr Partridges, one paper, only a letter for Coleridge—I expected a letter from Wm. It was a sweet morning, the ashes in the valleys nearly in full leaf but still to be distinguished, quite bare on the higher grounds. I was warm in returning, & becoming cold with sitting in the house —I had a bad head-ach—went to bed after dinner, & lay till after 5—not well after tea. I worked in the garden, but did not walk further. A delightful evening before the Sun set but afterwards it grew colder. Mended stockings &c.

*Wednesday [28th].* In the morning walked up to the rocks above Jenny Dockeray's—sate a long time upon the grass the prospect divinely beautiful. If I had three hundred pounds & could afford to have a bad interest for my money I would buy that estate, & we would build a cottage there to end our days in—I went into her garden & got white & yellow lilies, periwinkle, &c, which I planted. Sate under the trees with my work—no fire in the morning. Worked till between 7 & 8, & then watered the garden, & was about to go up to Mr Simpson's, when Miss S & her visitors passed the door. I went home with them, a beautiful evening the crescent moon hanging above helm crag.

*Thursday [29th].* In the morning worked in the garden a little, read King John. Miss Simpson & Miss Falcon & Mr S came very early—went to Mr Gells boat before tea—we fished upon the lake & amongst us caught 13 Bass. Miss Simpson brought gooseberries & *cream* left the water at near nine o clock, very cold. Went part of the way home with the party.

*Friday* [*30th*]. In the morning went to Ambleside, forgetting that the post does not come till the evening—how was I grieved when I was so informed—I walked back resolving to go again in the evening. It rained very mildly & sweetly in the morning as I came home, but came on a wet afternoon & evening—luckily I caught Mr Ollifs Lad as he was going for letters, he brought me one from Wm & 12 papers. I planted London pride upon the wall & many things on the Borders. John sodded the wall. As I came past Rydale in the morning I saw a Heron swimming with only its neck out of water—it beat & struggled amongst the water when it flew away & was long in getting loose.

*Saturday* [*31st*]. A sweet mild rainy morning. Grundy the carpet man called I paid him 1–10/–Went to the Blind man's for plants. I got such a load that I was obliged to leave my Basket in the Road & send Molly for it. Planted &c. After dinner when I was putting up vallances Miss Simpson & her Visitors called—I went with them to Brathay Bridge. We got Broom in returning, strawberries &c, came home by Ambleside—Grasmere looked divinely beautiful. Mr, Miss Simpson & Tommy drank tea at 8 o clock—I walked to the Potters with them.

*Sunday June 1st*. Rain in the night—a sweet mild morning—Read Ballads, went to church. Singers from Wytheburn. Went part of the way home with Miss Simpson. Walked upon the hill above the house till dinner-time—went again to church —a Christening & singing which kept us very late. The pew-side came down with me. Walked with Miss Simpson nearly home. After tea went to Ambleside, round the lakes—a very fine warm evening. I lay upon the steep of Loughrigg my heart dissolved in what I saw when I was not startled but recalled from my reverie by a noise as of a child paddling without shoes. I looked up and saw a lamb close to me—it approached nearer & nearer as if to examine me & stood a long time. I did not move—at last it ran past me & went bleating along the pathway seeming to be seeking its mother. I saw a hare in the high road. The post was not come in—I waited in the Road till Johns apprentice came with a letter from Coleridge & 3 papers. The moon shone upon the water—reached home at 10 o clock—went to bed immediately. Molly brought Daisies &c which we planted.

*Monday* [*2nd*]. A cold dry windy morning. I worked in the garden & planted flowers &c—Sate under the trees after dinner till tea time. John Fisher stuck the peas, Molly weeded & washed. I went to Ambleside after tea, crossed the stepping-stones at the foot of Grasmere & pursued my way on the other side of Rydale & by Clappersgate. I sate a long time to watch the hurrying waves & to hear the regularly irregular sound of the dashing waters. The waves round about the little [Island] seemed like a dance of spirits that rose out of the water, round its small circumference of shore. Inquired about lodgings for Coleridge, & was accompanied by Mrs Nicholson as far as Rydale. This was very kind, but God be thanked I want not society by a moonlight lake—It was near 11 when I reached home. I wrote to Coleridge & went late to bed.

*Tuesday* [*3rd*]. Sent off my letter by the Butcher—a boisterous drying day. Worked in the garden before dinner. Read R[ichar]d Second—was not well after dinner & lay down. Mrs Simpsons grandson brought me some gooseberries —I got up & walked with him part of the way home, afterwards went down rambling by the lake side—got Lockety goldings, strawberries &c, & planted. After tea the wind fell I walked towards Mr Simpsons. Gave the newspapers to the Girl, reached home at 10. No letter, no William—a letter from R[ichar]d to John.

*Wednesday* [*4th*]. A very fine day. I sate out of doors most of the day, wrote to Mr Jackson. Ambleside fair. I walked to the lake side in the morning, took up plants & sate upon a stone reading Ballads. In the Evening I was watering plants when Mr & Miss Simpson called—I accompanied them home—& we went to the waterfall at the head of the valley—it was very interesting in the Twilight. I brought home lemon thyme &

several other plants, & planted them by moonlight. I lingered out of doors in the hope of hearing my Brothers tread.

*Thursday* [*5th*]. I sate out of doors great part of the day & worked in the Garden—had a letter from Mr Jackson, & wrote an answer to Coleridge. The little birds busy making love & pecking the blossoms & bits of moss off the trees, they flutter about & about & thrid the trees as I lie under them. Molly went out to tea—I would not go far from home expecting my Brothers—I rambled on the hill above the house gathered wild thyme & took up roots of wild Columbine. Just as I was returning with my 'load', Mr & Miss Simpson called. We went again upon the hill, got more plants, set them, & then went to the Blind Mans for London Pride for Miss Simpson. I went up with them as far as the Blacksmith's. A fine lovely moonlight night.

*Friday* [*6th*]. Sate out of doors reading the Whole Afternoon, but in the morning I wrote to my aunt Cookson. In the Evening I went to Ambleside with Coleridge's letter—it was a lovely night as the day had been. I went by Loughrigg & Clappersgate & just met the post at the turnpike—he told me there were two letters but none for me. So I was in no hurry & went round again by Clappersgate, crossed the Stepping stones & entered Ambleside at Matthew Harrisons—A letter from Jack Hutchinson, & one from Montagu enclosing a 3£ note—No William! I slackened my pace as I came near home fearing to hear that he was not come. I listened till after one o'clock to every barking dog, Cock fighting, & other sports: it was Mr Borricks opening. Foxgloves just coming into blossom.

*Saturday* [*7th*]. A very warm cloudy morning, threatening to rain. I walked up to Mr Simpsons to gather gooseberries—it was a very fine afternoon—little Tommy came down with me, ate gooseberry pudding & drank tea with me. We went up the hill to gather sods & plants & went down to the lake side & took up orchises &c—I watered the garden & weeded. I did not leave home in the expectation of Wm & John, & sitting at work till after 11 o clock I heard a foot go to the front of the house, turn round, & open the gate. It was William— —after our first joy was over we got some tea. We did not go to bed till 4 o clock in the morning so he had an opportunity of seeing our improvements—the birds were singing, & all looked fresh though not gay. There was a greyness on earth & sky. We did not rise till near 10 in the morning. We were busy all day in writing letters to Coleridge, Montagu, Douglass, Richard. Mr & Miss Simpson called in the Evening, the little Boy carried our letters to Ambleside. We walked with Mr & Miss S home on their return the evening was cold & I was afraid of the tooth-ach for William. We met John on our return home.

*Monday 9th.* In the morning W cut down the winter cherry tree I sowed French Beans & weeded. A coronetted Landau went by when we were sitting upon the sodded wall. The ladies (evidently Tourists) turned an eye of interest upon our little garden & cottage. We went to R Newtons for pikefloats & went round to Mr Gell's Boat & on to the Lake to fish we caught nothing—it was extremely cold. The Reeds & Bulrushes or Bullpipes of a tender soft green making a plain whose surface moved with the wind. The reeds not yet tall. The lake clear to the Bottom, but saw no fish. In the evening I stuck peas, watered the garden & planted Brocoli—Did not walk for it was very cold. A poor Girl called to beg who had no work at home & was going in search of it to Kendal. She slept in Mr Bensons Lathe—& went off after Breakfast in the morning with 7d & a letter to the Mayor of Kendal.

*Tuesday 10th.* A cold, yet sunshiny morning. John carried letters to Ambleside. I made tarts, pies &c—Wm stuck peas. After dinner he lay down—John not at home—I stuck peas alone—Molly washing. Cold showers with hail & rain, but at half past five after a heavy rain the lake became calm—& very beautiful. Those parts of the water which were perfectly unruffled lay like green islands of various shapes. W & I walked to Ambleside to seek lodgings for C. No letters—no papers. It was a very cold cheerless evening. John had been fishing in Langdale & was gone to bed.

On Tuesday, May 27th, a very tall woman, tall much beyond the measure of tall women, called at the door. She had on a very long brown cloak, & a very white cap without Bonnet—her face was excessively brown, but it had plainly once been fair. She led a little bare footed child about 2 years old by the hand & said her husband who was a tinker was

gone before with the other children. I gave her a piece of
Bread. Afterwards on my road to Ambleside, beside the
Bridge at Rydale, I saw her husband sitting by the road-side,
his two asses feeding beside him & the two young children at
play upon the grass. The man did not beg—I passed on &
about ¼ of a mile further I saw two boys before me, one about
10 the other about 8 years old at play chasing a butterfly. They
were wild figures, not very ragged, but without shoes &
stockings; the hat of the elder was wreathed round with yellow
flowers, the younger whose hat was only a rimless crown, had
stuck it round with laurel leaves. They continued at play till I
drew very near & then they addressed me with the Begging
cant & the whining voice of sorrow—I said I served your
Mother this morning (The Boys were so like the woman who
had called at the door that I could not be mistaken)—O! says
the elder you could not serve my mother for she's dead & my
father's on at the next town—he's a potter—I persisted in my
assertion & that I would give them nothing. Says the elder
Come lets 'away' & away they flew like lightning. They had
however sauntered so long in their road that they did not
reach Ambleside before me, & I saw them go up to Matthew
Harrison's house with their wallet upon the elder's shoulder,
& creeping with a Beggars complaining foot. On my return
through Ambleside I met in the street the mother driving her
asses; in the two Panniers of one of which were the two little
children whom she was chiding & threatening with a wand
which she used to drive on her asses, while the little things
hung in wantonness over the Panniers edge. The woman had
told me in the morning that she was of Scotland, which her
accent fully proved, but that she had lived (I think at Wigton)
that they could not keep a house, & so they travelled.

*Wednesday 13th June* [*11th*]. A very cold morning—we went
on the lake to set pike floats with John's fish—W & J went first
alone—Mr Simpson called & I accompanied him to the Lake
side—My Brothers & I again went upon the water, &
returned to dinner—we landed upon the Island where I saw
the whitest Hawthorn I have seen this year, the generality of
hawthorns are bloomless—I saw wild roses in the hedges.
Went to bed in the afternoon & slept till after six—a

threatening of the tooth-ach. Wm & John went to the pike floats—they brought in 2 pikes. I sowed Kidney-beans & spinnach, a cold evening. Molly stuck the peas. I weeded a little. Did not walk.

*Thursday 14th June [12th]*. William & I went upon the water to set pike floats—John fished under Loughrigg. We returned to dinner—2 pikes boiled & roasted—a very cold air but warm sun. W & I again went upon the water—we walked to Rydale after tea, & up to the potter's—a cold night, but warmer.

*Friday [13th]*. A rainy morning. W & J went upon the Lake —very warm, & pleasant gleams of sunshine. Went upon the water after tea, caught a pike 7½ [lbs.] Mr Simpson trolling. Mr Gell & his party come.

*Saturday [14th]*. A fine morning but cloudy—W & John went upon the lake—I staid at home. We drank tea at Mr Simpsons. Stayed till after 10 o clock.

*Sunday [15th]*. John walked to Coniston. W & I sauntered in the Garden. Afterwards walked by the lake side: a cold air— we pushed through the wood—walked behind the fir grove & returned to dinner. We lay down after dinner. Parker, the Tanner & the Blacksmith from Hawkshead called.

*Monday [16th]*. Wm & I went to Brathay by Little Langdale & Collath & Skelleth. It was a warm mild morning with threatenings of rain. The vale of Little Langdale looked bare & unlovely. Collath was wild & interesting, from the Peat carts & peat gatherers—the valley all perfumed with the Gale & wild thyme. The woods about the waterfall veined with rich yellow Broom. A succession of delicious views from Skelleth to Brathay. We met near Skelleth a pretty little Boy with a wallet over his shoulder he came from Hawkshead & was going to 'late' a lock of meal. He spoke gently & without complaint. When I asked him if he got enough to eat he looked surprized & said 'Nay'. He was 7 years old but seemed not more than 5. We drank tea at Mr Ibbetsons & returned by Ambleside. Sent 3–9–0 to the Potter at Kendal. Met John on our return home at about 10 o clock. Saw a primrose in blossom.

*Tuesday [17th]*. We put the new window in. I ironed &

worked about a good deal in house & garden. In the Evening
we walked for letters. Found one for Coleridge at Rydale, & I
returned much tired.

*Wednesday [18th]*. We walked round the lake in the morning
& in the evening to the lower waterfall at Rydale—it was a
warm dark, lowering evening.

*Thursday [19th]*. A very hot morning—Wm & I walked up to
Mr Simpsons. W & old Mr S. went to fish in Wytheburn
water. I dined with John, & lay under the trees. The afternoon
changed from clear to cloudy & to clear again—John & I
walked up to the waterfall & to Mr Simpsons, & with Miss
Simpson met the fishers—W caught a pike weighing 4¾ lbs.
There was a gloom almost terrible over Grasmere water &
vale—a few drops fell but not much rain. No Coleridge whom
we fully expected.

*Friday [20th]*. I worked in the garden in the morning. Wm
prepared Pea sticks. Threatening for rain but yet it comes not.
On Wednesday evening a poor man called, a hatter—he had
been long ill, but was now recovered & his wife was lying-in
of her 4th child. The parish would not help him because he
had implements of trade &c—&c—We gave him 6d.

*Saturday [21st]*. In the morning W & I went to Ambleside to
get his tooth drawn, & put in—a fine clear morning but cold
—Ws tooth drawn with very little pain he slept till 3 o'clock.
Young Mr S. drank tea & supped with us they fished in
Rydale water & they caught 2 small fishes, W no bite, John 3.
Miss Simpson & 3 children called—I walked with them to
Rydale. The evening cold & clear & frosty, but the wind was
falling as I returned. I staid at home about an hour & then
walked up the hill to Rydale lake. Grasmere looked so
beautiful that my heart was almost melted away. It was quite
calm only spotted with sparkles of light. The church visible.
On our return all distant objects had faded away—all but the
hills. The reflection of the light bright sky above Black quarter
was very solemn. Mr S did not go till 12 o clock.

*Sunday [22nd]*. In the morning W & I walked towards
Rydale & up into the wood but finding it not very pleasant we
returned—sauntered in the garden—a showery day. In the
evening I planted a honeysuckle round the yew tree. In the

evening we walked for letters. No letters, no news of Coleridge.
Jimmy Benson came home drunk beside us.

*Monday [23rd]*. Mr Simpson called in the morning Tommys
Father dead. W & I went into Langdale to fish. The morning
was very cold. I sate at the foot of the lake till my head ached
with cold. The view exquisitely beautiful, through a gate &
under a sycamore tree beside the first house going into
Loughrigg—Elter water looked barren, & the view from the
church less beautiful than in winter. When W went down to
the water to fish I lay under the wind my head pillowed upon a
mossy rock & slept about 10 minutes which relieved my
headach. We ate our dinner together & parted again. Wm was
afraid he had lost his line & sought me. An old Man saw me
just after I had crossed the stepping stones & was going thro' a
copse—Ho, where were you going? To Elterwater Bridge—
Why says he its well I saw you, ye were gane to Little
Langdale by Wrynose, & several other places—which he ran
over, with a mixture of triumph, good-nature, & wit. Its well
I saw you or youd ha been lost— —The evening grew very
pleasant we sate on the side of the hill looking to Elterwater. I
was much tired & returned home to tea—W went to fish for
pike in Rydale. John came in when I had done tea, & he & I
carried a jug of tea to William. We met him in the old road
from Rydale—he drank his tea upon the turf—the setting sun
threw a red purple light upon the rocks & stone walls of
Rydale which gave them a most interesting & beautiful
appearance.

*Tuesday [24th]*. W went to Ambleside—John walked out—I
made tarts &c—Mr B Simpson called & asked us to tea—I
went to the view of Rydale to meet William. John went to him
—I returned—W & I drank tea at Mr Simpsons, brought
down Lemon Thyme, greens &c—The old woman was very
happy to see us & we were so in the pleasure we gave. She was
an affecting picture of Patient disappointment suffering under
no particular affliction.

*Wednesday [25th]*. A very rainy day—I made a shoe—Wm &
John went to fish in Langdale. In the evening I went above the
house, & gathered flowers which I planted, fox-glove &c. On
Sunday [29 June] Mr & Mrs Coleridge & Hartley came. The

day was very warm we sailed to the foot of Loughrigg. They staid with us three weeks & till the Thursday following, ie. till the 23 [24th] of July. On the Friday preceding their departure we drank tea at the island. The weather very delightful—& on the Sunday we made a great fire, & drank tea in Bainriggs with the Simpsons—I accompanied Mrs C. to Wytheburne & returned with W—to tea at Mr Simpsons—it was excessively hot. But the day after Friday July 24th [25th] still hotter. All the morning I was engaged in unpacking our Somersetshire goods & in making pies. The house was a hot oven but yet we could not bake the pies—I was so weary I could not walk so I went & sate with Wm in the orchard—we had a delightful half hour, in the warm still evening.

*Saturday 25th [26th]*. Still hotter. I sate with W. in the orchard all the morning & made my shoe. In the afternoon from excessive heat I was ill in the headach & toothach & went to bed—I was refreshed with washing myself after I got up, but it was too hot to walk till near dark, & then I sate upon the wall finishing my shoes.

*Sunday Mor. 26th [27th]*. Very warm—Molly ill—John bathed in the lake. I wrote out Ruth in the afternoon, in the morning I read Mr Knight's Landscape. After tea we rowed down to Loughrigg Fell, visited the white foxglove, gathered wild strawberries, & walked up to view Rydale we lay a long time looking at the lake, the shores all embrowned with the scorching sun. The Ferns were turning yellow, that is here & there one was quite turned. We walked round by Benson's wood home. The lake was now most still & reflected the beautiful yellow & blue & purple & grey colours of the sky. We heard a strange sound in the Bainriggs wood as we were floating on the water it *seemed* in the wood, but it must have been above it, for presently we saw a raven very high above us —it called out & the Dome of the sky seemed to echoe the sound—it called again & again as it flew onwards, & the mountains gave back the sound, seeming as if from their center a musical bell-like answering to the birds hoarse voice. We heard both the call of the bird & the echoe after we could see him no longer. We walked up to the top of the hill again in view of Rydale—met Mr & Miss Simpson on horseback. The crescent moon which had shone upon the water was now gone down. Returned to supper at 10 o clock.

*Monday morning [28th].* Received a letter from Coleridge enclosing one from Mr Davy about the Lyrical Ballads—intensely hot I made pies in the morning. Wm went into the wood & altered his poems. In the Evening it was so very warm that I was too much tired to walk.

*Tuesday [29th].* Still very hot. We gathered peas for dinner. We walked up in the Evening to find out Hewetson's cottage but it was too dark. I was sick & weary.

*Wednesday [30th].* Gathered peas for Mrs Simpson—John & I walked up with them—very hot—Wm had intended going to Keswick. I was obliged to lie down after dinner from excessive heat & headach. The Evening excessively beautiful—a rich reflection of the moon, the moonlight clouds & the hills, & from the Rays gap a huge rainbow pillar. We sailed upon the lake till it was 10 o clock.

*Thursday [31st].* All the morning I was busy copying poems—gathered peas, & in the afternoon Coleridge came very hot, he brought the 2nd volume of the Anthology— —The men went to bathe & we afterwards sailed down to Loughrigg read poems on the water & let the boat take its own course—we walked a long time upon Loughrigg & returned in the grey twilight. The moon just setting as we reached home.

*Friday 1st August.* In the morning I copied The Brothers—Coleridge & Wm went down to the lake. They returned & we all went together to Mary Point where we sate in the breeze & the shade & read Wms poems altered 'The Whirlblast &c'—Mr Simpson came to tea & Mr B Simpson afterwards—we drank tea in the orchard.

*Saturday Morning 2nd.* Wm & Coleridge went to Keswick. John went with them to Wytheburn & staid all day fishing & brought home 2 small pikes at night. I accompanied them to Lewthwaite's cottage & on my return papered Wm's room—I afterwards lay down till tea time & after tea worked at my shifts in the orchard. A grey evening—about 8 o'clock it gathered for rain & I had the scatterings of a shower, but afterwards the lake became of a glassy calmness & all was still. I sate till I could see no longer & then continued my work in the house.

*Sunday Morning 3rd*. I made pies & stuff'd the pike—baked a loaf. Headach after dinner—I lay down, a letter from Wm rouzed me, desiring us to go to Keswick. After writing to Wm we walked as far as Mr Simpson's & ate black cherries—a Heavenly warm evening with scattered clouds upon the hills. There was a vernal greenness upon the grass from the rains of the morning & afternoon—peas for dinner.

*Monday 4th*. Rain in the night. I tied up Scarlet beans, nailed the honeysuckles &c &c—John was prepared to walk to Keswick all the morning—he seized a returned chaise & went after dinner. I pulled a large basket of peas & sent to Keswick by a returned chaise—a very cold evening—assisted to spread out linen in the morning.

*Tuesday 5th*. Dried the linen in the morning, the air still cold. I pulled a bag full of peas for Mrs Simpson. Miss Simpson drank tea with me & supped on her return from Ambleside. A very fine evening. I sate on the wall making my shifts till I could see no longer—walked half-way home with Miss Simpson.

*Wednesday 6th August*. A rainy morning. I ironed till dinner time—sewed till near dark—then pulled a basket of peas, & afterwards boiled & picked gooseberries. William came home from Keswick at 11 o clock a very fine night.

*Thursday Morning 7th August*. Packed up the mattrass, & sent to Keswick—boiled gooseberries—NB 2 lbs of sugar in the first panfull 3 quarts all good measure—3 lbs in the 2nd 4 quarts—2½ lbs in the 3rd—a very fine day. William composing in the wood in the morning—in the evening we walked to Mary Point—a very fine sunset.

*Friday Morning [8th]*. We intended going to Keswick, but were prevented by the excessive heat. Nailed up scarlet beans in the morning—Drank tea at Mr Simpsons; & walked over the mountains by Wattenlath—very fine gooseberries at Mr S's—a most enchanting walk—Wattenlath a heavenly scene. Reached Coleridge's at 11 o clock.

*Saturday Morning [9th]*. I walked with Coleridge in the Windy Brow woods.

*Sunday [10th]*. Very hot the Cs went to church. We sailed upon Derwent in the evening.

*Monday afternoon* [*11th*]. Walked to Windy Brow.

*Tuesday* [*12th*]. Drank tea with the Cockins—Wm & I walked along the Cockermouth road—he was altering his poems.

*Wednesday* [*13th*]. Made the Windy Brow seat.

*Thursday Morning* [*14th*]. Called at the Speddings. In the Evening walked in the wood with W—very very beautiful the moon.

*Friday Morning* [*15th*]. W in the wood—I went with Hartley to see the Cockins & to buy Bacon. In the evening we walked to Water End—feasted on gooseberries at Silver hill.

*Saturday Morning* [*16th*]. Worked for Mrs C—& walked with Coleridge intending to gather Raspberries—joined by Miss Spedding.

*Sunday 16th August* [*17th*]. Came home—Dined in Borrowdale. A rainy morning but a fine evening—saw the Bristol prison & Bassenthwaite at the same time—Wm read us the 7 Sisters on a stone.

*Monday* [*18th*]. Putting linen by & mending. Walked with John to Mr Simpson's & met Wm in returning a fine warm day.

*Tuesday* [*19th*]. Mr & Mrs Simpson dined with us—Miss S & Brother drank tea in the orchard.

*Wednesday* [*20th*]. I worked in the morning. Cold in the evening & rainy. Did not walk.

*Thursday* [*21st*]. Read Wallenstein & sent it off—worked in the morning—walked with John round the two lakes—gathered white foxglove seeds & found Wm in Bain-riggs at our return.

*Friday 21st* [*22nd*]. Very cold—baking in the morning—gathered pea seeds & took up—lighted a fire upstairs. Walked as far as Rydale with John intending to have gone on to Ambleside but we found the papers at Rydale—Wm walking in the wood all the time. John & he went out after our return —I mended stockings. Wind very high shaking the corn.

*Saturday 22nd* [*23rd*]. A very fine morning. Wm was composing all the morning—I shelled peas, gathered beans, & worked in the garden till ½ past 12 then walked with William in the wood. The Gleams of sunshine & the stirring trees &

gleaming bright chearful lake, most delightful. After dinner we walked to Ambleside—showery, went to see Mr Partridges house. Came home by Clappersgate. We had intended going by Rydale woods, but it was cold—I was not well, & tired, got tea immediately, & had a fire—did not reach home till 7 o clock—mended stockings—& W read Peter Bell. He read us the Poem of Joanna beside the Rothay by the roadside.

*Sunday 23rd [24th]*. A fine cool pleasant breezy day walked in the wood in the morning. Mr Twining called. John walked up to Mr Simpsons in the evening. I staid at home & wrote to Mrs Rawson & my aunt Cookson—I was ill in the afternoon & lay down—got up restored by a sound sleep.

*Monday 24th [25th]*. A fine day—walked in the wood in the morning & to the firgrove—walked up to Mr Simpsons in the evening.

*Tuesday 25th [26th]*. We walked in the evening to Ambleside, Wm not quite well. I bought sacking for the mattrass. A very fine solemn evening. The wind blew very free from the islands at Rydale—we went on the other side of Rydale, & sate a long time looking at the mountains which were all black at Grasmere & very bright in Rydale—Grasmere exceedingly dark & Rydale of a light yellow green.

*Wednesday 27th*. In the morning we walked—John Baty passed us. We walked along the shore of the lake in the Evening & went over into Langdale & down to Loughrigg tarn—a very fine evening calm & still.

*Thursday 27 August [28th]*. Still very fine weather I baked bread & cakes. In the Evening we walked round the Lake by Rydale & Mr Simpson came to fish.

*Friday evening [29th]*. We walked to Rydale to inquire for letters. We walked over the hill by the Firgrove. I sate upon a rock & observed a flight of swallows gathering together high above my head they flew towards Rydale. We walked through the wood over the stepping stones—The lake of Rydale very beautiful, partly still. John & I left Wm to compose an Inscription—that about the path. We had a very fine walk by the gloomy lake. There was a curious yellow reflection in the water as of corn fields—there was no light in the clouds from which it appeared to come.

*Saturday Morning 28th August [30th]*. I was baking Bread pies & dinner. It was very warm. Wm finished his Inscription of the Pathway. Then walked in the wood & when John returned he sought him & they bathed together. I read a little of Boswells Life of Johnson. I had a headache & went to lie down in the orchard. I was rouzed by a shout that Anthony Harrison was come. We sate in the orchard till tea time, drank tea early & rowed down the lake which was stirred by Breezes. We looked at Rydale which was soft, chearful, & beautiful. We then went to peep into Langdale. The Pikes were very grand. We walked back to the view of Rydale, which was now a dark mirror. We rowed home over a lake still as glass & then went to George Mackareth's to hire a horse for John. A fine moonlight night. The beauty of the Moon was startling as it rose to us over Loughrigg Fell. We returned to supper at 10 o'clock. Thomas Ashburner brought us our 8th Cart of coals since May 17th.

*Sunday 29th [31st]*. Anthony Harrison & John left us at ½ past seven—a very fine morning. A great deal of corn is cut in the vale, & the whole prospect though not tinged with a general autumnal yellow, yet softened down into a mellowness of colouring which seems to impart softness to the forms of hills & mountains. At 11 o'clock Coleridge came when I was walking in the still, clear moonshine in the garden—he came over Helvellyn—Wm was gone to bed & John also, worn out with his ride round Coniston. We sate & chatted till ½ past three W in his dressing gown. Coleridge read us a part of Christabel. Talked much about the mountains &c &c Miss Thrale's hatred—Losh's opinion of Southey—the first of poets.

*Monday Morning 1st September*. We walked in the wood by the Lake. W read Joanna & the Firgrove to Coleridge. They bathed. The morning was delightful with somewhat of an autumnal freshness. After dinner Coleridge discovered a rock seat in the orchard, cleared away the brambles. Coleridge obliged to go to bed after tea. John & I followed Wm up the hill & then returned to go to Mr Simpsons—we borrowed some bottles for bottling rum. The evening somewhat frosty & grey but very pleasant. I broiled Coleridge a mutton chop which he ate in bed. Wm was gone to bed—I chatted with John & Coleridge till near 12.

*Tuesday 2nd.* In the morning they all went to Stickel Tarn. A very fine, warm sunny beautiful morning. I baked a pie &c for dinner—little Sally was with me. The fair day. Miss Simpson & Mr came down to tea we walked to the fair. There seem'd very few people & very few stalls yet I believe there were many cakes & much beer sold. My Brothers came home to dinner at 6 o'clock. We drank Tea immediately after by Candlelight. It was a lovely moonlight night. We talked much about a house on Helvellyn. The moonlight shone only upon the village it did not eclipse the village lights & the sound of dancing & merriment came along the still air—I walked with Coleridge & Wm up the Lane & by the Church, I then lingered with Coleridge in the garden. John & Wm were both gone to bed & all the lights out.

*Wednesday 3rd September.* Coleridge Wm & John went from home to go upon Helvellyn with Mr Simpson. They set out after breakfast. I accompanied them up near the Blacksmith's. A fine coolish morning. I ironed till ½ past three—now very hot. I then went to a funeral at John Dawsons. About 10 men & 4 women. Bread cheese & ale—they talked sensibly & chearfully about common things. The dead person 56 years of age buried by the parish—the coffin was neatly lettered & painted black & covered with a decent cloth. They set the corpse down at the door & while we stood within the threshold the men with their hats off sang with decent & solemn countenances a verse of a funeral psalm. The corpse was then borne down the hill & they sang till they had got past the Town-end. I was affected to tears while we stood in the house, the coffin lying before me. There were no near kindred, no children. When we got out of the dark house the sun was shining & the prospect looked so divinely beautiful as I never saw it. It seemed more sacred than I had ever seen it, & yet more allied to human life. The green fields, neighbours of the churchyard, were green as possible & with the brightness of the sunshine looked quite Gay. I thought she was going to a quiet spot & I could not help weeping very much. When we came to the bridge they began to sing again & stopped during

4 lines before they entered the church-yard. The priest met us —he did not look as a man ought to do on such an occasion— I had seen him half drunk the day before in a pot-house. Before we came with the corpse one of the company observed he wondered what sort of cue 'our Parson would be in.' NB it was the day after the Fair. I had not finished ironing till 7 o'clock. The wind was now high & I did not walk—writing my journal now at 8 o clock. Wm & John came home at 10 o clock.

*Thursday 4th September.* A fine warm day—I was busy all the morning making a mattrass. Mr Simpson called in the afternoon. Wm walked in the wood in the morning & in the evening as we set forward to walk a letter from Mrs Clarkson. We walked into the black quarter. The patches of corn very interesting.

*Friday Morning* [*5th*]. Finished the mattrass, ironed the white bed in the afternoon. When I was putting it up Mr & Mrs Losh arrived while Wm & John were walking.

*Saturday Morning 6th September.* Breakfasted with the Loshes —very warm—returned through Rydale woods. The Clarksons dined. After tea we walked round Rydale, a little rain.

*Sunday Morning 7th.* Rainy. Walked before dinner over the stepping stones to Langdale & home on the other side of the lake. I lay down after dinner. Wm poorly. Walked into the Black quarter.

*Monday Morning 8th September.* Very rainy. The Clarksons left us after dinner—still rainy. We walked towards Rydale, & then to Mr Olliff's gate a fine evening.

*Tuesday Morning 9th.* Mr Marshall came—he dined with us. My Brothers walked with him round the lakes after dinner— windy we went to the island. W & I after to tea. John & I went to the B quarter, before supper went to seek a horse at Dawsons—fir grove—After supper talked of Wms Poems.

*Wednesday Sept. 10th.* After Breakfast Mr Marshall, Wm & John went on horseback to Keswick—I wrote to Mrs Marshall—a fine autumn day. I had a fire. Paid Mr Bousfield 8–2–11. After tea walked with French Beans to Mr Simpsons —went up to the Forest side above a deserted house, sat till twilight came on. Mr & Miss S came down with me & supped.

*Thursday 11th.* All the morning mending white gown—washed my head—Molly washing. Drank tea at Mr Simpsons. Found Wm at home at my return he was unable to go on with Mr Marshall & parted from him in Borrowdale. Made tea after my return.

*Friday 12th Sept.* I worked in the morning cut my thumb. Walked in the Fir-grove before dinner—after dinner sate under the trees in the orchard. A rainy morning but very fine afternoon. Miss Simpson called for my packing needle. The Fern of the mountains now spreads yellow veins among the trees. The coppice wood turns brown. William observed some affecting little things in Borrowdale—a decayed house with this inscription [

            ] in the church-yard, the tall silent rocks seen thro' the broken windows—a kind of rough column put upon the gavel end of a house with a ball stone smooth from the river placed upon it for ornament—near it one stone like it upon an old mansion carefully hewn.

*Saturday Morning 13th September.* William writing his preface did not walk. Jones & Mr Palmer came to tea—we walked with them to Borricks—a lovely evening but the air frosty—worked when I returned home. Wm walked out. John came. horse from Mr Marshall sent backward to Mrs Clarkson.

*Sunday Morning 14th.* Made bread—a sore thumb from a cut —a lovely day—read Boswell in the house in the morning & after dinner under the bright yellow leaves of the orchard—the pear trees a bright yellow, the apple trees green still, a sweet lovely afternoon.

Here I have long neglected my Journal. John came home in the evening after Jones left us. Jones returned again on the Friday the 19th September—Jones stayed with us till Friday, 26th September. Coleridge came on Tuesday 23rd & went home with Jones. Charles Lloyd called on Tuesday 23rd, & on Sunday 27th we drank tea & supped with him, & on that day heard of the Abergavennys arrival. While Jones was with us we had much rainy weather. On Sunday the 21st Tom Myers & Father called, & on the 28th Mr & Miss Smith.

On Monday 29th John left us. Wm & I parted with him in

sight of Ulswater. It was a fine day, showery but with sunshine
& fine clouds—poor fellow my heart was right sad—I could
not help thinking we should see him again because he was only
going to Penrith.

On Tuesday 30th September Charles Lloyd dined with us.
We walked homewards with him after dinner. It rained very
hard. Rydale was extremely wild & we had a fine walk. We
sate quietly & comfortably by the fire. I wrote—the last sheet
of notes & preface—Went to bed at 12 o'clock.

*Wednesday 1st October.* A fine morning—a showery night the
lake still in the morning—in the forenoon flashing light from
the beams of the sun, as it was ruffled by the wind. We
corrected the last sheet.

*Thursday 2nd October.* A very rainy morning—We walked
after dinner to observe the torrents—I followed Wm to
Rydale, he afterwards went to Butterlip How. I came home to
receive the Lloyds. They walked with us to see Churnmilk
force & the Black quarter. The black quarter looked marshy,
& the general prospect was cold, but the Force was very
grand. The Lychens are now coming out afresh, I carried
home a collection in the afternoon. We had a pleasant
conversation about the manners of the rich—Avarice, inordinate desires, & the effeminacy unnaturalness & the unworthy
objects of education. After the Lloyds were gone we walked—
a showery evening. The moonlight lay upon the hills like
snow.

*Friday 3rd October.* Very rainy all the morning—little Sally
learning to mark. Wm walked to Ambleside after dinner. I
went with him part of the way—he talked much about the
object of his Essay for the 2nd volume of LB. I returned
expecting the Simpsons—they did not come. I should have
met Wm but my teeth ached & it was showery & late—he
returned after 10. Amos Cottle's death in the Morning Post.
wrote to S Lowthian.

N.B. When Wm & I returned from accompanying Jones we
met an old man almost double, he had on a coat thrown over
his shoulders above his waistcoat & coat. Under this he
carried a bundle & had an apron on & a night cap. His face
was interesting. He had Dark eyes & a long nose—John who

afterwards met him at Wythburn took him for a Jew. He was of Scotch parents but had been born in the army. He had had a wife '& a good woman & it pleased God to bless us with ten children'—all these were dead but one of whom he had not heard for many years, a Sailor—his trade was to gather leeches but now leeches are scarce & he had not strength for it —he lived by begging & was making his way to Carlisle where he should buy a few godly books to sell. He said leeches were very scarce partly owing to this dry season, but many years they have been scarce—he supposed it owing to their being much sought after, that they did not breed fast, & were of slow growth. Leeches were formerly 2/6 100; they are now 30/. He had been hurt in driving a cart his leg broke his body driven over his skull fractured—he felt no pain till he recovered from his first insensibility. It was then 'late in the evening—when the light was just going away.'

*Saturday October 4th 1800.* A very rainy, or rather showery & gusty morning for often the sun shines. Thomas Ashburner could not go to Keswick. Read a part of Lambs play. The language is often very beautiful, but too imitative in particular phrases, words &c. The characters except Margarets unintelligible, & except Margarets do not shew themselves in action. Coleridge came in while we were at dinner very wet.—We talked till 12 o clock—he had sate up all the night before writing Essays for the newspaper.—His youngest child had been very ill in convulsion fits. Exceedingly delighted with the 2nd part of Christabel.

*Sunday Morning 5th October.* Coleridge read a 2nd time Christabel—we had increasing pleasure. A delicious morning. Wm & I were employed all the morning in writing an addition to the preface. Wm went to bed very ill after working after dinner—Coleridge & I walked to Ambleside after dark with the letter. Returned to tea at 9 o'clock. Wm still in bed & very ill. Silver How in both lakes.

*Monday* [6th]. A rainy day—Coleridge intending to go but did not get off. We walked after dinner to Rydale. After tea read The Pedlar. Determined not to print Christabel with the LB.

*Tuesday* [7th]. Coleridge went off at 11 o clock—I went as far as Mr Simpson's returned with Mary. She drank tea here. I was very ill in the Evening at the Simpsons—went to bed—supped there. Returned with Miss S & Mrs J—heavy showers. Found Wm at home. I was still weak & unwell—went to bed immediately.

*Wednesday [8th]*. A threatening bad morning—We dried the Linen frequent threatenings of showers. Received a 5£ note from Montagu. Wm walked to Rydale. I copied a part of The Beggar in the morning—I was not quite well in the Evening therefore I did not walk—Wm walked a very mild moonlight night. Glowworms everywhere.

*Thursday [9th]*. I was ironing all the day till tea-time. Very rainy—Wm & I walked in the evening—intending to go to Lloyds but it came on so very rainy that we were obliged to shelter at Flemings. A grand Ball at Rydale. After sitting some time we went homewards & were again caught by a shower & sheltered under the Sycamores at the boat house—a very cold snowlike rain. A man called in a soldiers dress—he was thirty years old—of Cockermouth, had lost a leg & thigh in battle was going to his home. He could earn more money in travelling with his ass than at home.

*Friday 10th October*. In the morning when I arose the mists were hanging over the opposite hills & the tops of the highest hills were covered with snow. There was a most lovely combination at the head of the vale—of the yellow autumnal hills wrapped in sunshine, & overhung with partial mists, the green & yellow trees & the distant snow-topped mountains. It was a most heavenly morning. The Cockermouth Traveller came with thread hardware mustard, &c. She is very healthy, has travelled over the mountains these thirty years. She does not mind the storms if she can keep her goods dry. Her husband will not travel with an ass, because it is the tramper's badge—she would have one to relieve her from the weary load. She was going to Ulverston & was to return to Ambleside Fair. After I had finished baking I went out with Wm Mrs Jameson & Miss Simpson towards Rydale—the fern among the Rocks exquisitely beautiful—we turned home & walked to Mr Gells. After dinner Wm went to bed—I read Southey's letters. Miss Simpson & Mrs Jameson came to tea.

After tea we went to Lloyds—a fine Evening as we went but rained in returning—we were wet—found them not at home. I wrote to Mrs Clarkson—sent off The Beggar &c by Thomas Ashburner who went to fetch our 9th Cart of Coals. William sat up after me writing Point Rash judgment.

*Saturday 11th.* A fine October morning—sat in the house working all the morning. Wm composing—Sally Ashburner learning to mark. After Dinner we walked up Greenhead Gill in search of a Sheepfold. We went by Mr Ollifs & through his woods. It was a delightful day & the views looked excessively chearful & beautiful chiefly that from Mr Oliff's field where our house is to be built. The Colours of the mountains soft & rich, with orange fern—The Cattle pasturing upon the hill-tops Kites sailing as in the sky above our heads—Sheep bleating & in lines & chains & patterns scattered over the mountains. They come down & feed on the little green islands in the beds of the torrents & so may be swept away. The Sheepfold is falling away it is built nearly in the form of a heart unequally divided. Look down the brook & see the drops rise upwards & sparkle in the air, at the little falls, the higher sparkles the tallest. We walked along the turf of the mountain till we came to a Cattle track—made by the cattle which come upon the hills. We drank tea at Mr Simpson's returned at about nine—a fine mild night.

*Sunday 12th October.* Beautiful day. Sate in the house writing in the morning while Wm went into the Wood to compose. Wrote to John in the morning—copied poems for the LB, in the evening wrote to Mrs Rawson. Mary Jameson & Sally Ashburner dined. We pulled apples after dinner, a large basket full. We walked before tea by Bainriggs to observe the many coloured foliage the oaks dark green with yellow leaves —The birches generally still green, some near the water yellowish. The Sycamore crimson & crimson-tufted—the mountain ash a deep orange—the common ash Lemon colour but many ashes still fresh in their summer green. Those that were discoloured chiefly near the water. William composing in the Evening. Went to bed at 12 o clock.

*Monday October 13th.* A grey day—Mists on the hills. We did not walk in the morning. I copied poems on the naming of places a fair at Ambleside—walked in the black quarter at night.

*Tuesday 14th.* Wm lay down after dinner—I read Southeys Spain. The wind rose very high at Evening. Wm walked out just at bed time—I went to bed early. We walked before dinner to Rydale.

*Wednesday [15th].* A very fine clear morning. After Wm had composed a little, I persuaded him to go into the orchard—we walked backwards & forwards, the prospect most divinely beautiful from the seat—all colours, all melting into each other. I went in to put bread in the oven & we both walked within view of Rydale. Wm again composed at the sheep-fold after dinner—I walked with him to Wytheburn, & he went on to Keswick. I drank tea & supped at Mr Simpsons—a very cold frosty air, & a spangled sky in returning. Mr & Miss S came with me. Wytheburn looked very wintry but yet there was a foxglove blossoming by the road-side.

*Thursday 16th October.* A very fine morning—starched & hung out linen a very fine day—John Fisher, TA, SA & Molly working in the garden. Wrote to Miss Nicholson. I walked as far as Rydale between 3 & 4—Ironed till six—got tea & wrote to Mr Griffith. A letter from Mr Clarkson.

*Friday 17th.* A very fine grey morning. The swan hunt. Sally working in the garden. I walked round the lake between 1/4 past 12 & 1/2 past one—wrote to MH. After dinner I walked to Lloyds—carried my letters to Miss N & MH. The Lloyds not in—I waited for them. Charles not well. Letters from MH, Biggs & John. In my walk in the morning, I observed Benson's Honeysuckles in flower, & great beauty. It was a very fine mild evening. Ll's servants came with me to Parkes. I found Wm at home where he had been almost ever since my departure—Coleridge had done nothing for the LB—Working hard for Stuart. Glowworms in abundance.

*Saturday [18th].* A very fine October morning. William worked all the morning at the Sheep-fold but in vain. He lay down in the afternoon till 7 o clock but could not sleep—I slept. My head better—he unable to work. We did not walk all day.

*Sunday Morning [19th].* We rose late & walked directly after breakfast. The tops of G[ras]mere mountains cut off. Rydale was very very beautiful the surface of the water quite still like a dim mirror. The colours of the large island exquisitely beautiful & the trees still fresh & green were magnified by the mists. The prospects on the west side of the Lake were very beautiful, we sate at the two points looking up to Park's. The lowing of the Cattle was echoed by a hollow voice in Knab Scar. We went upon Loughrigg Fell—& were disappointed with G[ras]mere, it did not look near so beautiful as Rydale. We returned home over the stepping-stones Wm got to work —we are not to dine till 4 o clock— —Dined at ½ past 5—Mr Simpson dined & drank tea with us. We went to bed immediately after he left us.

*Monday 20th.* William worked in the morning at the sheep-fold. After dinner we walked to Rydale crossed the stepping stones & while we were walking under the tall oak trees the Lloyds called out to us. They went with us on the western side of Rydale. The lights were very grand upon the woody Rydale Hills. Those behind dark & topp'd with clouds. The two lakes were divinely beautiful—Grasmere excessively solemn & the whole lake was calm & dappled: with soft grey dapple—The Lloyds stayed with us till 8 o clock. We then walked to the top of the hill at Rydale—very mild & warm—about 6 glow-worms shining faintly. We went up as far as the grove. When we came home the fire was out. We ate our supper in the dark & went to bed immediately. William was disturbed in the night by the rain coming into his room, for it was a very rainy night. The Ash leaves lay across the Road.

*Tuesday 21st.* We walked in the morning past Mr Gells—a very fine clear & sharp sunny morning. We drank tea at the Lloyds—it was very cold in the evening quite frosty, & starlight. Wm had been unsuccessful in the morning at the sheep-fold. The reflection of the ash scattered, & the tree stripped.

*Wednesday Morning [22nd].* We walked to Mr Gells a very fine morning. Wm composed without much success at the Sheep-fold. Coleridge came in to dinner. He had done nothing. We were very merry. C. & I went to look at the prospect from his seat. In the evening Stoddart came in when we were at tea, &

after tea Mr & Miss Simpson with large potatoes & plumbs. Wm read after supper, Ruth &c—Coleridge Christabel.

*Thursday 23rd.* Coleridge & Stoddart went to Keswick—we accompanied them to Wytheburn. A wintry grey morning from the top of the Rays Grasmere looked like winter & Wytheburn still more so—We called upon Mrs Simpson & sate 10 minutes in returning. Wm was not successful in composition in the Evening.

*Friday 24th.* A very fine morning we walked before Wm began to work to the Top of the Rydale Hill. He was afterwards only partly successful in composition. After dinner we walked round Rydale Lake, rich, calm, streaked, very beautiful. We went to the top of Loughrigg—Grasmere sadly inferior. We were much tired Wm went to bed till ½ past seven. The ash in our garden green, one close to it bare the next nearly so.

*Saturday [25th].* A very rainy day. Wm again unsuccessful. We could not walk it was so very rainy. We read Rogers, Miss Seward, Cowper &c.

*Sunday [26th].* Heavy rain all night. A fine morning after 10 o clock. Wm composed a good deal—in the morning. The Lloyds came to dinner & were caught in a shower. Wm read some of his poems after dinner—a terrible night I went with Mrs Lloyd to Newtons to see for Lodgings. Mr Simpson in coming from Ambleside called in for a glass of rum, just before we went to bed.

*28th October, Monday [27th].* Not fine a rainy morning. The Hill tops covered with snow. Charles Lloyd came for his wife's glass. I walked home with him past Rydale. When he came I met him as I was carrying some cold meat to Wm in the Firgrove. I had before walked with him there for some time. It was a fine shelter from the wind. The Coppices now nearly of one brown. An oak tree in a sheltered place near John Fisher's —not having lost any of its leaves was quite brown & dry. We did not walk after dinner—it was a fine wild moonlight night. Wm could not compose much fatigued himself with altering.

*Tuesday 29th [28th].* A very rainy night. I was baking bread in the morning & made a giblet pie. We walked out before dinner to our favorite field. The mists sailed along the mountains & rested upon them enclosing the whole vale. In the evening the Lloyds came. We drank tea with them at Borricks & played a rubber at Whist, stayed supper—Wm looked very well. A fine moonlight night when we came home.

*Wednesday* [*29th*]. William working at his poem all the morning. After dinner Mr Clarkson called—We went down to Borrwicks & he & the Lloyds & Priscilla came back to drink tea with us. We met Stoddart upon the Bridge—Played at Cards. The Lloyds &c went home to supper—Mr Clarkson slept here.

*Thursday* [*30th*]. A rainy morning. Mr C went over Kirkstone. Wm talked all day & almost all night with Stoddart. Mrs & Miss Ll called in the morning I walked with them to Tail End—a fine pleasant morning but a very rainy afternoon. W & S in the house all day.

*Friday* [*31st*]. W & S did not rise till 1 o clock. W very sick & very ill. S & I drank tea at Lloyds & came home immediately after, a very fine moonlight night—The moonshine like herrings in the water.

*Saturday* [*1st*]. William better. We met as we walked to Rydale a Boy from Lloyds, coming for Don Quixote. Talk in the evening. Tom Ashburner brought our 10th Cart of coals.

*Sunday Morning* [*2nd*]. We walked into the Black Quarter a very fine morning, a succession of beautiful views mists &c &c. Much rain in the night. In the Evening drank tea at Lloyds—found them all ill in colds came home to supper.

*Monday Morning* [*3rd*]. Walked to Rydale a cold day. Wm & Stoddart still talking, frequent showers in our walk. In the evening we talked merrily over the fire. The Speddings stopped at the door.

*Tuesday* [*4th*]. Stoddart left us—I walked a little way with W & him, W went to the Tarn afterwards to the top of Seat Sandal—he was obliged to lie down in the tremendous wind—the snow blew from Helvellyn horizontally like smoke—the Spray of the unseen Waterfall like smoke— —Miss Lloyd called upon me—I walked with her past Rydale. Wm sadly tired, threatenings of the piles.

*Wednesday* [*5th*]. Wm not well. A very fine beautiful clear

winter's day. I walked after dinner to Lloyds—drank tea &
Mrs & Miss Lloyd came to Rydale with me—the moon was
rising but the sky all over cloud. I made tea for William. Piles.

*Thursday 6th November.* A very rainy morning & night—I was
baking bread dinner & parkins. Charles & P Lloyd called—
Wm somewhat better read Point Rash Judgment. The lake
calm & very beautiful a very rainy afternoon & night.

*Friday 7th November.* A cold rainy morning Wm still unwell. I
working & reading Amelia. The Michaelmas daisy droops.
The pansies are full of flowers. The Ashes opposite are green,
all but one but they have lost many of their leaves. The copses
are quite brown. The poor woman & child from Whitehaven
drank tea—nothing warm that day. Friday 7th. A very rainy
morning—it cleared up in the afternoon. We expected the
Lloyds but they did not come. Wm still unwell. A rainy night.

*Saturday 8th November.* A rainy morning—a whirlwind came
that tossed about the leaves & tore off the still green leaves of
the Ashes. A fine afternoon. Wm & I walked out at 4 o clock—
went as far as Rothay Bridge met the Butcher's man with a
l[ette]r from Monk Lewis. The country very wintry—some
oaks quite bare—others more sheltered with a few green
leaves, others with brown leaves—but the whole face of the
country in a winter covering. We went early to bed.

*Sunday* [*9th*]. Wm slept tolerably—better this morning. It
was a frosty night. We walked to Rydale after dinner, partly
expecting to meet the Lloyds. Mr Simpson brought newspapers but met Molly with them—W burnt the sheep fold—a
rainy night.

*Monday* [*10th*]. I baked bread a fine clear frosty morning. We
walked after dinner—to Rydale village. Jupiter over the Hill-
tops, the only star like a sun flashed out at intervals from
behind a black cloud.

*Tuesday Morning* [*11th*]. Walked to Rydale before dinner for
letters. William had been working at the sheep-fold. They
were salving sheep—a rainy morning. The Lloyds drank tea
with us. Played at Cards—Priscilla not well. We walked after
they left us to the Top of the Rydale Hill then towards Mr
Ollifs & towards the village. A mild night partly cloudy partly
starlight. The cottage lights the mountains not very distinct.

*Wednesday* [*12th*]. We sate in the house all the day. Mr Simpson called & found us at dinner—a rainy evening he staid the evening & supper—I lay down after dinner with a headach.

*Thursday* [*13th*]. A stormy night. We sate in the house all the morning rainy weather. Old Mr Simpson, Mrs J & Miss S. drank tea & supped played at cards, found us at dinner—a poor woman from Hawkshead begged—a widow of Grasmere —a merry African from Longtown.

*Friday* [*14th*]. I had a bad head-ach. Much wind but a sweet mild morning. I nailed up trees. Sent Molly Ashburner to excuse us to Lloyds. 2 letters from Coleridge—very ill. One from Sara H, one from S Lothian—I wrote to S Hutchinson & received 3£ from her.

*Saturday Morning* [*15th*]. A terrible rain so Wm prevented from going to Coleridges. The afternoon fine & mild I walked to the top of the hill for a head-ach. We both set forward at 5 o clock after tea—a fine wild but not cold night. I walked with him over the Rays—it was starlight. I parted with him very sad unwilling not to go on. The hills & the stars & the white waters with their ever varying yet ceaseless sound were very impressive. I supped at the Simpsons. Mr S. walked home with me.

*Sunday 16th November.* A very fine warm sunny morning, a Letter from Coleridge & one from Stoddart—Coleridge better — —My head aching very much I sent to excuse myself to Lloyds—then walked to the Cottage beyond Mr Gell's. One beautiful ash tree sheltered with yellow leaves—one low one quite green—some low ashes green—A noise of boys in the rocks hunting some animal. Walked a little in the garden when I came home, very pleasant. Now rain came on. Mr Jackson called in the evening when I was at tea brought me a letter from C & W—C better.

*Monday Morning* [*17th*]. A fine clear frosty morning with a sharp wind. I walked to Keswick, set off at 5 minutes past 10, & arrived at ½ past 2. I found them all well.

On Tuesday morning W & C set off towards Penrith. Wm met Sara Hutchinson at Threlkeld—they arrived at Keswick at tea-time.

*Wednesday [19th].* We walked by the lake side & they went to Mr Denton's. I called upon the Miss Cockyns.

*Thursday [20th].* We spent the morning in the Town. Mr Jackson & Mr Peach dined with us.

*Friday [21st].* A very fine day. Went to Mrs Greaves. Mrs C & I called upon the Speddings—a beautiful Crescent moon.

*Saturday Morning [22nd].* After visiting Mr Peaches Chinese pictures we set off to Grasmere—a threatening & rather rainy morning. Arrived at G—very dirty & a little wet at the closing in of Evening. Wm not quite well.

*Sunday [23rd].* Wm not well. I baked bread & pie for dinner. Sarah & I walked after dinner & met Mr Gawthorpe, paid his bill & he drank tea with us paid 5£ for Mr Bousfield.

*Monday [24th].* A fine morning. Sara & I walked to Rydale. After dinner we went to Lloyds & drank tea & supped—a sharp cold night with sleet & snow. I had the tooth-ach in the night—took Laudanum.

*Tuesday [25th].* Very ill—in bed all day—better in the Evening I read Tom Jones—very sleepy slept all night.

*Wednesday [26th].* Well in the morning—Wm very well. We had a delightful walk up into Eastdale. The Tops of the Mountains covered with snow—frosty & sunny—the roads slippery A letter from Mary. The Lloyds drank tea. We walked with them near to Ambleside, a beautiful moonlight night—Sara & I walked before home,—William very well & highly poetical.

*Thursday 27th November.* Wrote to Tom Hutchinson to desire him to bring Mary with him from Stockton—a thaw & the ground covered with snow. Sara & I walked before dinner.

*Friday [28th].* Coleridge walked over. Miss Simpson drank tea with us. William walked home with her. Coleridge was very unwell—he went to bed before Wm's return. Great Boils upon his neck.

*Saturday [29th].* A fine day.

*Sunday 29th November [30th].* A very fine clear morning. Snow upon the ground everywhere. Sara & I walked towards Rydale by the upper road & were obliged to return—because of the snow walked by moonlight.

*Monday [1st].* A thaw in the night & the snow was entirely

gone. Sara & I had a delighttul walk by the upper Rydale Road & Mr King's. Coleridge unable to go home for his health. We walked by moonlight. Baking day little loaves.

*Tuesday December 2nd.*—A Rainy morning—Coleridge was obliged to set off. Sara & I met C Lloyd & P—turned back with them. I walked round the 2 lakes with Charles very pleasant—passing lights—I was sadly wet when we came home & very cold. Priscilla drank tea with us—we all walked to Ambleside—a pleasant moonlight evening but not clear. Supped upon a hare—it came on a terrible evening hail & wind & cold & rain.

*Wednesday December 3rd.* We lay in bed till 11 o clock. Wrote to John & MH—William & Sara & I walked to Rydale after tea—a very fine frosty night. Sara & W walked round the other side—I was tired & returned home. We went to bed early.

*Thursday [4th].* Coleridge came in just as we finished dinner —Pork from the Simpsons. Sara & I walked round the 2 lakes —a very fine morning. C. ate nothing to cure his boils. We walked after tea by moonlight to look at Langdale covered with snow—the pikes not grand, but the old man very impressive—cold & slippery but exceedingly pleasant. Sat up till ½ past one.

*Friday Morning [5th].* Terribly cold & rainy Coleridge & Wm set forward towards Keswick but the wind in Coleridge's eyes made him turn back. Sara & I had a grand bread & cake baking we were very merry in the evening but grew sleepy soon tho' we did not go to bed till 12 o clock.

*Saturday [6th].* Wm accompanied Coleridge to the foot of the Rays—a very pleasant morning—Sara & I accompanied him half way to Keswick. Thirlemere was very beautiful—even more so than in summer. William was not well had laboured unsuccessfully. Charles Lloyd had called. Sara & I drank tea with Mrs Simpson. A sharp shower met us—it rained a little when we came home. Mr BS accompanied us—Miss S at Ambleside. William tired & not well. A letter from MH.

*Sunday [7th].* A fine morning. I read. Sara wrote to Hartley, Wm to Mary, I to Mrs C. We walked just before dinner to the Lake-side & found out a seat in a tree windy but pleasant.

Sara & Wm walked to the waterfalls at Rydale. I was unwell & went to bed till 8 o clock—a pleasant mild evening. Went to bed at 12. Miss Simpson called.

*Monday 8th December.* A sweet mild morning—I wrote to Mrs Cookson & Miss Griffith.

*Tuesday 9th.* I dined at Lloyds—Wm drank tea walked home a pleasant starlight frosty evening—reached home at one o clock. Wm finished his poem today.

*Wednesday 10th.* Walked to Keswick. Snow upon the ground. A very fine day ate bread & ale at John Stanley's. Found Coleridge better. Stayed at Keswick till Sunday 14th December.

*Monday [15th].* Baking & starching.

*Tuesday [16th].* Ironing—the Lloyds called.

*Wednesday [17th].* A very fine day—Writing all the morning for William.

*Thursday [18th].* Mrs Coleridge & Derwent came—sweeping chimneys.

*Friday [19th].* Baking.

*Saturday [20th].* Coleridge came—very ill rheumatic, fever-ish. Rain—incessantly.

*Monday [22nd].* S & Wm went to Lloyds. Wm dined, it rained very hard when he came home at . . .

## II. *10 October 1801 to 14 February 1802*

*Saturday 10th October 1801.* Coleridge went to Keswick after we had built Sara's seat.

*Sunday 11th.* Mr & Miss Simpson came in after tea & supped with us.

*Monday 12th.* We drank tea at Mr Simpson's.

*Tuesday 13th.* A thorough wet day.

*Thursday 15th.* We dined at Mr Luffs—a rainy morning. Coleridge came into Mr L's while we were at dinner. Wm & I walked up Loughrigg Fell then by the waterside. I held my head under a spout very sick & ill when I got home—went to bed in the sitting room took laudanum.

*Friday 16th.* Tom Hutchinson came—it rained almost all day—Coleridge poorly.

*Saturday 17th.* We walked into Easedale. Coleridge poorly after dinner.

*Sunday 18th.* I have forgotten.

*Monday 19th.* Coleridge went home. Tom & William walked to Rydale a very fine day. I was ill in bed all day. Mr Simpson tea & supper.

*Tuesday 20th.* We went to the Langdales & Colleth a very fine day—a heavy shower in the afternoon in Langdale.

*Wednesday 21st.* Dined at Bowness, slept at penny bridge—in danger of being cast away on Windermere. A very fine day, but windy a little—a moonlight night.

*Thursday 22nd.* Breakfasted at Penny Bridge dined at Coniston—a grand stormy day—drank tea at home.

*Friday 23rd.* A sweet delightful morning. I planted all sorts of plants, Tom helped me. He & W then rode to Hawkshead. I baked bread & pies. Tom brought me 2 shrubs from Mr Curwen's nursery.

*Saturday 24th.* Attempted Fairfield but misty & we went no further than Green Head Gill to the sheepfold—mild misty beautiful soft. Wm & Tom put out the Boat brought the coat from Mr Luff's. Mr Simpson came in at dinner-time—drank tea with us & played at cards.

*Sunday 25th.* Rode to Legberthwaite with Tom—expecting Mary—sweet day—went upon Helvellyn, glorious glorious sights—The sea at Cartmel—The Scotch mountains beyond the sea to the right—Whiteside large & round & very soft & green behind us. Mists above & below & close to us, with the Sun amongst them—they shot down to the coves. Left John Stanely's at 10 minutes past 12 returned thither ¼ past 4— drank tea ate heartily—before we went on Helvellyn we got bread & cheese—paid 4/- for the whole—reached home at 9 o clock a soft grey evening—the light of the moon but she did not shine on us.

*Monday 26th October.* Omitted. They went to Buttermere.

*Tuesday 27th October.* Omitted, drank tea at Mr Simpsons.

*Wednesday 28th.* The Clarksons came.

*Thursday 29th.* Rain all day.

*Friday 30th.* Rain all day.

*Saturday 31st*. We walked to Rydale a soft & mild morning but threatening for rain.

*Sunday Nov[embe]r 1st*. Very cold—we walked in the evening to Butterlip How.

*Monday 2nd*. Very rainy.

*Tuesday 3rd*. We dined at Lloyds cold & clear day.

*Wedenesday 4th*. Mr C & Wm rode out—very cold.

*Thursday [5th]*. [The Clarksons] left us.

*Friday [6th]*. [Coleridge] came.

[*Monday 9th*.] [Walked with Coleridge to Keswick.] . . . the mountains for ever varying, now hid in the Clouds & now with their tops visible while perhaps they were half concealed below —Legberthwaite beautiful. We ate Bread & Cheese at John Stanleys & reached Keswick without fatigue just before Dark. We enjoyed ourselves in the study & were *at home*. Supped at Mr Jacksons. Mary & I sate in C's room a while.

*Tuesday 10th*. Poor C left us & we came home together. We left Keswick at 2 o'clock & did not arrive at G till 9 0 clock— drank tea at John Stanleys very comfortably. I burnt myself with Coleridge's Aquafortis. Mary's feet sore. C had a sweet day for his ride—every sight & every sound reminded me of him dear dear fellow—of his many walks to us by day & by night—of all dear things. I was melancholy & could not talk, but at last I eased my heart by weeping—nervous blubbering says William. It is not so—O how many, many reasons have I to be anxious for him.

*Wednesday 11th*. Baked bread & giblet pie put books in order —mended stockings, put aside dearest C's letters & now at about 7 o'clock we are all sitting by a nice fire—W with his book & a Candle & Mary writing to Sara.

*Thursday 12th*. A beautiful still sunshiny morning. We rose very late. I put the rag Boxes into order. We walked out while the Goose was roasting—we walked to the top of the Hill. M & I followed Wm he was walking upon the Turf between John's Grove & the Lane—it was a most sweet noon—we did not go into John's Grove but we walked among the Rocks & there we sate. Mr Olliff passed Mary & me upon the Road Wm still among the Rocks. The Lake beautiful from the

Orchard. Wm & I walked out before tea—The Crescent moon
—we sate in the Slate quarry I sate there a long time alone.
Wm reached home before me—I found them at Tea. There
were a thousand stars in the Sky.

*Friday Morning* [*13th*]. Dullish, damp & cloudy—a day that
promises not to dry our clothes— —We spent a happy
evening—went to bed late—& had a restless night, Wm
better than I expected.

*Saturday Morning* [*14th*]. Still a cloudy dull day, very dark. I
lay in bed all the Day very unwell, they made me some broth
& I rose better after it was dark. We spent a quiet evening by
the fire.

*Sunday* [*15th*]. I walked in the morning to Churnmilk Force
nearly, & went upon Heifer crags. The valley of its winter
yellow, but the bed of the brook still in some places almost
*shaded* with leaves—the oaks brown in general but one that
might be almost called green—the whole prospect was very
soft & the distant view down the vale very impressive, a long
vale down to Ambleside—the hills at Ambleside in mist &
sunshine—all else grey. We sate by the fire & read Chaucer
(Thomson, Mary read) & Bishop Hall. Letters from Sara &
Mrs Clarkson late at night.

*Monday 16th November*. A very dankish misty, wettish
morning—Mary & Molly ironed all day. I made bread &
called at Mr Olliffs—Mrs O at home—the prospect soft from
the windows. Mrs O observed that it was beautiful *even* in
winter! The Luffs passed us. We walked backwards &
forwards in the Church field. Wm somewhat weakish, but
upon the whole pretty well—he is now at 7 o clock reading
Spenser, Mary is writing beside me. The little Syke murmurs.
We are quiet & happy, but poor Peggy Ashburner is very ill &
in pain. She coughs as if she would cough her life away. I am
going to write to Coleridge & Sara. Poor C! I hope he was in
London yesterday. Molly has been very witty with Mary all
day. She says 'Ye may say what ye will but there's nothing like
a gay auld man for behaving weel to a young wife. Ye may
laugh but this wind blows no favour—& where there's no love
there's no favour.' On Sunday I lectured little John Dawson
for telling lies. I told him I had heard that he charged Jenny

Baty falsely with having beaten him. Says Molly—'she says it's not so that she never lifted hand till him, & she *should* speak truth you would think in her condition'—She is with child. Two Beggars today.

*Tuesday 17th.* A very rainy morning we walked into Easedale before dinner. Miss S. came in at dinner time—we went to Mr Gell's cottage—then returned the coppices a beautiful brown the oaks having a very fine leafy shade. We stood a long time to look at the corner Birch tree, the wind was among the light thin twigs & they yielded to it this way & that. Drank tea & supped at the Simpsons a moonlight wettish night dirty roads.

*Wednesday 18th.* We sate in the house in the morning reading Spenser. I was unwell & lay in bed all the afternoon. Wm & Mary walked to Rydale—very pleasant moonlight the Lakes beautiful. The church an image of Peace—Wm wrote some lines upon it. I in bed when they came home. Mary & I walked as far as Saras Gate before Supper—we stood there a long time, the whole scene impressive, the mountains indistinct the Lake calm & partly ruffled—large Island, a sweet sound of water falling into the quiet Lake. A storm was gathering in Easedale so we returned but the moon came out & opened to us the Church & village. Helm Crag in shade, the larger Mountains Dappled like a sky—we stood long upon the bridge. Wished for Wm—he had stayed at home being sickish —found him better. We went to bed.

*Thursday 19th Nov[embe]r.*—A beautiful sunny, frosty morning. We did not walk all day. Wm said he would put it off till the fine moonlight night & then it came on a heavy rain & wind. Charles & Olivia Lloyd called in the morning.

*Friday 20th.* I wrote to Coleridge in the morning. We walked in the morning to Easedale. In the evening we had chearful letters from Coleridge & Sara.

*Saturday 21st.* We walked in the morning & payed one pound & 4d for letters. William out of spirits. We had a pleasant walk & spent a pleasant evening. There was a furious wind & cold at night. Mr Simpson drank tea with us & helped William out with the Boat. Wm & Mary walked to the Swan homewards with him. A keen clear frosty night—I went into the orchard while they were out.

*Sunday 22nd.*—We wrote to Coleridge—sent our letter by the Boy. Mr & Miss Simpson came in at tea time we went with them to the Blacksmiths & returned by Butterlip How—a frost & wind with bright moonshine. The vale looked spacious & very beautiful—the level meadows seemed very large, & some nearer us, unequal ground heaving like Sand—the Cottages beautiful & quiet, we passed one near which stood a cropped ash with upright forked Branches like the Devils horns frightening a guilty conscience. We were happy & chearful when we came home—we went early to bed.

*Monday 23rd.* A beautiful frosty morning. Mary was making Williams woollen waistcoat. Wm unwell & did not walk. Mary & I sate in our cloaks upon the Bench in the Orchard. After dinner I went to bed unwell—Mary had a head-ach at night—we all went to bed soon.

*Tuesday 24th.* A rainy morning. We all were well except that my head ached a little & I took my Breakfast in bed. I read a little of Chaucer, prepared the goose for dinner, & then we all walked out—I was obliged to return for my fur tippet & Spenser it was so cold. We had intended going to Easedale but we shaped our course to Mr Gell's cottage. It was very windy & we heard the wind everywhere about us as we went along the Lane but the walls sheltered us—John Greens house looked pretty under Silver How—as we were going along we were stopped at once, at the distance perhaps of 50 yards from our favorite Birch tree it was yielding to the gusty wind with all its tender twigs, the sun shone upon it & it glanced in the wind like a flying sunshiny shower—it was a tree in shape with stem & branches but it was like a Spirit of water—The sun went in & it resumed its purplish appearance the twigs still yielding to the wind but not so visibly to us. The other Birch trees that were near it looked bright & chearful—but it was a Creature by its own self among them. We could not get into Mr Gells grounds—the old tree fallen from its undue exaltation above the Gate. A shower came on when we were at Bensons. We went through the wood—it became fair, there was a rainbow which spanned the lake from the Island house to the foot of Bainriggs. The village looked populous & beautiful. Catkins are coming out palm trees budding—the

alder with its plumb coloured buds. We came home over the
stepping stones the Lake was foamy with white waves. I saw a
solitary butter flower in the wood. *I* found it not easy to get
over the stepping stones—reached home at dinner time. Sent
Peggy Ashburner some goose. She sent me some honey—with
a thousand thanks—'alas the gratitude of men has &c' I went
in to set her right about this & sate a while with her. She
talked about Thomas's having sold his land—'Ay' says she I
said many a time 'He's not come fra London to buy our Land
however' then she told me with what pains & industry they
had made up their taxes interest &c &c—how they all got up
at 5 o clock in the morning to spin & Thomas carded, & that
they had paid off a hundred pound of the interest. She said she
used to take such pleasure in the cattle & sheep—'O how
pleased I used to be when they fetched them down, & when I
had been a bit poorly I would gang out upon a hill & look
ower t' fields & see them & it used to do me so much good you
cannot think'—Molly said to me when I came in 'poor Body!
she's very ill but one does not know how long she may last.
Many a fair face may gang before her.' We sate by the fire
without work for some time then Mary read a poem of Daniell
upon Learning. After tea Wm read Spenser now & then a little
aloud to us. We were making his waistcoat. We had a note
from Mrs C, with bad news from poor C very ill. William
walked to John's grove—I went to meet him—moonlight but
it rained. I met him before I had got as far as John Batys he
had been surprized & terrified by a sudden rushing of winds
which seemed to bring earth sky & lake together, as if the
whole were going to enclose him in—he was glad that he was
in a high Road.

In speaking of our walk on Sunday Evening the 22nd
November I forgot to notice one most impressive sight—it was
the moon & the moonlight seen through hurrying driving
clouds immediately behind the Stone man upon the top of the
hill on the Forest side. Every tooth & every edge of Rock was
visible, & the Man stood like a Giant watching from the Roof
of a lofty Castle. The hill seemed perpendicular from the
darkness below it. It was a sight that I could call to mind at
any time it was so distinct.

*Wednesday 25th November*. It was a showery morning & threatened to be a wettish day, but the sun shone once or twice. We were engaged to the Lloyds & Wm & Mary were determined to go that it might be over. I accompanied them to the Thorn beside Rydale Water. I parted from them first at the top of the hill & they called me back.—it rained a little & rained afterwards all the afternoon. I baked pies & bread, & wrote to Sara Hutchinson & Coleridge—I passed a pleasant evening but the wind roared so & it was such a storm that I was afraid for them. They came in at nine o'clock no worse for their walk & chearful blooming & happy.

*Thursday 26th*. Mr Olliff called before Wm was up to say that they would drink tea with us this afternoon. We walked into Easedale to gather mosses & to fetch cream. I went for the cream & they sate under a wall. It was piercing cold, & a hail Storm came on in the afternoon. The Olliffs arrived at 5 o clock—we played at Cards & passed a decent evening. It was a very still night but piercing cold when they went away at 11 o clock—a shower came on.

*Friday 27th*. Snow upon the ground thinly scattered. It snowed after we got up & then the sun shone & it was very warm though frosty—now the Sun shines sweetly. A woman came who was travelling with her husband he had been wounded & was going with her to live at Whitehaven. She had been at Ambleside the night before, offered 4d at the Cock for a bed—they sent her to one Harrison's where she & her husband had slept upon the hearth & bought a pennyworth of Chips for a fire. Her husband was gone before very lame— 'Aye' says she 'I was once an officers wife I, as you see me now. My first Husband married me at Appleby I had 18£ a year for teaching a school & because I had no fortune his father turned him out of doors. I have been in the West Indies —I lost the use of this Finger just before he died he came to me & said he must bid farewell to his dear children & me—I had a Muslin gown on like yours—I seized hold of his coat as he went from me & slipped the joint of my finger—He was shot directly. I came to London & married this man. He was clerk to Judge Chambray, *that man* that man thats going on the Road now. If he, Judge Chambray, had been at Kendal he

would [have] given us a guinea or two & made nought of it, for
he is very generous.' Before dinner we set forward to walk
intending to return to dinner. But as we had got as far as
Rydale Wm thought he would go on to Mr Luffs we
accompanied him under Loughrigg, & parted near the
stepping stones—it was very cold. Mary & I walked quick
home. There was a fine gleam of Sunshine upon the eastern
side of Ambleside Vale, we came up the old road & turning
round we were struck with the appearance. Mary wrote to her
aunt. We expected the Simpsons. I was sleepy & weary &
went to bed—before tea. It came on wet in the Evening & was
very cold. We expected letters from C & Sara—Sara's came
by the Boy. But none from C—a sad disappointment. We did
not go to meet Wm as we had intended—Mary was at work at
Wms warm waistcoat.

*Saturday 28th November.*—A very fine sunny morning. Soldiers still going by—I should have mentioned that yesterday
when we went with Wm to Mr Luff's we met a soldier & his
wife, he with a child in his arms, she carrying a bundle & his
gun—we gave them some halfpence it was such a pretty sight.
William having slept ill lay in bed till after one o'clock. Mary
& I walked up to Mr Simpsons between 20 minutes before 2 &
20 minutes before 3 to desire them not to come—we drank tea
& supped at Mr Olliffs—a keen frost with sparkling stars
when we came home at ½ past 11.

*Sunday 29th.* Baking bread apple pies, & Giblet pie—a bad
giblet pie—it was a most beautiful morning. George Olliff
brought Wm's stick. The sun shone all the day—but we never
walked. In the evening we had intended going for letters but
the Lad said he would go. We sate up till after one—no letters!
—very cold—hard frost.

*Monday 30th.* A fine sharp morning. The Lad brought us a
Letter from Montague & a short one from Coleridge—C very
well—promised to write tomorrow. We walked round the
Lake Wm & Mary went first over the stepping stones. I
remained after them & went into the prospect field above
Benson's to sit—Mary joined me there—clear & frosty
without wind. William went before to look at Langdale—we
saw the pikes & then came home. They have cropped the tree

which overshadowed the gate beside that cottage at the turning of the hill which used to make a frame for Loughrigg Tarn & Windermere. We came home & read. Mary wrote to Joanna—I wrote to Richard, & Mrs Coleridge.

*Tuesday 1st December 1801.* A fine sunny & frosty morning. Mary & I walked to Rydale for letters, William was not well & staid at home reading after having lain long in bed. We found a Letter from Coleridge, a short one—he was pretty well. We were overtaken by two soldiers on our return—one of them being very drunk we wished them to pass us, but they had too much liquor in them to go very fast so we contrived to pass them—they were very merry & very civil. They fought with the mountains with their sticks. Aye says one, that will upon us—One might stride over that &c. They never saw such a wild country though one of them was a Scotchman—they were honest looking fellows—The Corporal said he was frightened to see the Road before them. We met Wm at Sara's gate, he went back intending to go round the lake but having attempted to cross the water & not succeeding he came back. The Simpsons Mr & Miss drank tea with us—Wm was very poorly & out of spirits. They stayed supper.

*Wednesday 2nd.* A fine grey frosty morning. Wm rose late. I read the tale of Phœbus & the Crow which he afterwards attempted to translate & did translate a large part of it today. Mrs Olliff brought us some yeast & made us promise to go there the next day to meet the Luffs. We were sitting by the fire in the evening when Charles & Olivia Lloyd came in. I had not been very well so I did not venture out with them when they went away—Mary & William went as far as Rydale village, it snowed after it was dark, & there was a thin covering over the ground which made it light & soft. They looked fresh & well when they came in. I wrote part of a letter to Coleridge. After his return William went on a little with Chaucer.

*Thursday 3rd December 1801.* I was not well in the morning. We baked bread—after dinner I went to bed—William walked into Easedale. Rain, hail & snow. I rose at ½ past 7, got tea, then went to sup at Mr Olliffs—I had a glorious sleep & was quite well. A light night roads very slippery—we spent a pleasant evening—Mr & Mrs Luff there—Mrs L poorly. I wrote a little bit of my letter to Coleridge before I went to Mr O's. We went to bed immediately after our return—Molly gone.

*Friday 4th.* My head bad & I lay long. Mrs Luff called— Mary went with her to the Slate quarry. Mr Simpson & Charles Lloyd called for the yeast Receipt. William translating the Prioress's tale. William & Mary walked after tea to Rydale —it snowed & rained & they came in wet. I finished the Letter to Coleridge & we received a letter from him & Sara. S's letter written in good spirits—C's also. A letter of Lambs about George Dyer with it.

*Saturday 5th.* My head bad & I lay long. Mr Luff called before I rose—we put off walking in the morning: dull & misty & grey very rainy in the afternoon & we could not go out— William finished the Prioress's tale, & after tea Mary & he wrote it out Wm not well.—No parcel from Mrs Coleridge.

*Sunday 6th.* A very fine beautiful sunshiny morning— William worked a while at Chaucer then we set forward to walk into Easedale. We met Mr & Mrs Olliff who were going to call upon us. They turned back with us & we parted at the White Bridge. We went up in to Easedale & walked backwards & forwards in that flat field which makes the second circle of Easedale with that beautiful Rock in the field beside us & all the rocks & the woods &c the mountains enclosing us round. The Sun was shining among them, the snow thinly scattered upon the tops of the mountains. In the afternoon we sate by the fire—I read Chaucer aloud, & Mary read the first Canto of the Fairy Queen. After tea Mary & I walked to Ambleside for letters—reached home by 11 o clock —we had a sweet walk, it was a sober starlight evening, the stars not shining as it were with all their brightness when they were visible & sometimes hiding themselves behind small greyish clouds that passed soberly along. We opened C's letter at Wilcocks door we thought we saw that he wrote in good spirits so we came happily homewards where we arrived 2 hours after we left home. It was a sad melancholy letter & prevented us all from sleeping.

*Monday Morning 7th.* We rose by candlelight, a showery

unpleasant morning after a downright rainy night we determined however to go to Keswick if possible, & we set off at a
little after 9 o'clock. When we were upon the Rays it snowed
very much & the whole prospect closed in upon us like a
moorland valley upon a moor—very wild—but when we were
at the top of the Rays we saw the mountains before us the sun
shone upon them here & there & Wytheburn vale though wild
looked soft. The rain went on chearfully & pleasantly now &
then a hail shower attacked us but we kept up a good heart for
Mary is a famous Jockey—We met Miss Barcroft—she had
been unwell in the '*Liverpool* complaint' & was riding out for
the benefit of her health. She had not seen Mrs C 'The weather
had been such as to preclude all intercourse between
neighbours'—. We reached Greta Hall at about one o clock.
Met Mrs C in the field, Derwent in the cradle asleep, Hartley
at his dinner—Derwent pale the image of his Father, Hartley
well. We wrote to C. Mrs C left us at ½ past 2—we drank tea
by ourselves, the children playing about us. Mary said to
Hartley, Shall I take Derwent with me? No says H I cannot
spare my little Brother in the sweetest tone possible & he can't
Do without his Mama. Well says Mary, why cannot I be his
Mama. Can't he have more Mamas than one? No says H.
What for? because they do not love as Mothers do. What is the
difference between Mothers & Mamas, looking at his sleeves,
Mothers wear sleeves like this pulling his own tight down &
Mamas (pulling them up & making a bustle about his
shoulders) so—. We parted from them at 4 o clock. It was a
little of the Dusk when we set off. Cotton mills lighted up—the
first star at Nadel fell, but it was never dark—we rode very
briskly snow upon the Rays—reached home far sooner than
we expected, at 7 o clock. William at work with Chaucer, The
God of Love sate latish—I wrote a little to C.

  *Tuesday 8th November* [*December*] 1801. A dullish rainyish
morning. Wm at work with Chaucer. I read Bruce's Lochleven & Life. Going to bake bread & pies, after dinner I felt
myself unwell having not slept well in the night so, after we
had put up the Book cases which Charles Lloyd sent us I lay
down I did not sleep much but I rose refreshed. Mary &
William walked to the Boat house at Rydale while he [I] was

in bed. It rained very hard all night—no company Wm worked at the Cuckow & the Nightingale till he was tired, Mary very sleepy & not quite well—We both slept sound. Letter from Rd with news of John dated 7th August.

*Wednesday Morning 9th December.* William slept well but his tongue fevrish. I read Palamon & Arcite—Mary read Bruce— William writing out his alteration of Chaucers Cuckow & Nightingale. After dinner it was agreed that we should walk, when I had finished a letter to C, part of which I had written in the morning by the kitchen-fire while the mutton was roasting. William did not go with us but Mary & I walked into Easedale & backwards & forwards in that Large field under George Rawnson's white cottage. We had intended gathering mosses & for that purpose we turned into the green Lane behind the Tailors but it was too dark to see the mosses. The river came galloping past the Church as fast as it could come & when we got into Easedale we saw Churn Milk force like a broad stream of snow. At the little foot-Bridge we stopped to look at the company of rivers which came hurrying down the vale this way & that; it was a valley of streams & Islands, with that great waterfall at the head & lesser falls in different parts of the mountains coming down to these Rivers. We could hear the sound of those lesser falls but we could not *see* them—we walked backwards & forwards till all distant objects except the white shape of the waterfall, & the lines of the mountains were gone. We had the Crescent Moon when we went out, & at our return there were a few stars that shone dimly, but it was a grey cloudy night.

*Thursday 10th December.* A very fine sunny morning—not frosty we walked into Easedale to gather mosses, & then we went past to Aggy Fleming's & up the gill, beyond that little waterfall—it was a wild scene of crag & mountain. One craggy point rose above the rest irregular & ragged & very impressive it was. We called at Aggy Fleming's she told us about her miserable house she looked shockingly with her head tyed up. Her mother was there—the children looked healthy. We were very unsuccessful in our search after mosses. Just when the evening was closing in Mr Clarkson came to the door—it was a fine frosty Evening. We played at cards.

*Friday 11th.* Baked pies & cakes. It was a stormy morning with Hail showers. The Luffs dined with us—Mrs L came with Mrs Olliff in the Gig. We sate lazily round the fire after dinner. Mr & Mrs Olliff drank tea & supped with us—a hard frost when they came.

*Saturday 12th.* A fine frosty morning—snow upon the ground —I made bread & pies. We walked with Mrs Luff to Rydale, & came home on the other side of the Lake. Met Townley with his dogs—all looked chearful & bright—Helm Crag rose very bold & craggy, a being by itself, & behind it was the large Ridge of mountain smooth as marble & snow white—all the mountains looked like solid stone on our left going from Grasmere i.e. White Moss & Nab scar. The snow hid all the grass & all signs of vegetation & the Rocks shewed themselves boldly everywhere & seemed more stony than Rock or stone. The Birches on the Crags beautiful, Red brown & glittering—the ashes glittering spears with their upright stems—the hips very beautiful, & so good!! & dear Coleridge —I ate twenty for thee when I was by myself. I came home first—they walked too slow for me. William went to look at Langdale Pikes. We had a sweet invigorating walk. Mr Clarkson came in before tea. We played at Cards—sate up late. The moon shone upon the water below Silver-how, & above it hung, combining with Silver how on one side, a Bowl-shaped moon the curve downwards—the white fields, glittering Roof of Thomas Ashburner's house, the dark yew tree, the white fields—gay & beautiful. Wm lay with his curtains open that he might see it.

*Sunday 13th.* Mr Clarkson left us leading his horse. Went to Brathay & Luffs. We drank tea at Betty Dixons—very cold & frosty—a pleasant walk home. William had been very unwell but we found him better. The Boy brought letters from Coleridge & from Sara. Sara in bad spirits about C.

*Monday 14th December.* Wm & Mary walked to Ambleside in the morning to buy mouse-traps. Mary fell & hurt her wrist. I accompanied them to the top of the hill—clear & frosty. I wrote to Coleridge, a very long letter while they were absent. Sate by the fire in the evening reading.

*Tuesday 15th.* Wm & I walked to Rydale for letters—found

one from Joanna. We had a pleasant walk but coldish—it thawed a little.

*Wednesday 16th.* A very keen frost, extremely slippery. After dinner Wm & I walked twice up to the Swan & back again— met Miss Simpson. She came with us to Olliffs & we went back with her—very cold.

*Thursday 17th.* Snow in the night & still snowing we went to Mr Luffs to dine—met Mrs King. Hard frost & as light as day we had a delightful walk & reached home a little after twelve. Mrs Luff ill. Ambleside looked excessively beautiful as we came out—like a village in another country. The light chearful mountains were seen in the long long distance as bright & as clear as at midday with the blue sky above them. We heard waterfowl calling out by the lake side. Jupiter was very glorious above the Ambleside hills & one large star hung over the Coombe of the hills on the opposite side of Rydale water.

*Friday 18th December 1801.* Mary & Wm walked round the two lakes. I stayed at home to make bread, cakes & pies. I went afterwards to meet them, & I met Wm near Bensons. Mary had gone to look at Langdale pikes. It was a chearful glorious day. The Birches & all trees beautiful—hips bright red—mosses green. I wrote to Coleridge for money.

*Saturday 19th.* I was not quite well & did not rise to Breakfast. We walked by Brathay to Ambleside, called at the Lloyds—they were at Kendal, dined with the Luffs—& came home in the evening—the evening cloudy & promising snow. The day very beautiful, Brathay vale scattered & very chearful & interesting.

*Sunday 20th December.* It snowed all day—in the evening we went to tea at Thomas Ashburners. It was a very deep snow. The Brooms were very beautiful—arched feathers with wiry stalks pointed to the End, smaller & smaller. They waved gently with the weight of the snow. We stayed at Thomas A's till after 8 o clock. Peggy better—the Lasses neat & clean & rosy.

*Monday 21st*, being the shortest day. Mary walked to Ambleside for letters, it was a wearisome walk for the snow lay deep upon the Roads & it was beginning to thaw. I stayed at home & clapped the small linen. Wm sate beside me & read the Pedlar, he was in good spirits & full of hope of what he should do with it. He went to meet Mary & they brought 4 letters, 2 from Coleridge, one from Sara & one from France. Coleridge's were very melancholy letters, he had been very ill in his bowels. We were made very unhappy. Wm wrote to him & directed the letter into Somersetshire. I finished it after tea. In the afternoon Mary & I ironed—afterwards she packed her clothes up & I mended Wm's stockings while he was reading the Pedlar. I then packed up for Mr Clarkson's— we carried the Boxes cross the Road to Fletcher's peat house, after Mary had written to Sara & Joanna.

*Tuesday 22nd.* Still Thaw. I washed my head. Wm & I went to Rydale for letters, the road was covered with dirty snow, rough & rather slippery. We had a melancholy letter from C, for he had been very ill, tho' he was better when he wrote. We walked home almost without speaking—Wm composed a few lines of the Pedlar. We talked about Lamb's Tragedy as we went down the White Moss. We stopped a long time in going to watch a little bird with a salmon coloured breast—a white cross or T upon its wings, & a brownish back with faint stripes. It was pecking the scattered Dung upon the road—it began to peck at the distance of 4 yards from us & advanced nearer & nearer till it came within the length of Wm's stick without any apparent fear of us. As we came up the White Moss we met an old man, who I saw was a beggar by his two bags hanging over his shoulder, but from a half laziness, half indifference & a wanting to *try* him if he would speak I let him pass. He said nothing, & my heart smote me. I turned back & said You are begging? 'Ay' says he—I gave him a halfpenny. William, judging from his appearance joined in I suppose you were a Sailor? 'Ay' he replied, 'I have been 57 years at sea, 12 of them on board a man-of-war under Sir Hugh Palmer.' Why have you not a pension? 'I have no pension, but I could have got into Greenwich hospital but all my officers are dead.' He was 75 years of age, had a freshish colour in his cheeks, grey hair, a decent hat with a binding round the edge, the hat worn brown & glossy, his shoes were small thin shoes low in the quarters, pretty good—they had belonged to a gentleman. His coat was blue, frock shaped coming over his thighs, it had been joined up at the seams behind with paler blue to let it out, & there were three Bell-shaped patches of darker blue behind where the Buttons had been. His breeches were either of fustian or grey cloth, with strings hanging down, whole & tight & he had a checked shirt on, & a small coloured handkerchief tyed round his neck. His bags were hung over each shoulder & lay on each side of him, below his breast. One was brownish & of coarse stuff, the other was white with meal on the outside, & his blue waistcoat was whitened with meal. In the coarse bag I guessed he put his scraps of meat &c. He walked with a slender stick decently stout, but his legs bowed outwards. We overtook old Fleming at Rydale, leading his little Dutchman-like grandchild along the slippery road. The same pace seemed to be natural to them both, the old man & the little child, & they went hand in hand, the Grandfather cautious, yet looking proud of his charge. He had two patches of new cloth at the shoulder blades of his faded claret coloured coat, like eyes at each shoulder, not worn elsewhere. I found Mary at home in her riding-habit all her clothes being put up. We were very sad about Coleridge. Wm walked further. When he came home he cleared a path to the necessary— called me out to see it but before we got there a whole housetop full of snow had fallen from the roof upon the path & it echoed in the ground beneath like a dull beating upon it. We talked of going to Ambleside after dinner to borrow money of Luff, but we thought we would defer our visit to Eusemere a day.—Half the Seaman's nose was reddish as if he had been in his youth somewhat used to drinking, though he was not injured by it.—We stopped to look at the Stone seat at the top of the Hill. There was a white cushion upon it round at the edge like a cushion & the Rock behind looked soft as velvet, of a vivid green & so tempting! The snow too looked as soft as a down cushion. A young Foxglove, like a Star in the Centre. There were a few green lichens about it & a few withered Brackens of Fern here & there & upon the ground near. All else was a thick snow—no foot mark to it, not the foot of a sheep.—When we were at Thomas Ashburner's on Sunday Peggy talked about the Queen of Patterdale. She had been brought to drinking by her husband's unkindness &

Avarice. She was formerly a very nice tidy woman. She had
taken to drinking but 'that was better than if she had taken to
something worse' (by this I suppose she meant killing herself).
She said that her husband used to be out all night with other
women & she used to *hear* him come in in the morning for they
never slept together—'Many a poor Body a Wife like me, has
had a working heart for her, as much stuff as she had'. We sate
snugly round the fire. I read to them the Tale of Custance &
the Syrian Monarch, also some of the Prologues. It is the Man
of Lawes Tale. We went to bed early. It snowed & thawed.

*Wednesday 23rd.* A downright thaw but the snow not gone off
the ground except on the steep hillsides—it was a thick black
heavy air—I baked pies & bread. Mary wrote out the Tales
from Chaucer for Coleridge. William worked at The Ruined
Cottage & made himself very ill. I went to bed without dinner,
he went to the other bed—we both slept & Mary lay on the
Rug before the Fire. A broken soldier came to beg in the
morning. Afterwards a tall woman, dressed somewhat in a
tawdry style with a long checked Muslin apron a beaver hat,
and throughout what are called *good Clothes*. Her Daughter
had gone before with a soldier & his wife. She had buried her
husband at Whitehaven & was going back into Cheshire.

*Thursday 24th.* Still a thaw. We walked to Rydale, Wm Mary
& I—left the patterns at Thomas Flemings for Mrs King. The
Roads uncomfortable & slippery. We sate comfortably round
the fire in the Evening & read Chaucer. Thoughts of last year
—I took out my old journal.

*Friday 25th.* Christmas day—a very bad day. We drank tea
at John Fisher's. We were unable to walk. I went to bed after
dinner. The roads very slippery. We received a letter from
Coleridge while we were at John Fisher's. A terrible night—
little John brought the letter. Coleridge poorly but better—his
letter made us uneasy about him. I was glad I was not by
myself when I received it.

*Saturday 26th.* My head ached & I lay long in bed & took my
breakfast there. Soon after I had breakfasted we went to call at
Mr Olliff's. They were not at home. It came on very wet.
Mary went in to the house, & Wm & I went up to Tom
Dawsons to speak about his Grandchild. The rain went off &

we walked to Rydale—it was very pleasant—Grasmere Lake a beautiful image of stillness, clear as glass, reflecting all things—the wind was up & the waters sounding. The lake of a rich purple, the field a soft yellow, the Island yellowish-green, the copses Red Brown the mountains purple. The Church & buildings, how quiet they were! Poor Coleridge, Sara, & dear little Derwent here last year at this time. After tea we sate by the fire comfortably. I read aloud—The Miller's Tale. Wrote to Coleridge. The Olliffs passed in chaise & gig. Wm wrote part of the poem to Coleridge.

*Sunday 27th*. A fine soft beautiful, mild day with gleams of sunshine. I lay in bed till 12 o clock, Mr Clarkson's man came, we wrote to him. We walked up within view of Rydale. William went to take in his Boat. I sate in John's Grove a little while. Mary came home. Mary wrote some lines of the 3rd part of Wm's poem which he brought to read to us when we came home. Mr Simpson came in at dinner-time & stayed tea. They fetched in the Boat. I lay down upon the Bed in the mean time. A sweet evening.

*Monday 28th December*. William, Mary & I set off on foot to Keswick. We carried some cold mutton in our pockets, & dined at John Stanley's where they were making Christmas pies. The sun shone, but it was coldish. We parted from Wm upon the Rays—he joined us opposite Sara's rock—he was busy in composition & sate down upon the Wall. We did not see him again till we arrived at John Stanley's. There we roasted apples in the oven. After we had left John Stanley's Wm discovered that he had lost his gloves he turned back but they were gone. We were tired & had bad head aches. We rested often—once Wm left his Spenser & Mary turned back for it & found it upon the Bank where we had last rested. We reached Greta Hall at about ½ past 5 o clock. The Children & Mrs C well. After Tea message came from Wilkinson who had passed us on the road inviting Wm to sup at the Oak—he went—met a young man (a predestined Marquis) called Johnston—he spoke to him familiarly of the LB—he had seen a copy presented by the Queen to Mrs Harcourt—said he saw them everywhere & wondered they did not sell. We all went weary to bed. My Bowels very bad.

*Tuesday 29th.* A fine morning—a thin fog upon the hills which soon disappeared—the sun shone. Wilkinson went with us to the top of the hill—we turned out of the road at the 2nd mile stone & passed a pretty cluster of houses at the foot of St John's Vale. The houses were among tall trees partly of Scotch fir, & some naked forest trees. We crossed a Bridge just below these houses & the river winded sweetly along the meadows. Our road soon led us along the sides of dreary bare hills, but we had a glorious prospect to the left of Saddleback, half way covered with snow & underneath the comfortable white houses & the village of Threlkeld. These houses & the village want trees about them. Skiddaw was behind us & dear Coleridge's desert home— —As we ascended the hills it grew very cold & slippery. Luckily the wind was at our backs & helped us on. A sharp hail shower gathered at the head of Martindale & the view upwards was very grand—the wild cottages seen through the hurrying hail shower—the wind drove & eddied about & about & the hills looked large & swelling through the storm. We thought of Coleridge. O the bonny nooks & windings & curlings of the Beck down at the bottom of the steep green mossy Banks. We dined at the publick house on porridge, with a second course of Christmas pies. We were well received by the Landlady, & her little Jewish daughters were glad to see us again. The husband a very handsome man. While we were eating our dinners a traveller came in—he had walked over Kirkstone that morning. We were much amused by the curiosity of the Landlord & Landlady to learn who he was, & by his mysterious manner of letting out a little bit of his errand & yet telling nothing. He had business further up in the vale. He left them with this piece of information to work upon & I doubt not they discovered who he was & all his business before the next day at that hour. The woman told us of the Riches of a Mr Walker formerly of Grasmere. We said What does he do nothing for his relations? He has a sickly sister at Grasmere. 'Why' said the Man 'I daresay if they had any sons to put forward he would do it for them, but he has Children of his own'. NB.—his fortune is above 60,000£ & he has two children!! The Landlord went about 1 mile & a ½ with us to put us in the right way. The road was often very slippery, the wind high, & it was nearly dark before we got into the right Road. I was often obliged to crawl upon all fours, & Mary fell many a time. A stout young man whom we met on the hills & who knew Mr Clarkson very kindly set us into the right road & we inquired again near some houses & were directed by a miserable poverty struck looking woman, who had been fetching water, to go down a nasty miry lane. We soon got into the main Road & reached Mr Clarksons at Tea time. Mary H. spent the next day with us & we walked in Dunmallet before dinner but it snowed a little. The day following being New Year's Eve we accompanied Mary to Stainton Bridge—met Mr Clarkson with a Calf's head in a Basket—we turned with him & parted from Mary.

*New Year's Day* [*1802*]. We walked Wm & I towards Martindale.

*2nd January* [*Saturday*]. It snowed all day—we walked near to Dalemain in the snow.

*3rd January Sunday*. Mary brought us letters from Sara & Coleridge & we went with her homewards to Sockbridge, parted at the style on the Poolley side. Thomas Wilkinson dined with us, & stayed supper.

I do not recollect how the rest of our time was spent exactly —we had a very sharp frost which broke on Friday the 15th January or rather on the morning of Saturday 16th.— —On Sunday the 17th we went to meet Mary it was a mild gentle Thaw she stayed with us till Friday 22nd January. She was to have left us on Thursday 23rd [21st] but it was too stormy. On Thursday we dined at Mr Myers's & on Friday 24th [22nd] we parted from Mary. Before our parting we sate under a wall in the sun near a cottage above Stainton Bridge. The field in which we sate sloped downwards to a nearly level meadow round which the Emont flowed in a small half circle, as at Sockburn. The opposite bank is woody, steep as a wall, but not high, & above that Bank the fields slope gently & irregularly down to it. These fields are surrounded by tall hedges with trees among them, & there are *Clumps* or grovelets of tall trees here & there. Sheep & cattle were in the fields. Dear Mary! there we parted from her—I daresay, as often as she passes that road she will turn in at the Gate to look at this sweet prospect. There was a Barn & I think two or three cottages to be seen among the trees & slips of lawn & irregular fields. During our stay at Mr Clarksons we walked every day, except that stormy Thursday & then Wm dined at Mr Myers's & I went after dinner on a double horse. Mrs Clarkson was poorly all the time we were there. We dined at Thomas Wilkinsons on Friday the 15th & walked to Penrith for Mary. The trees were covered with hoar frost, grasses & trees & hedges beautiful—a glorious sunset frost keener than ever—next day thaw. Mrs Clarkson amused us with many stories of her family & of persons whom she had known—I wish I had set them down as I heard them, when they were fresh in my memory. She had two old Aunts who lived at Norwich. The son of one of them (Mrs Barnard) had had a large fortune left him. The other sister rather piqued that her Child had not got it says to her 'Well, we have one Squire in the family however' Mrs Barnard replied with tears rushing out 'Sister Harmer Sister Harmer there you sit. My Son's no more a Squire than yours I take it very unkindly of you Sister Harmer.' She used to say 'Well I wish it may do him any good'. When her son wished to send his carriage for her she said 'Nay I can walk to the Tabernacle, & surely I may walk to see him.' She kept two maids yet she white-washed her kitchen herself. The two sisters lived together. She had a grand cleaning day twice a week & the sister had a fire made up stairs that all below might be thoroughly cleaned. She gave a great deal away in Charity, visited the sick & was very pious. Mrs Clarkson knew a Clergyman & his wife who brought up ten children upon a Curacy, sent 2 sons to college, & he left 1000£ when he died. The wife was very generous gave to all poor people victuals & drink. She had a passion for feeding animals, she killed a pig with feeding it over much. When it was dead she said 'To be sure it's a great loss but I thank God it did not die *clemmed*' the Cheshire word for starved. Her husband was very fond of playing Backgammon & used to play whenever he could get any Body to play with him. She had played much in her youth & was an excellent player but her husband knew nothing of this till one day she said to him

'You're fond of Backgammon come play with me'. He was surprized. She told him that she had kept it to herself while she had a young family to attend to but that now she would play with him. So they began to play & played afterwards every night. Mr C told us many pleasant stories. His journey from London to Wisbech on foot when a schoolboy, Irish murderer's knife & stick, Postboy, &c, the white horse sleeping at the turnpike gate, snoring of the turnpike man, clock ticking. The Burring story, the story of the mastiff, Bull-baitings by men at Wisbech. On Saturday January 23rd we left Eusemere at 10 o clock in the morning, I behind Wm Mr C on his Galloway. The morning not very promising the wind cold. The mountains large & dark but only thinly streaked with snow—a strong wind. We dined in Grisdale on ham bread & milk. We parted from Mr C at one o clock—it rained all the way home. We struggled with the wind & often rested as we went along—A hail-shower met us before we reached the Tarn & the way often was difficult over the snow but at the Tarn the view closed in—we saw nothing but mists & snow & at first the ice on the Tarn below us, cracked & split yet without water, a dull grey white: we lost our path & could see the Tarn no longer. We made our way out with difficulty guided by a heap of stones which we well remembered—we were afraid of being bewildered in the mists till the Darkness should overtake us—we were long before we knew that we were in the right track but thanks to William's skill we knew it long before we could see our way before us. There was no footmark upon the snow either of man or beast. We saw 4 sheep before we had left the snow region. The Vale of Grasmere when the mists broke away looked soft & grave, of a yellow hue—it was dark before we reached home. We were not very much tired. My inside was sore with the cold. We had both of us been much heated upon the mountains but we caught no cold— —O how comfortable & happy we felt ourselves sitting by our own fire when we had got off our wet clothes & had dressed ourselves fresh & clean. We found 5£ from Montague & 20£ from Chris'. We talked about the Lake of Como, read in the descriptive Sketches, looked about us, & felt that we were happy. We indulged all dear thoughts about home—poor Mary! we were sad to think of the contrast for her.

*Sunday 24th.* We went into the orchard as soon as breakfast was over laid out the situation for our new room, & sauntered a while. We had Mr Clarkson's turkey for dinner, the night before we had broiled the gizzard & some mutton & made a nice piece of cookery for Wms supper. Wm walked in the morning I wrote to Coleridge. After dinner I lay down till tea time. I rose fresher & better. Wm could not beat away sleep when I was gone—We went late to bed.

*Monday 25th January.* We did not rise so soon as we intended. I made bread & apple pies. We walked at dusk to Rydale—no letters! it rained all the way. I wrote to Chris$^r$. & Mrs Clarkson & Mrs Coleridge, & sent off C's letter to Mary. William tired with composition. We both went to bed at 10 o clock.

*Tuesday 26th.* A dull morning. I have employed myself in writing this journal & reading newspapers till now (½ past 1 o'clock) we are going to walk, & I am ready & waiting by the kitchen fire for Wm. We set forward, intending to go into Easedale but the wind being rather loudish, & blowing down Easedale we turned under Silver How for a sheltered walk. We went a little beyond the Wyke—Then up to John's Grove, where the storm of Thursday has made sad ravages, two of the finest trees are uprooted one lying with the turf about its root as if the whole together had been pared by a knife. The other is a larch, several others are blown aside, one is snapped in two. We gathered together a faggot. William had tired himself with working—he resolved to do better. We received a letter from Mary by Fletcher with an account of C's arrival in London—I wrote to Mary before bed-time. We sate nicely together & talked by the fire till we were both tired, for Wm wrote out part of his poem & endeavoured to alter it, & so made himself ill. I copied out the rest for him. We went late to bed. Wm wrote to Annette.

*Wednesday 27th.* A beautiful mild morning—the sun shone, the lake was still, & all the shores reflected in it. I finished my letter to Mary, Wm wrote to Stuart. I copied out sonnets for him. Mr Olliff called & asked us to tea tomorrow. We stayed

in the house till the sun shone more dimly & we thought the
afternoon was closing in but, though the calmness of the Lake
was gone with the bright sunshine, yet it was delightfully
pleasant. We found no letter from Coleridge. One from Sara,
which we sate upon the wall to read—a sweet long letter, with
a most interesting account of Mr Patrick. We had ate up the
cold turkey before we walked so we cooked no dinner—sate a
while by the fire & then drank tea at Frank Batys. As we went
past the Nab, I was surprized to see the youngest child
amongst the rest of them running about by itself with a canny
round fat face, & rosy cheeks. I called in. They gave me some
nuts—everybody surprized that we should come over Grisdale. Paid £1–3–3 for letters come since December 1st—paid
also about 8 shillings at Penrith. The Bees were humming
about the hive. William raked a few stones off the garden, his
first garden labour this year. I cut the shrubs. When we
returned from Franks William wasted his mind in the
Magazines. I wrote to Coleridge & Mrs C, closed the letters
up to Ianson. Then we sate by the fire & were happy only our
tender thoughts became painful—went to bed at ½ past 11.

*Thursday 28th*. A downright rain, a wet night. Wm slept
better—better this morning—he had [written an] epitaph &
altered one that he wrote when he was a Boy. It cleared up
after dinner. We were both in miserable spirits, & very
doubtful about keeping our engagement to the Olliffs. We
walked first within view of Rydale, then to Lewthwaites then
we went to Mr Olliffs. We talked a while. William was tired,
we then played at Cards. Came home in the rain—very dark,
came with a Lantern. William out of spirits & tired. After we
went to bed I heard him continually he called at ¼ past 3 to
know the hour.

*Friday 29th January*. William was very unwell, worn out with
his bad nights rest—he went to bed, I read to him to
endeavour to make him sleep. Then I came into the other
room, & read the 1st Book of Paradise Lost. After dinner we
walked to Ambleside, found Lloyds at Luffs—we stayed &
drank tea by ourselves—A heart-rending letter from Coleridge—we were sad as we could be. Wm wrote to him. We
talked about Wms going to London. It was a mild afternoon—

there was an unusual softness in the prospects as we went—a rich yellow upon the fields, & a soft grave purple on the waters. When we returned, many stars were out, the clouds were moveless, in the sky soft purple, the Lake of Rydale calm, Jupiter behind, Jupiter at least *we* call him, but William says we always call the largest star Jupiter. When we came home we both wrote to C—I was stupefied.

*Saturday January 30th*. A cold dark morning. William chopped wood—I brought it in in a basket—a cold wind—Wm slept better but he thinks he looks ill—he is shaving now. He asks me to set down the story of Barbara Wilkinsons Turtle Dove. Barbara is an old maid. She had 2 turtle Doves. One of them died the first year I think. The other bird continued to live alone in its cage for 9 years, but for one whole year it had a companion & daily visitor, a little mouse that used to come & feed with it, & the Dove would caress it, & cower over it with its wings, & make a loving noise to it. The mouse though it did not testify equal delight in the Dove's company yet it was at perfect ease. The poor mouse disappeared & the Dove was left solitary till its death. It died of a short sickness & was buried under a tree with funeral ceremony by Barbara & her maiden & one or two others.

On *Saturday 30th*, William worked at the Pedlar all the morning, he kept the dinner waiting till 4 o clock—he was much tired. We were preparing to walk when a heavy rain came on.

*Sunday 31st*. William had slept very ill, he was tired & had a bad headache. We walked round the two lakes—Grasmere was very soft & Rydale was extremely beautiful from the pasture side. Nab Scar was just topped by a cloud which cutting it off as high as it could be cut off made the mountain look uncommonly lofty. We sate down a long time in different places. I always love to walk that way because it is the way I first came to Rydale & Grasmere, & because our dear Coleridge did also. When I came with Wm 6½ years ago it was just at sunset. There was a rich yellow light on the waters & the Islands were reflected there. Today it was grave & soft but not perfectly calm. William says it was much such a day as when Coleridge came with him. The sun shone out before we reached Grasmere. We sate by the roadside at the foot of the Lake close to Mary's dear name which she had cut herself upon the stone. William employed cut at it with his knife to make it plainer. We amused ourselves for a long time in watching the Breezes some as if they came from the bottom of the lake spread in a circle, brushing along the surface of the water, & growing more delicate, as it were thinner & of a *paler* colour till they died away—others spread out like a peacocks tail, & some went right forward this way & that in all directions. The lake was still where these breezes were not, but they made it all alive. I found a strawberry blossom in a rock, the little slender flower had more courage than the green leaves, for *they* were but half expanded & half grown, but the blossom was spread full out. I uprooted it rashly, & I felt as if I had been committing an outrage, so I planted it again—it will have but a stormy life of it, but let it live if it can. We found Calvert here. I brought a handkerchief full of mosses which I placed on the chimneypiece when C was gone—he dined with us & carried away the Encyclopaedias. After they were gone I spent some time in trying to reconcile myself to the change, & in rummaging out & arranging some other books in their places. One good thing is this—there is a nice Elbow place for William, & he may sit for the picture of John Bunyan any day. Mr Simpson drank tea with us. We payed our rent to Benson. William's head bad after Mr S was gone I petted him on the carpet & began a letter to Sara.

*Monday February 1st.* Wm slept badly. I baked pies & bread. William worked hard at the Pedlar & tired himself—he walked up with me towards Mr Simpsons. There was a purplish light upon Mr Olliff's house which made me look to the other side of the vale when I saw a strange stormy mist coming down the side of Silver How of a reddish purple colour. It soon came on a heavy rain. We parted presently. Wm went to Rydale—I drank tea with Mrs S, the two Mr Simpsons both tipsy. I came home with Jenny as far as the Swan—a cold night, dry & windy—Jupiter above the Forest Side. Wm pretty well, but he worked a little. In the morning a Box of clothes with Books came from London. I sate by his bedside, & read in the Pleasures of Hope to him, which came in the Box—he could not fall asleep, but I found in the morning that he had slept better than he expected. No letters.

*Tuesday 2nd February*. A fine clear morning but sharp & cold. William went into the orchard after breakfast to chop wood. I walked backwards & forwards on the platform. Molly called me down to Charles Lloyd, he brought me flower seeds from his Brother. William not quite well—we walked into Easedale —were turned back in the open field by the sight of a cow. Every horned cow puts me in terror. We walked as far as we could having crossed the foot-bridge, but it was dirty, & we turned back—walked backwards & forwards between Goody Bridge & Butterlip How. William wished to break off composition, & was unable, & so did himself harm. The sun shone but it was cold. After dinner Wm worked at The Pedlar. After tea I read aloud the 11th Book of Paradise Lost we were much impressed & also melted into tears. The papers came in soon after I had laid aside the Book—a good thing for my William. I worked a little today at putting the Linen into repair that came in the Box. Molly washing.

*Wednesday 3rd*. A rainy morning. We walked to Rydal for letters, found one from Mrs Cookson & Mary H—it snowed upon the hills. We sate down on the wall at the foot of White Moss. Sate by the fire in the evening—William tired & did not compose he went to bed soon & could not sleep. I wrote to Mary H, sent off the letter by Fletcher. Wrote also to Coleridge, read Wm to sleep after dinner, & read to him in bed till ½ past one.

*Thursday 4th*. I was very sick, bad headach & unwell—I lay in bed till 3 o clock that is I lay down as soon as breakfast was over. It was a terribly wet day. William sate in the house all day. Fletchers Boy did not come home. I worked at Montagu's shirts. William thought a little about the Pedlar. I slept in the sitting room read Smollets life.

*Friday 5th*. A cold snowy morning. Snow & hail showers— we did not walk. William cut wood a little. I read the story of Snell in Wanly Penson. Sara's parcel came with waistcoat. The Chaucer not only misbound but a leaf or two wanting. I wrote about it to Mary & wrote to Soulby. We received the waistcoats, shoes & gloves from Sara by the Waggon. William not well—sate up late at the pedlar.

*Saturday 6th February.* William had slept badly—it snowed in the night, & was, on Saturday, as Molly expressed it, a Cauld Clash. William went to Rydale for letters, he came home with two very affecting letters from Coleridge—resolved to try another Climate. I was stopped in my writing, & made ill by the letters. William a bad headach—he made up a bed on the floor, but could not sleep—I went to his bed & slept not, better when I rose. Wrote again after tea & translated 2 or 3 of Lessing's Fables.

*Sunday 7th.* A fine clear frosty morning. The Eaves drop with the heat of the sun all day long. The ground thinly covered with snow—the Road Black, rocks black—Before night the Island was quite green, the sun had melted all the snow upon it. Mr Simpson called before William had done shaving— William had had a bad night & was working at his poem. We sate by the fire & did not walk, but read the pedlar thinking it done but lo, though Wm could find fault with no one part of it —it was uninteresting & must be altered. Poor William!

*Monday Morning 8th February 1802.* It was very windy & rained very hard all the morning. William worked at his poem & I read a little in Lessing & the Grammar. A chaise came past to fetch Ellis the Carrier who had hurt his head. After dinner (i.e we set off at about ½ past 4) we went towards Rydale for letters it was a cold '*Cauld Clash*'—the Rain had been so cold that it hardly melted the snow. We stopped at Park's to get some straw in William's shoes. The young mother was sitting by a bright wood fire with her youngest child upon her lap & the other two sate on each side of the chimney. The light of the fire made them a beautiful sight, with their innocent countenances, their rosy cheeks & glossy curling hair. We sate & talked about poor Ellis, & our journey over the Hawes. It had been reported that we came over in the night. Willy told us of 3 men who were once lost in crossing that way in the night, they had carried a lantern with them— the lantern went out at the Tarn & they all perished. Willy had seen their cloaks drying at the public house in Patterdale the day before their funeral. We walked on very wet through the clashy cold roads in bad spirits at the idea of having to go as far as Rydale, but before we had come again to the shore of the Lake, we met our patient, bow-bent Friend with his little wooden box at his Back. 'Where are you going?' said he, 'To Rydale for letters'—'I have two for you in my Box.' We lifted up the Lid & there they lay—Poor Fellow, he straddled & pushed on with all his might but we soon out-stripped him far away when we had turned back with our letters. We were very thankful that we had not to go on, for we should have been sadly tired. In thinking of this I could not help comparing lots with him! he goes at that slow pace every morning, & after having wrought a hard days work returns at night, however weary he may be, takes it all quietly, & though perhaps he neither feels thankfulness, nor pleasure when he eats his supper, & has no luxury to look forward to but falling asleep in bed, yet I daresay he neither murmurs nor thinks it hard. He seems mechanized to labour. We broke the seal of Coleridge's letter, & I had light enough just to see that he was not ill. I put it in my pocket but at the top of the White Moss I took it to my bosom, a safer place for it. The night was wild. There was a strange Mountain lightness when we were at the top of the White Moss. I have often observed it there in the evenings, being between the two valleys. There is more of the sky there than any other place. It has a strange effect sometimes along with the obscurity of evening or night. It seems almost like a peculiar *sort* of light. There was not much wind till we came to John's Grove, then it roared right out of the grove, all the trees were tossing about. C's letter somewhat damped us, it spoke with less confidence about France. William wrote to him. The other letter was from Montagu with 8£. William was very unwell, tired when he had written, he went to bed, & left me to write to MH, Montagu & Calvert, & Mrs Coleridge. I had written in his letter to Coleridge. We wrote to Calvert to beg him not to fetch us on Sunday. Wm left me with a *little* peat fire—it grew less—I wrote on & was starved. At 2 o clock I went to put my letters under Fletcher's door. I never felt such a cold night. There was a strong wind & it froze very hard. I collected together all the clothes I could find (for I durst not go into the pantry for fear of waking William). At first when I went to bed I seemed to be warm, I suppose because the cold air which I had just left no longer touched my body, but I soon found that I was mistaken. I could not sleep from sheer cold. I had baked pies & bread in the morning. Coleridge's letter contained prescriptions.

NB. The moon came out suddenly when we were at Johns Grove & 'a star or two beside'.

*Tuesday* [9th]. William had slept better. He fell to work, & made himself unwell. We did not walk. The funeral came by of a poor woman who had drowned herself, some say because she was hardly treated by her husband, others that he was a very decent respectable man & *she* but an indifferent wife. However this was she had only been married to him last Whitsuntide & had had very indifferent health ever since. She had got up in the night & drowned herself in the pond. She had requested to be buried beside her Mother & so she was brought in a hearse. She was followed by several decent-looking men on horse-back, her Sister, Thomas Flemings wife, in a Chaise, & some others with her, & a cart full of women. Molly says folks thinks o' their Mothers—Poor Body *she* has been little thought of by any body else. We did a little of Lessing. I attempted a fable, but my head ached my bones were sore with the cold of the day before & I was downright stupid. We went to bed but not till William had tired himself.

*Wednesday 10th*. A very snowy morning—it cleared up a little however for a while but we did not walk. We sent for our letters by Fletcher & for some writing paper &c—he brought us word there were none. This was strange for I depended upon Mary. While I was writing out the Poem as we hope for a final writing, a letter was brought me by John Dawsons Daughter, the letter written at Eusemere.—I paid Wm Jackson's Bill by John Fisher. Sent off a letter to Montagu by Fletcher. After Molly went we read the first part of the poem & were delighted with it—but Wm afterwards got to some ugly places & went to bed tired out. A wild, moonlight night.

*Thursday 11th*. A very fine clear sunny frost the ground white with snow—William rose before Molly was ready for him. I rose at a little after nine. William sadly tired & working still at the Pedlar. Miss Simpson called when he was worn out—he escaped & sate in his own room till she went. She was very faint & ill, had had a tooth drawn & had suffered greatly. I walked up with her past Goans—the sun was very warm till we got past Lewthwaites, then it had little power, & had not melted the roads. As I came back again I felt the vale like a different Climate. The vale was bright & beautiful. Molly had linen hung out. We had pork to dinner sent us by Mrs Simpson. William still poorly—we made up a good fire after dinner, & William brought his Mattrass out, & lay down on the floor I read to him the life of Ben Johnson & some short Poems of his which were too *interesting* for him, & would not let him go to sleep. I had begun with Fletcher, but he was too *dull* for me. Fuller says in his life of Jonson, (speaking of his plays) 'If his latter be not so spriteful & vigorous as his first pieces all that are old, & all who desire to be old, should excuse him therein'. He says he had '*beheld*' wit combats between Shakespeare & Jonson, & compares Shakespeare to an English man of war, Jonson to a Spanish great Galleon. There is one affecting line in Jonson's Epitaph on his first Daughter

> Here lies to each her Parents ruth,
> *Mary the Daughter of their youth*
> At six months end she parted hence
> In safety of her Innocence.

I have been writing this journal while Wm has had a nice little sleep. Once he was waked by Charles Lloyd who had come to see about Lodgings for his children in the hooping cough. It is now 7 o'clock—I have a nice coal fire—Wm is still on his bed —2 beggars today. I continued to read to him—we were much delighted with the Poem of Penshurst. William rose better. I was chearful & happy but he got to work again & went to bed unwell.

*Friday 12th.* A very fine bright clear hard frost—William working again. I recopied the Pedlar, but poor William all the time at work. Molly tells me 'What! little Sally's gone to visit at Mr Simpsons. They say she's very smart she's got on a new bed-gown that her Cousin gave her. Its a very bonny one they tell me, but I've not seen it. Sally & me's in Luck.' In the afternoon a poor woman came, *she said* to beg some rags for her husbands leg which had been wounded by a slate from the Roof in the great wind—but she has been used to go a-begging, for she has often come here. Her father lived to the age of 105. She is a woman of strong bones with a complexion that has been beautiful, & remained very fresh last year, but now she looks broken, & her little Boy, a pretty little fellow, & whom I have loved for the sake of Basil, looks thin & pale. I observed this to her. Aye says she we have all been ill. Our house was unroofed in the storm recently & *so* we lived in it for more than a week. The Child wears a ragged drab coat & a fur cap, poor little fellow, I think he seems scarcely at all grown since the first time I saw him. William was with me—we met him in a lane going to Skelwith Bridge he looked very pretty, he was walking lazily in the deep narrow lane, overshadowed with the hedge-rows, his meal poke hung over his shoulder. He said he was going 'a laiting'. He now wears the same coat he had on at that time. Poor creatures! When the woman was gone, I could not help thinking that we are not half thankful enough that we are placed in that condition of life in which we are. We do not so often bless god for this as we wish for this 50£ that 100£ &c &c. We have not, however to reproach ourselves with ever breathing a murmur. This woman's was but a *common* case.—The snow still lies upon the ground. Just at the closing in of the Day I heard a cart pass the door, & at the same time the dismal sound of a crying Infant. I went to the window & had light enough to see that a man was driving a cart which seemed not to be very full, & that a woman with an infant in her arms was following close behind & a dog close to her. It was a wild & melancholy sight.— William rubbed his Table after candles were lighted, & we sate a long time with the windows unclosed. I almost finished writing The Pedlar, but poor William wore himself & me out with Labour. We had an affecting conversation. Went to bed at 12 o clock.

*Saturday 13th.* It snowed a little this morning—still at work at the Pedlar, altering & refitting. We did not walk though it was a very fine day. We received a present of Eggs & milk from Janet Dockeray, & just before she went the little Boy from the Hill brought us a letter from Sara H, & one from the Frenchman in London. I wrote to Sara after tea & Wm took out his old newspapers, & the new ones came in soon after. We sate, after I had finished the letter, talking & William read parts of his Recluse aloud to me—we did not drink tea till ½ past 7.

*Sunday 14th February*. A fine morning the sun shines but it has been a hard frost in the night. There are some little snowdrops that are afraid to pop their white heads quite out, & a few blossoms of Hepatica that are half starved. William left me at work altering some passages of the Pedlar, & went into the orchard—the fine day pushed him on to resolve & as soon as I had read a letter to him which I had just received from Mrs Clarkson he said he would go to Penrith, so Molly was dispatched for the horse—I worked hard, got the backs pasted the writing finished, & all quite trim. I wrote to Mrs Clarkson & put up some letters for Mary H—& off he went in his blue Spenser & a pair of *new* pantaloons fresh from London. He turned back when he had got as far as Franks to ask if he had his letters safe, then for some apples—then fairly off. We had money to borrow for him.— —It was a pleasant afternoon. I ate a little bit of cold mutton without laying cloth & then sate over the fire reading Ben Jonson's Penshurst, & other things. Before sunset I put on my shawl & walked out. The snow-covered mountains were spotted with rich sunlight, a palish buffish colour. The roads were very dirty, for though it was a keen frost the sun had melted the snow & water upon them. I stood at Saras gate & when I came in view of Rydale I cast a long look upon the mountains beyond. They were very white but I concluded that Wm would have a very safe passage over Kirkstone, & I was quite easy about him.

## III. *14 February 1802 to 2 May 1802*

*Sunday 14th February 1802.* See the morning former book. After dinner a little before sunset I walked out. About 20 yards above glowworm Rock I met a Carman, a High[land]er I suppose, with 4 Carts, the first 3 belonging to himself, the last evidently to a man & his family who had joined company with him & who I guessed to be Potters. The Carman was cheering his horses & talking to a little Lass about 10 years of age who seemed to make him her companion. She ran to the Wall & took up a large stone to support the wheel of one of his carts & ran on before with it in her arms to be ready for him. She was a beautiful Creature & there was something uncommonly impressive in the lightness & joyousness of her manner. Her business seemed to be all pleasure—pleasure in her own motions—& the man looked at her as if he too was pleased & spoke to her in the same tone in which he spoke to his horses. There was a wildness in her whole figure, not the wildness of a Mountain lass but a *Road* lass, a traveller from her Birth, who had wanted neither food nor clothes. Her Mother followed the last cart with a lovely child, perhaps about a year old, at her Back & a good-looking girl about 15 years old walked beside her. All the children were like the mother. She had a very fresh complexion, but she was blown with fagging up the hill with the steepness of the hill & the Bairn that she carried. Her husband was helping the horse to drag the cart up by pushing it with his Shoulder. I got tea when I reached home & read German till about 9 o clock. Then Molly went away & I wrote to Coleridge. Went to bed at about 12 o clock. I slept in Wm's bed, & I slept badly, for my thoughts were full of William.

*Monday 15th February 1802*. I was starching small linen all the morning. It snowed a good deal & was terribly cold. After dinner it was fair, but I was obliged to run all the way to the foot of the White Moss to get the least bit of warmth into me. I found a letter from C—he was much better—this was very satisfactory but his letter was not an *answer* to William's which I expected. A letter from Annette. I got tea when I reached home & then set on to reading German. I wrote part of a letter to Coleridge, went late to bed & slept badly.

*Tuesday 16th*. A fine morning but I had persuaded myself not to expect William, I believe because I was afraid of being disappointed—I ironed all day—he came in just at Tea time, had only seen Mary H—for a couple of hours between Emont Bridge & Hartshorn tree— —Mrs C better. He had had a difficult journey over Kirkstone, & came home by Threlkeld—

his mouth & breath were very cold when he kissed me. We spent a sweet Evening—he was better—had altered the pedlar. We went to bed pretty soon & we slept better than we expected & had no bad dreams. Mr Graham said he wished William had been with him the other day—he was riding in a post chaise & he heard a strange cry that he could not understand, the sound continued & he called to the chaise driver to stop. It was a little girl that was crying as if her heart would burst. She had got up behind the chaise & her cloak had been caught by the wheel & was jammed in & it hung there. She was crying after it. Poor thing. Mr Graham took her into the Chaise & the cloak was released from the wheel but the Childs misery did not cease for her Cloak was torn to rags; it had been a miserable cloak before, but she had no other & it was the greatest sorrow that could befal her. Her name was Alice Fell. She had no parents, & belonged to the next Town. At the next Town Mr G left money with some respectable people in the Town to buy her a new cloak.

*Wednesday 17th.* A miserable clashy snowy morning. We did not walk. But the old man from the Hill brought us a short letter from Mary H. I copied the 2nd part of Peter Bell. William pretty well.

*Thursday 18th.* A foggy morning but it cleared up in the afternoon & Wm went to Mrs Simpson's to Tea. I went with him to Goan Mackareth's. Roads very dirty. I copied third part of Peter Bell in his absence & began a letter to Coleridge. Wm came in with a letter from Coleridge that came by Keswick. We talked together till 11 o clock. Then Wm got to work & was the worse for it Hard frost.

*Friday 19th.* Hard frost this morning—but it soon snowed then thawed, a miserable afternoon. Williamson came & cut William's hair—I wrote to C—he carried the letter to Ambleside. Afterwards I wrote to Mary & Sara, tired & went early to bed.

*Saturday 20th.* A very rainy morning, but it cleared up a little we walked to Rydale. There were no letters. The Roads were very dirty—we met little Dawson on horseback & desired him to bring us paper from Mrs Jamesons. After Tea I wrote the first part of Peter Bell—William better.

*Sunday 21st.* A very wet morning. I wrote the 2nd prologue to Peter Bell, then went to Mrs Olliffs. After dinner I wrote the 1st Prologue. William walked to the Tailor's while I was at Mrs O's it rained all the time. Snowdrops quite out, but cold & winterly—yet for all this a thrush that lives in our orchard has shouted & sung its merriest all day long. In the evening I wrote to Mrs Clarkson, & my Br Richard. Wm went to bed exhausted.

*Monday 22nd.* A wet morning. I lay down as soon as breakfast was over very unwell. I slept. Wm brought me 4 letters to bed—from Annette & Caroline, Mary & Sara, & Coleridge—C had had another attack in his Bowels— otherwise mending. M & S both well—M reached Middle- ham the Monday night before at 12 o clock. Tom there.—In the evening we walked to the Top of the hill, then to the bridge, we hung over the wall, & looked at the deep stream below; it came with a full steady yet very rapid flow down to the lake. The sykes made a sweet sound everywhere, & looked very interesting in the twilight. That little one above Mr Olliffs house was very impressive, a ghostly white serpent line —it made a sound most distinctly heard of itself. The mountains were black & steep—the tops of some of them having yet snow visible, but it rained so hard last night that much of it has been washed away. After tea I was just going to write to Coleridge when Mr Simpson came in. Wm began to read Peter Bell to him so I carried my writing to the kitchen fire. Wm called me up stairs to read the 3rd part. Mr S had brought his first engraving to let us see—he supped with us. William was tired with reading & talking & went to bed in bad spirits.

*Tuesday 23rd.* A misty rainy morning—the lake calm. I baked bread & pies. Before dinner worked a little at Wm's waistcoat—after dinner read German Grammar. Before tea we walked into Easedale we turned aside in the Parson's field a pretty field with 3 pretty prospects. Then we went to the first large field, but such a cold wind met us that we turn'd again. The wind seemed warm when we came out of our own door. That Dear thrush was singing upon the topmost of the smooth branches of the Ash tree at the top of the orchard. How long it had been perched on that same tree I cannot tell but we had heard its dear voice in the orchard the day through, along with a chearful undersong made by our winter friends the Robins. We came home by Goan's. I picked up a few mosses by the Roadside, which I left at home. We then went to John's Grove, there we sate a little while looking at the fading landscape. The lake, though the objects on the shore were fading, seemed brighter than when it is perfect day, & the Island pushed itself upwards, distinct & large—all the shores marked. There was a sweet sea-like sound in the trees above our heads, we walked backwards & forwards some time for dear John's sake. Then walked to look at Rydale. Darkish when we reached home & we got tea immediately with Candles.—William now reading in Bishop Hall—I going to read German, we have a nice singing fire, with one piece of wood. Fletcher's carts are arrived but no papers from Mrs Coleridge.

*Wednesday 24th.* A rainy Day. We were busy all day unripping William's Coats for the tailor. William wrote to Annette, to Coleridge & the Frenchman. I received a letter from Mrs Clarkson, a very kind affecting letter which I answered telling her I would go to Eusemere when William went to Keswick. I wrote a little bit to Coleridge—we sent off these letters by Fletcher. It was a tremendous night of wind & Rain. Poor Coleridge! A sad night for a traveller such as he. God be praised he was in safe quarters. Wm went out & put the letters under the door—he never felt a colder night.

*Thursday 25th.*—A fine mild grey beautiful morning. The tailor here—I worked at unripping. William wrote to Montagu in the morning. After dinner he went to Lloyds—I accompanied him to the gate in the corner or turning of the Vale close to the River side beyond Lenty Flemings Cottage. It was coldish & like for frost—a clear evening. I reached home just before dark, brought some mosses & ivy, then got tea, & fell to work at German. I read a good deal of Lessing's Essay. William came home between nine & 10 o clock. We sate nicely together by the fire till bed-time. William not very much tired I was bad in my Bowels.

*Friday 26th.* A grey morning till 10 o'clock. Then the sun shone beautifully. Mrs Lloyds children & Mrs Luff came in a

chaise, were here at 11 o'clock then went to Mrs Olliffs—Wm
& I accompanied them to the gate. I prepared dinner,
sought out Peter Bell, gave Wm some cold meat, & then we
went to walk. We walked first to Butterlip How, where we sate
& overlooked the Vale, no sign of spring but the Red tints of
the upper twigs of the Woods & single trees—sate in the sun
—met Charles Lloyd near the Bridge. Got dinner, I lay down
unwell—got up to tea. Mr & Mrs Luff walked home. The
Lloyds stayed till 8 o'clock. We always get on better with
conversation at home than elsewhere—discussion about Mrs
King & Mrs Olliff.—The Chaise driver brought us a letter
from M H—a short one from C. We were perplexed about
Saras coming. I wrote to Mary. Wm closed his letter to
Montagu, & wrote to Calvert & to Mrs Coleridge. Birds sang
divinely today. Bowels & head bad. William better.

*Saturday 27th*. We walked in the afternoon towards Rydale
returning to tea. Mr Barth Simpson called after supper a little
tipsy. Fletcher said he had had no papers. Wm was not very
well. I sate in the orchard after dinner—we walked in the
evening towards Rydale.

*Sunday 28th February*. Wm very ill, employed with the pedlar.
We got papers in the morning. William shaved himself. I was
obliged to go to bed after dinner—rose better—Wrote to Sara
H & Mrs Clarkson—no walk—disaster pedlar.

*Monday [1st March]*. A fine pleasant day, we walked to
Rydale. I went on before for the letters, brought 2 from M &
S. H—we climbed over the wall & read them under the shelter
of a mossy rock. We met Mrs Lloyd in going—Mrs Olliffs
child ill. The Catkins are beautiful in the hedges. The ivy is
very green. Robert Newtons Paddock is greenish—that is all
we see of spring. Finished & sent off the Letter to Sara & wrote
to Mary. Wrote again to Sara, & William wrote to Coleridge.
Mrs Lloyd called when I was in bed.

*Tuesday [2nd]*. A fine grey morning. I was baking bread &
pies. After dinner I read german & a little before dinner—Wm
also read. We walked on Butterlip How under the wind it
rained all the while, but we had a pleasant walk. The
mountains of Easedale, black or covered with snow at the tops,
gave a peculiar softness to the valley. The clouds hid the tops

of some of them. The valley was populous, & enlivened with streams.—Mrs Lloyd drove past without calling.

*Wednesday* [*3rd*]. I was so unlucky as to propose to rewrite The Pedlar. Wm got to work & was worn to death, we did not walk I wrote in the afternoon.

*Thursday* [*4th*]. Before we had quite finished Breakfast Calvert's man brought the horses for Wm. We had a deal to do to shave—pens to make—poems to put in order for writing, to settle the dress pack up &c & The man came before the pens were made & he was obliged to leave me with only two— Since he has left me (at ½ past 11) it is now 2 I have been putting the Drawers into order, laid by his clothes which we had thrown here & there & everywhere, filed two months' newspapers & got my dinner 2 boiled Eggs & 2 apple tarts. I have set Molly on to clear the garden a little, & I myself have helped. I transplanted some snowdrops—The Bees are busy —Wm has a rich bright day—It was hard frost in the night— The Robins are singing sweetly—Now for my walk. I *will* be busy, I *will* look well & be well when he comes back to me. O the Darling! here is one of his bitten apples! I can hardly find in my heart to throw it into the fire. I must wash myself, then off—I walked round the two Lakes crossed the stepping stones at Rydale Foot. Sate down where we always sit I was full of thoughts about my darling. Blessings on him. I came home at the foot of our own lake under Loughrigg. They are making sad ravages in the woods—Benson's Wood is going & the wood above the River. The wind has blown down a small fir tree on the Rock that terminates John's path—I suppose the wind of Wednesday night. I read German after my return till tea time. After tea I worked & read the LB, enchanted with the Idiot Boy. Wrote to Wm then went to Bed. It snowed when I went to Bed.

*Friday* [*5th*]. First walked in the Garden & Orchard—a frosty sunny morning. After dinner I gathered mosses in Easedale. I saw before me sitting in the open field upon his Sack of Rags the old Ragman that I know—his coat is of Scarlet in a thousand patches his Breeches knees were untied —the Breeches have been given him by some one—he has a round hat pretty good, small crowned but large rimmed.

When I came, to me He said Is there a Brigg yonder that'll carry me ower t'watter? He seemed half stupid. When I came home Molly had shook the Carpet & cleaned every thing up stairs. When I see her so happy in her work & exulting in her own importance I often think of that affecting expression which she made use of to me one evening lately—talking of her good luck in being in this house, 'Aye Mistress them 'at's Low laid would have been a proud creature could they but have [seen] where I is now fra what they thought mud be my Doom.'—I was tired when I reached home, I sent Molly Ashburner to Rydale. No letters! I was sadly mortified. I expected one fully from Coleridge—wrote to William. Read the LB, got into sad thoughts, tried at German but could not go on—Read LB.—Blessings on that Brother of mine! Beautiful new moon over Silver How.

*Saturday Morning* [*6th*]. I awoke with a bad head ache & partly on that account partly for ease I lay in bed till one o clock. At one I pulled off my nightcap—½ past one sate down to breakfast—a very cold sunshiny frost. I wrote the Pedlar & finished it before I went to Mr Simpsons to drink tea. Miss S at Keswick but she came home. Mrs Jameson came in I stayed supper. Fletcher's carts went past & I let them go with William's letter. Mr BS. came nearly home with me. I found letters from Wm, Mary & Coleridge. I wrote to C. Sate up late & could not fall asleep when I went to bed.

*Sunday Morning* [*7th*]. A very fine clear frost. I stitched up the Pedlar—wrote out Ruth—read it with the alterations. Then wrote Mary H. Read a little German—got my dinner. Mrs Lloyd called at the door; & in came William. I did not expect him till tomorrow—How glad I was. After we had talked about an hour I gave him his dinner a Beef Steak, we sate talking & happy. Mr & Miss Simpson came in at Tea time. William came home very well—he had been a little fatigued with reading his poems—he brought two new stanzas of Ruth. We went to bed pretty soon & slept well. A mild grey evening.

*Monday Morning* [*8th*]. A soft Rain & mist we walked to Rydale for letters. The Vale looked very beautiful, in excessive simplicity yet at the same time in uncommon obscurity. The Church stood alone no mountains behind. The meadows looked calm & rich bordering on the still lake; nothing else to be seen but Lake & Island—Found a very affecting letter from Montague also one from Mary—We read Montagu's in walking on, sate down to read Marys. I came home with a bad head-ach & lay down. I slept but rose little better. I have got tea & am now much relieved. On friday Evening the Moon hung over the Northern side of the highest point of Silver How, like a gold ring snapped in two & shaven off at the Ends it was so narrow. Within this Ring lay the Circle of the Round moon, as *distinctly* to be seen as ever the enlightened moon is— — William had observed the same appearance at Keswick perhaps at the very same moment hanging over the Newlands fells. Sent off a letter to Mary H also to Coleridge & Sara, & rewrote in the Evening the alterations of Ruth which we sent off at the same time.

*Tuesday Morning* [*9th*]. William was reading in Ben Jonson— he read me a beautiful poem on Love. We then walked, the first part of our walk was melancholy—we went within view of Rydale then we sate in Saras seat. We walked afterwards into Easedale. It was cold when we returned—We met Sally Newton & her Water Dog. We sate by the fire in the evening & read the Pedlar over. William worked a little and altered it in a few places. I was not very well mended stockings.

*Wednesday* [*10th*]. A fine mildish morning that is, not frost— Wm read in Ben Jonson in the morning. I read a little German altered Saras waistcoats. We then walked to Rydale—No letters!—they are slashing away in Benson's wood—We walked round by the Church, through Olliffs' field when we returned, then home & went up into the orchard. We sate on the Seat, talked a little by the fire, & then got our tea— William has since Tea been talking about publishing the Yorkshire Wolds poem with the Pedlar.

*Thursday* [*11th*]. A fine morning William worked at the poem of the Singing Bird. Just as we were sitting down to dinner we heard Mr Clarkson's voice I ran down, William followed. He was so finely mounted that William was more intent upon the Horse than the Rider an offence easily forgiven for Mr Clarkson was as proud of it himself as he well could be. We ate our dinner after Mr Clarkson came. We walked with him round by the White Bridge after dinner. The vale in mist, rather the mountains, big with the rain soft & beautiful. Mr C was sleepy & went soon to bed.

*Friday* [*12th*]. A very fine morning we went to see Mr Clarkson off. Then we went up towards Easedale but a shower drove us back. The Sun shone while it rained, & the Stones of the walls & the pebbles on the Road glittered like silver. When William was at Keswick I saw Jane Ashburner driving the Cow along the high road from the well where she had been watering it she had a stick in her hand & came tripping along in the Jig step, as if she were dancing—Her presence was bold & graceful, her cheeks flushed with health & her countenance was free & gay. William finished his poem of the singing bird. In the meantime I read the remainder of Lessing. In the Evening after tea William wrote Alice Fell—he went to bed tired with a wakeful mind & a weary Body—a very sharp clear night.

*Saturday Morning* [*13th*]. It was as cold as ever it has been all winter very hard frost. I baked pies Bread, & Seed-cake for Mr Simpson—William finished Alice Fell, & then he wrote the Poem of the Beggar woman taken from a Woman whom I had seen in May—(now nearly 2 years ago) when John & he were at Gallow Hill— —I sate with him at Intervals all the morning, took down his stanzas &c—After dinner we walked to Rydale, for letters, it was terribly cold we had 2 or 3 brisk hail showers. The hail stones looked clean & pretty upon the dry clean Road. Little Peggy Simpson was standing at the door catching the Hail-stones in her hand. She grows very like her Mother. When she is sixteen years old I daresay, that to her Grandmothers eye she will seem as like to what her Mother was as any rose in her garden is like the Rose that grew there years before. No letters at Rydale. We drank tea as soon as we reached home. After tea I read to William that account of the little Boys belonging to the tall woman & an unlucky thing it was for he could not escape from those very words, & so he could not write the poem, he left it unfinished & went tired to Bed. In our walk from Rydale he had got warmed with the subject & had half cast the Poem.

*Sunday Morning* [*14th*]. William had slept badly—he got up

at 9 o clock, but before he rose he had finished the Beggar Boys
—& while we were at Breakfast that is (for I had Breakfasted)
he, with his Basin of Broth before him untouched & a little
plate of Bread & butter he wrote the Poem to a Butterfly!—He
ate not a morsel, nor put on his stockings but sate with his
shirt neck unbuttoned, & his waistcoat open while he did it.
The thought first came upon him as we were talking about the
pleasure we both always feel at the sight of a Butterfly. I told
him that I used to chase them a little but that I was afraid of
brushing the dust off their wings, & did not catch them—He
told me how they used to kill all the white ones when he went
to school because they were frenchmen. Mr Simpson came in
just as he was finishing the Poem. After he was gone I wrote it
down & the other poems & I read them all over to him. We
then called at Mr Olliffs. Mr O walked with us to within sight
of Rydale—the sun shone very pleasantly, yet it was extremely
cold. We dined & then Wm went to bed. I lay upon the fur
gown before the fire but I could not sleep—I lay there a long
time—it is now half past 5 I am going to write letters. I began
to write to Mrs Rawson—William rose without having slept
we sate comfortably by the fire till he began to try to alter the
butterfly, & tired himself he went to bed tired.

*Monday Morning* [*15th*]. We sate reading the poems & I read
a little German. Mr Luff came in at one o clock, he had a long
talk with William—he went to Mr Olliffs after dinner &
returned to us to tea. During his absence a sailor who was
travelling from Liverpool to Whitehaven called he was faint &
pale when he knocked at the door, a young Man very well
dressed. We sate by the kitchen fire talking with him for 2
hours—he told us most interesting stories of his life. His name
was Isaac Chapel—he had been at sea since he was 15 years
old. He was by trade a sail-maker. His last voyage was to the
Coast of Guinea, he had been on board a Slave Ship the
Captain's name Maxwell where one Man had been killed a
Boy put to lodge with the pigs & was half eaten, one Boy set to
watch in the hot sun till he dropped down dead. He had been
cast away in North America & had travelled 30 days among
the Indians where he had been well treated—He had twice
swum from a King's ship in the Night & escaped, he said he
would rather be in hell than be pressed. He was now going to

wait in England to appear against Captain Maxwell—'O he's a Rascal, Sir, he ought to be put in the papers!' The poor man had not been in bed since Friday Night—he left Liverpool at 2 o'clock on Saturday morning, he had called at a farm house to beg victuals & had been refused. The woman said she would give him nothing—'Won't you? Then I cant help it.' He was excessively like my Brother John. A letter was brought us at tea time by John Dawson from MH—I wrote to her, to Sara about Mr Olliff's Gig, & to Longman & Rees—I wrote to Mrs Clarkson by Mr Luff.

*Tuesday* [*16th*]. A very fine morning Mrs Luff called—William went up into the orchard while she was here & wrote a part of The Emigrant Mother. After dinner I read him to sleep—I read Spenser while he leaned upon my shoulder. We walked to look at Rydale. Then we walked towards Goans. The Moon was a good height above the Mountains. She seemed far & distant in the sky there were two stars beside her, that twinkled in & out, & seemed almost like butterflies in motion & lightness. They looked to be far nearer to us than the Moon.

*Wednesday* [*17th*]. William went up into the Orchard and finished the Poem. Mrs Luff & Mrs Olliff called I went with Mrs O to the top of the White Moss—Mr O met us & I went to their house he offered me manure for the garden. I went & sate with W & walked backwards & forwards in the Orchard till dinner time—he read me his poem. I broiled Beefsteaks. After dinner we made a pillow of my shoulder, I read to him & my Beloved slept—I afterwards got him the pillows & he was lying with his head on the table when Miss Simpson came in. She stayed tea. I went with her to Rydale. No letters! a sweet Evening as it had been a sweet day, a grey evening, & I walked quietly along the side of Rydale Lake with quiet thoughts—the hills & the Lake were still!—the Owls had not begun to hoot, & the little Birds had given over singing. I looked before me & I saw a red light upon Silver How as if coming out of the vale below

> 'There was a light of most strange birth
> A Light that came out of the earth
> And spread along the dark hill-side.'

Thus I was going on when I saw the shape of my Beloved in
the Road at a little distance—we turned back to see the light
but it was fading—almost gone. The owls hooted when we
sate on the Wall at the foot of White Moss. The sky broke
more & more & we saw the moon now & then. John Green
passed us with his cart—we sate on. When we came in sight of
our own dear Grasmere, the Vale looked fair & quiet in the
moonshine, the Church was there & all the cottages. There
were high slow-travelling Clouds in the sky that threw large
Masses of Shade upon some of the Mountains. We walked
backwards & forwards between home & Olliffs till I was tired
William kindled & began to write the poem. We carried
Cloaks into the orchard & sate a while there I left him & he
nearly finished the poem. I was tired to death & went to bed
before him—he came down to me & read the Poem to me in
bed— —A sailor begged here today going to Glasgow he
spoke chearfully in a sweet tone.

*Thursday* [*18th*]. A very fine morning the Sun shone but it
was far colder than yesterday. I felt myself weak, & William
charged me not to go to Mrs Lloyds—I seemed indeed, to
myself unfit for it but when he was gone I thought I would get
the visit over if I could—so I ate a Beef-steak thinking it
would strengthen me so it did, & I went off—I had a very
pleasant walk. Rydale vale was full of life & motion. The wind
blew briskly & the lake was covered all over with Bright silver
waves that were there each the twinkling of an eye, then others
rose up & took their place as fast as they went away. The
Rocks glittered in the sunshine, the crows & the Ravens were
busy, & the thrushes & little Birds sang—I went through the
fields, & sate ½ an hour afraid to pass a Cow. The Cow looked
at me & I looked at the cow & whenever I stirred the cow gave
over eating. I was not very much tired when I reached Lloyds,
I walked in the garden. Charles is all for Agriculture. Mrs Ll
in her kindest way. A parcel came in from Birmingham, with
Lamb's play for us & for C. They came with me as far as
Rydale. As we came along Ambleside vale in the twilight—it
was a grave evening—there was something in the air that
compelled me to serious thought—the hills were large, closed
in by the sky. It was nearly dark when I parted from the

Lloyds that is, night was come on & the moon was overcast. But as I climbed Moss the moon came out from behind a Mountain Mass of Black Clouds—O the unutterable darkness of the sky & the Earth below the Moon! & the glorious brightness of the moon itself! There was a vivid sparkling streak of light at this end of Rydale water but the rest was very dark & Loughrigg fell & Silver How were white & bright as if they were covered with hoar frost. The moon retired again & appeared & disappeared several times before I reached home. Once there was no moonlight to be seen but upon the Island house & the promontory of the Island where it stands, 'That needs must be a holy place' &c—&c. I had many many exquisite feelings when I saw this lowly Building in the waters among the dark & lofty hills, with that bright soft light upon it —it made me more than half a poet. I was tired when I reached home I could not sit down to reading & tried to write verses but alas! I gave up expecting William & went soon to bed. Fletcher's carts came home late.

*Friday* [*19th*]. A very rainy morning—I went up into the lane to collect a few green mosses to make the Chimney gay against my darling's return. Poor C! I did not wish for, or expect him it rained so. Mr Luff came in before my dinner. We had a long talk. He left me before 4 o clock, & about ½ an hour after Coleridge came in—his eyes were a little swoln—with the wind—I was much affected with the sight of him—he seemed half Stupefied—William came in soon after. Coleridge went to bed late, & Wm & I sate up till 4 o clock. A letter from Sara sent by Mary. They disputed about Ben Jonson. My spirits were agitated very much.

*Saturday* [*20th*]. A tolerably fine morning after 11 o clock but when I awoke the whole vale was covered with snow. William & Coleridge walked to Borwicks. I followed but did not find them—came home & they were here—We had a little talk about going abroad. We sate pleasantly enough. After tea Wm read the Pedlar. After supper we talked about various things —Christening the Children &c &c went to bed at 12 o clock.

*Sunday* [*21st*]. A showery day. Coleridge & William lay long in bed. We sent up to G Mackareth's for the horse to go to Keswick but we could not have it—Went with C to Borwicks where he left us. William was very unwell this evening—We had a sweet & tender conversation. I wrote to Mary & Sara.

*Monday* [*22nd*]. A rainy day—William very poorly. Mr Luff came in after dinner & brought us 2 letters from Sara H. & one from poor Annette. I read Sara's letters while he was here. I finished my letters to M & S & wrote to my Br Richard. We talked a good deal about C & other interesting things we resolved to see Annette, & that Wm should go to Mary. We wrote to Coleridge not to expect us till Thursday or Friday.

*Tuesday* [*23rd*]. A mild morning William worked at the Cuckow poem. I sewed beside him. After dinner he slept I read German, & at the closing in of day went to sit in the Orchard—he came to me, & walked backwards & forwards, we talked about C—Wm repeated the poem to me—I left him there & in 20 minutes he came in rather tired with attempting to write—he is now reading Ben Jonson I am going to read German it is about 10 o clock, a quiet night. The fire flutters & the watch ticks I hear nothing else save the Breathings of my Beloved & he now & then pushes his book forward & turns over a leaf. Fletcher is not come home. No letter from C.

*Wednesday* [*24th*]. We walked to Rydale for letters. It was a beautiful spring morning—warm & quiet with mists. We found a letter from MH. I made a vow that we would not leave this County for G Hill, Sara & Tom not being going to the Wolds. I wrote to Mary in the Evening. I went to bed after dinner. William walked out & wrote Peggy Ashburner. I rose better. Wm altered the Butterfly as we came from Rydale.

*Thursday* [*25th*]. We did not walk though it was a fine day. Mr Simpson drank tea with us. No letter from Coleridge.

*Friday* [*26th*]. A beautiful morning. William wrote to Annette then worked at the Cuckow. I was ill & in bad spirits —after dinner I sate 2 hours in the Orchard. William & I walked together after tea first to the top of White Moss, then to Mr Olliffs. I left Wm & while he was absent wrote out poems I grew alarmed & went to seek him—I met him at Mr Olliffs he had been trying without success to alter a passage, in Silver How poem—he had written a conclusion just before he went out. While I was getting into bed he wrote the Rainbow.

*Saturday* [*27th*]. A divine morning—at Breakfast Wm wrote

part of an ode—Mr Olliff sent the Dung & Wm went to work in the garden we sate all day in the Orchard.

*Sunday* [*28th*]. We went to Keswick. Arrived wet to skin—a letter from Mary—C was not tired with walking to meet us—I lay down after dinner with a bad head ach.

*Monday* [*29th*]. A cold day. I went down to Miss Crosthwaite's to unpack the Box. Wm & C went to Ormathwaite—a letter from SH, had head ach & lay till after tea. Conversation with Mrs Coleridge.

*Tuesday 30th March.* We went to Calverts. I was somewhat better though not well.

*Wednesday 31st March 1802.* Very unwell. We walked to Portinscale lay upon the turf & saw into the Vale of Newlands, up to Borrowdale & down to Keswick a soft venetian view. I returned better. Calvert & Wilkinsons dined with us. I walked with Mrs W [to] the Quakers' meeting met Wm & we walked in the field together.

*Thursday 1st April.* Mrs C Wm C & I went to the How—a pleasant morning, we came home by Portinscale—sate for some time on the hill.

*Friday 2nd.* Wm & I sate all the morning in the field I nursed Derwent—drank tea with the Miss Cockins.

*Saturday 3rd.* Wm went on to Skiddaw with C. We dined at Calverts, fine day.

*Sunday 4th.* We drove in the gig to Water End. I walked down to Coleridge's. Mrs C came to Greta Bank to Tea. Wm walked down with Mrs C. I repeated his verses to them. We sate pleasantly enough after supper.

*Monday 5th.* We came to Eusemere—Coleridge walked with us to Threlkeld, reached Eusemere to tea. The schoolmistress at Dacre & her scholars. Mrs C at work in the garden she met us.

*Tuesday 6th.* Mrs C, Wm & I walked to Water side. Wm & I walked together in the Evening towards Dalemain—the moon & stars.

*Wednesday 7th.* Wms Birthday. Wm went to Middleham—I walked 6 miles with him—it rained a little but a fine day. Broth to supper & went soon to bed.

*Thursday 8*[*th*]. Mrs C & I walked to Woodside. We slept

after dinner on the Sofa—sate up till ½ past 10. Mrs C tired. I wrote to MH in the morning to Sara in the evening.

*Friday 9th*. Mrs C planting. Sent off letters. A windy morning —rough lake—sun shines very cold—a windy night. Walked in Dunmallet marked our names on a tree.

*Saturday 10th April*. Very cold—a stormy night wrote to C a letter from Wm & SH.

*Sunday 11th*. Very stormy & cold I did not walk.

*Monday 12th*. Had the mantua-maker the ground covered with snow. Walked to T Wilkinson's & sent for letters. The Woman brought me one from Wm & Mary. It was a sharp windy night. Thomas Wilkinson came with me to Barton, & questioned me like a catechizer all the way, every question was like the snapping of a little thread about my heart I was so full of thoughts of my half-read letter & other things. I was glad when he left me. Then I had time to look at the moon while I was thinking over my own thoughts—the moon travelled through the clouds tinging them yellow as she passed along, with two stars near her, one larger than the other. These stars grew or diminished as they passed from or went into the clouds. At this time William as I found the next day was riding by himself between Middleham & Barnard Castle having parted from Mary. I read over my letter when I got to the house. Mr & Mrs C were playing at Cards.

*Tuesday 13th April*. I had slept ill & was not well & obliged to go to bed in the afternoon—Mrs C waked me from sleep with a letter from Coleridge. After tea I went down to see the Bank & walked along the Lake side to the field where Mr Smith thought of building his house. The air was become still the lake was of a bright slate colour, the hills darkening. The Bays shot into the low fading shores. Sheep resting all things quiet. When I returned Jane met me—William was come. The surprize shot through me. He looked well but he was tired & went soon to bed after a dish of Tea.

*Wednesday 14th*. William did not rise till dinner time. I walked with Mrs C. I was ill out of spirits—disheartened. Wm & I took a long walk in the Rain.

*Thursday 15th*. It was a threatening misty morning—but mild. We set off after dinner from Eusemere—Mrs Clarkson went a short way with us but turned back. The wind was furious & we thought we must have returned. We first rested in the large Boat-house, then under a furze Bush opposite Mr Clarksons, saw the plough going in the field. The wind seized our breath the Lake was rough. There was a Boat by itself floating in the middle of the Bay below Water Millock—We rested again in the Water Millock lane. The hawthorns are black & green, the birches here & there greenish but there is yet more of purple to be seen on the Twigs. We got over into a field to avoid some cows—people working, a few primroses by the roadside, woodsorrel flowers, the anemone, scentless violets, strawberries, & that starry yellow flower which Mrs C calls pile wort. When we were in the woods beyond Gow-barrow park we saw a few daffodils close to the water side, we fancied that the lake had floated the seeds ashore & that the little colony had so sprung up—But as we went along there were more & yet more & at last under the boughs of the trees, we saw that there was a long belt of them along the shore, about the breadth of a country turnpike road. I never saw daffodils so beautiful they grew among the mossy stones about & about them, some rested their heads upon these stones as on a pillow for weariness & the rest tossed & reeled & danced & seemed as if they verily laughed with the wind that blew upon them over the Lake, they looked so gay ever glancing ever changing. This wind blew directly over the Lake to them. There was here & there a little knot & a few stragglers a few yards higher up but they were so few as not to disturb the simplicity & unity & life of that one busy highway—We rested again & again. The Bays were stormy & we heard the waves at different distances & in the middle of the water like the Sea —Rain came on, we were wet when we reached Luffs but we called in. Luckily all was chearless & gloomy so we faced the storm—we *must* have been wet if we had waited—put on dry clothes at Dobson's. I was very kindly treated by a young woman, the Landlady looked sour but it is her way. She gave us a goodish supper, excellent ham & potatoes. We paid 7/ when we came away. William was sitting by a bright fire when I came downstairs he soon made his way to the Library piled up in a corner of the window. He brought out a volume of

Enfield's Speaker, another miscellany, & an odd volume of Congreve's plays. We had a glass of warm rum & water—we enjoyed ourselves & wished for Mary. It rained & blew when we went to bed. NB deer in Gowbarrow park like to skeletons.

*Friday 16th April (Good Friday).* When I undrew my curtains in the morning, I was much affected by the beauty of the prospect & the change. The sun shone, the wind had passed away, the hills looked chearful. The river was very bright as it flowed into the lake. The Church rises up behind a little knot of Rocks, the steeple not so high as an ordinary 3 story house. Bees, in a row in the garden under the wall. After Wm had shaved we set forward. The valley is at first broken by little rocky woody knolls that make retiring places, fairy valleys in the vale, the river winds along under these hills travelling not in a bustle but not slowly to the lake. We saw a fisherman in the flat meadow on the other side of the water he came towards us & threw his line over the two arched Bridge. It is a Bridge of a heavy construction, almost bending inwards in the middle, but it is grey & there is a look of ancientry in the architecture of it that pleased me. As we go on the vale opens out more into one vale with somewhat of a cradle Bed. Cottages with groups of trees on the side of the hills we passed a pair of twin Children 2 years old—& sate on the next bridge which we crossed a single arch, we rested again upon the Turf & looked at the same Bridge—we observed arches in the water occasioned by the large stones sending it down in two streams—a Sheep came plunging through the river, stumbled up the Bank & passed close to us, it had been frightened by an insignificant little Dog on the other side, its fleece dropped a glittering shower under its belly—primroses by the roadside, pile wort that shone like stars of gold in the Sun, violets, strawberries, retired & half buried among the grass. When we came to the foot of Brothers water I left William sitting on the Bridge & went along the path on the right side of the Lake through the wood—I was delighted with what I saw—the water under the boughs of the bare old trees, the simplicity of the mountains & the exquisite beauty of the path. There was one grey cottage. I repeated the Glowworm as I walked along —I hung over the gate, & thought I could have stayed for ever. When I returned I found William writing a poem descriptive of the sights & sounds we saw and heard. There was the gentle flowing of the stream, the glittering lively lake, green fields without a living creature to be seen on them, behind us, a flat pasture with 42 cattle feeding, to our left the road leading to the hamlet, no smoke there, the sun shone on the bare roofs. The people were at work ploughing, harrowing & sowing—Lasses spreading dung, a dogs barking now & then, cocks crowing, birds twittering, the snow in patches at the top of the highest hills, yellow palms, purple & green twigs on the Birches, ashes with their glittering spikes quite bare. The hawthorn a bright green with black stems under, the oak & the moss of the oak glossy. We then went on, passed two sisters at work, *they first passed us*, one with two pitch forks in her hand. The other had a spade. We had some talk with them. They laughed aloud after we were gone perhaps half in wantonness, half boldness. William finished his poem before we got to the foot of Kirkstone. There were hundreds of cattle in the vale. There we ate our dinner. The walk up Kirkstone was very interesting. The Becks among the Rocks were all alive—Wm showed me the little mossy streamlet which he had before loved when he saw its bright green track in the snow. The view above Ambleside, very beautiful. There we sate & looked down on the green vale. We watched the Crows at a little distance from us become white as silver as they flew in the sunshine, & when they went still further they looked like shapes of water passing over the green fields. The whitening of Ambleside Church is a great deduction from the beauty of it seen from this point. We called at the Luffs, the Boddingtons there did not go in & went round by the fields. I pulled of my stockings intending to wade the Beck but I was obliged to put them on & we climbed over the wall at the Bridge. The post passed us. No letters! Rydale Lake was in its own evening brightness, the Islands & points distinct. Jane Ashburner came up to us when we were sitting upon the wall—we rode in her cart to Tom Dawsons—all well. The garden looked pretty in the half moonlight half daylight. As we went up the vale of Brothers Water more & more cattle feeding 100 of them.

*Saturday 17[th]*. A mild warm rain. We sate in the garden all the morning. William dug a little. I transplanted a honey suckle. The lake was still the sheep on the island reflected in the water, like the grey deer we saw in Gowbarrow park. We walked after tea by moonlight. I had been in bed in the afternoon & William had slept in his chair. We walked towards Rydale first then backwards & forwards below Mr Olliffs. The village was beautiful in the moonlight—helm crag we observed very distinct. The dead hedge round Benson's field bound together at the top by an interlacing of ash sticks which made a chain of silver when we faced the moon—a letter from C, & also from S.H. I saw a Robin chacing a scarlet Butterfly this morning.

*Sunday 18th.* I lay in bed late. Again a mild grey morning with rising vapours we sate in the orchard—William wrote the poem on the Robin & the Butterfly. I went to drink tea at Luffs but as we did not dine till 6 o clock it was late. It was mist & small rain all the way but very pleasant. William met me at Rydale—Aggy accompanied me thither. We sate up late. He met me with the conclusion of the poem of the Robin. I read it to him in Bed. We left out some lines.

*Monday 19th.* A mild rain very warm Wm worked in the garden, I made pies & bread. After dinner the mist cleared away & sun shone. William walked to Luff's I was not very well & went to bed. Wm came home pale & tired. I could not rest when I got to bed.

*Tuesday 20th.* A beautiful morning the sun shone—William wrote a conclusion to the poem of the Butterfly, 'I've watch'd you now a full half-hour'. I was quite out of spirits & went into the orchard—When I came in he had finished the poem. We sate in the orchard after dinner, it was a beautiful afternoon. The sun shone upon the Level fields & they grew greener beneath the eye—houses village all chearful, people at work. We sate in the Orchard & repeated the Glowworm & other poems. Just when William came to a Well or a Trough which there is in Lord Darlington's Park he began to write that poem of the Glow-worm not being able to ride upon the long Trot—interrupted in going through the Town of Stain-drop. Finished it about 2 miles & a half beyond Staindrop—he did not feel the jogging of the horse while he was writing but when he had done he felt the effect of it & his fingers were cold with his gloves. His horse fell with him on the other side of St Helen's, Auckland.—So much for the Glowworm: It was written coming from Middleham on Monday April 12th 1802. On Tuesday 20th when we were sitting after Tea Coleridge came to the door. I startled Wm with my voice—C came up palish but I afterwards found he looked well. William was not well & I was in low spirits.

*Wednesday 21st.* William & I sauntered a little in the garden. Coleridge came to us & repeated the verses he wrote to Sara— I was affected with them & was on the whole, not being well, in miserable spirits. The sunshine—the green fields & the fair sky made me sadder; even the little happy sporting lambs seemed but sorrowful to me. The pile wort spread out on the grass a thousand shining stars, the primroses were there & the remains of a few Daffodils. The well which we cleaned out last night is still but a little muddy pond, though full of water. I went to bed after dinner, could not sleep, went to bed again. Read Ferguson's life & a poem or two—fell asleep for 5 minutes & awoke better. We got tea. Sate comfortably in the Evening I went to bed early.

*Thursday 22nd.* A fine mild morning—we walked into Easedale. The sun shone. Coleridge talked of his plan of sowing the Laburnum in the woods—The waters were high for there had been a great quantity of rain in the night. I was tired & sate under the shade of a holly Tree that grows upon a Rock—I sate there & looked down the stream. I then went to the single holly behind that single Rock in the field & sate upon the grass till they came from the Waterfall. I saw them there & heard Wm flinging Stones into the River whose roaring was loud even where I was. When they returned William was repeating the poem 'I have thoughts that are fed by the Sun'. It had been called to his mind by the dying away of the stunning of the Waterfall when he came behind a stone. When we had got into the vale a heavy rain came on. We saw a family of little Children sheltering themselves under a wall before the rain came on, they sate in a Row making a canopy for each other of their clothes. The servant lass was planting potatoes near them. Coleridge changed his clothes—we were all wet—Wilkinson came in while we were at dinner. Coleridge & I after dinner drank black currants & water.

*Friday 23rd April 1802*. It being a beautiful morning we set off at 11 o clock intending to stay out of doors all the morning. We went towards Rydale & before we got to Tom Dawson's we determined to go under Nab Scar. Thither we went. The sun shone & we were lazy. Coleridge pitched upon several places to sit down upon but we could not be all of one mind respecting sun & shade so we pushed on to the Foot of the Scar. It was very grand when we looked up very stony, here & there a budding tree. William observed that the umbrella Yew tree that breasts the wind had lost its character as a tree & had become something like to solid wood. Coleridge & I pushed on before. We left William sitting on the stones feasting with silence—& C & I sate down upon a rock Seat—a Couch it might be under the Bower of William's Eglantine, Andrew's Broom. He was below us & we could see him—he came to us & repeated his poems while we sate beside him upon the ground. He had made himself a seat in the crumbly ground. After we had lingered long looking into the vales—Ambleside vale with the copses the village under the hill & the green fields—Rydale with a lake all alive & glittering yet but little stirred by Breezes, & our own dear Grasmere first making a little round lake of natures own with never a house never a green field—but the copses & the bare hills, enclosing it & the river flowing out of it. Above rose the Coniston Fells in their own shape & colour—not Man's hills but all for themselves the sky & the clouds & a few wild creatures. C went to search for something new. We saw him climbing up towards a Rock, he called us & we found him in a Bower, the sweetest that was ever seen—the Rock on one side is very high & all covered with ivy which hung loosely about & bore bunches of brown berries. On the other side it was higher than my head. We looked down upon the Ambleside vale that seemed to wind away from us the village *lying* under the hill. The Fir tree Island was reflected beautifully—we now first saw that the trees are planted in rows. About this bower there is mountain ash, common ash, yew tree, ivy, holly, hawthorn,

mosses & flowers, & a carpet of moss—Above at the top of the
Rock there is another spot—it is scarce a Bower, a little
parlour, one not *enclosed* by walls but shaped out for a resting
place by the rocks & the ground rising about it. It had a sweet
moss carpet—We resolved to go & plant flowers in both these
places tomorrow. We wished for Mary & Sara. Dined late.
After dinner Wm & I worked in the garden. C read. A letter
from Sara.

*Saturday 24th.* A very wet day. William called me out to see a
waterfall behind the Barberry tree—We walked in the evening
to Rydale—Coleridge & I lingered behind—C stopped up the
little runner by the Road side to make a lake. We all stood to
look at Glowworm Rock—a primrose that grew there & just
looked out on the Road from its own sheltered bower. The
clouds moved as William observed in one regular body like a
multitude in motion a sky all clouds over, not one cloud. On
our return it broke a little out & we saw here & there a star.
One appeared but for a moment in a lake pale blue sky.

*Sunday 25th April.* After breakfast we set off with Coleridge
towards Keswick. Wilkinson overtook us near the Potters &
interrupted our discourse. C got into a Gig with Mr Beck, &
drove away from us. A shower came on but it was soon over—
we spent the morning in the orchard. Read the Prothalamium
of Spenser—walked backwards & forwards. Mr Simpson
drank tea with us. I was not well before tea. Mr S sent us some
quills by Molly Ashburner & his Brother's book. The Luffs
called at the door.

*Monday 26th.* I copied Wm's poems for Coleridge. Letters
from Peggy & Mary H—wrote to Peggy & Coleridge. A
terrible rain & wind all day. Went to bed at 12 o clock.

*Tuesday 27th.* A fine morning. Mrs Luff called I walked with
her to the Boat-house—William met me at the top of the hill
with his fishing-rod in his hand. I turned with him & we sate
on the hill looking to Rydale. I left him intending to join him
but he came home, & said his lines would not stand the
pulling—he had had several bites. He sate in the orchard, I
made bread. Miss Simpson called I walked with her to Goans.
When I came back I found that he & John Fisher had

cleaned out the well—John had sodded about the Bee-stand. In the evening Wm began to write the Tinker. We had a Letter & verses from Coleridge.

*Wednesday 28th April.* A fine sunny but coldish morning. I copied the Prioress's tale. Wm was in the orchard—I went to him—he worked away at his poem, though he was ill & tired —I happened to say that when I was a Child I would not have pulled a strawberry blossom. I left him & wrote out the Manciple's Tale. At dinner-time he came in with the poem of 'Children gathering flowers'—but it was not quite finished & it kept him long off his dinner. It is now done he is working at the Tinker, he promised me he would get his tea & do no more but I have got mine an hour & a quarter & he has scarcely begun his. I am not quite well—We have let the bright sun go down without walking—now a heavy shower comes on & I guess we shall not walk at all—I wrote a few lines to Coleridge. Then we walked backwards & forwards between our house & Olliffs. We talked about T Hutchinson & Bell Addison. William left me sitting on a stone. When we came in we corrected the Chaucers but I could not finish them to-night, went to bed.

*Thursday 29th.* A beautiful morning. The sun shone & all was pleasant. We sent off our parcel to Coleridge by the waggon. Mr Simpson heard the Cuckow today. Before we went out, after I had written down the Tinker, which William finished this morning, Luff called. He was very lame, limped into the kitchen—he came on a little Pony. We then went to Johns Grove, sate a while at first. Afterwards William lay, & I lay in the trench under the fence—he with his eyes shut & listening to the waterfalls & the Birds. There was no one waterfall above another—it was a sound of waters in the air—the voice of the air. William heard me breathing & rustling now & then but we both lay still, & unseen by one another—he thought that it would be as sweet thus to lie so in the grave, to hear the *peaceful* sounds of the earth & just to know that ones dear friends were near. The Lake was still there was a Boat out. Silver how reflected with delicate purple & yellowish hues as I have seen Spar—Lambs on the island & Running races together by the half dozen in the round field near us. The

copses green*ish*, hawthorn green.—Came home to dinner then
went to Mr Simpson. We rested a long time under a wall.
Sheep & lambs were in the field—cottages smoking. As I lay
down on the grass, I observed the glittering silver line on the
ridges of the Backs of the sheep, owing to their situation
respecting the Sun—which made them look beautiful but with
something of strangeness, like animals of another kind—as if
belonging to a more splendid world. Met old Mr S at the door
—Mrs S poorly—I got mullens & pansies—I was sick & ill &
obliged to come home soon. We went to bed immediately—I
slept up stairs. The air coldish where it was felt somewhat
frosty.

    *Friday April 30th.* We came into the orchard directly after
Breakfast, & sate there. The lake was calm—the sky cloudy.
We saw two fishermen by the lake side. William began to write
the poem of the Celandine. I wrote to Mary H—sitting on the
fur gown. Walked backwards & forwards with William—he
repeated his poem to me—then he got to work again & would
not give over—he had not finished his dinner till 5 o clock.
After dinner we took up the fur gowns into The Hollins above.
We found a sweet seat & thither we will often go. We
spread the gown put on each a cloak & there we lay—William
fell asleep—he had a bad head ache owing to his having been
disturbed the night before with reading C's letter which
Fletcher had brought to the door—I did not sleep but I lay
with half shut eyes, looking at the prospect as in a vision
almost I was so resigned to it—Loughrigg Fell was the most
distant hill, then came the Lake slipping in between the copses
& above the copse the round swelling field, nearer to me a wild
intermixture of rocks trees, & slacks of grassy ground.—When
we turned the corner of our little shelter we saw the Church &
the whole vale. It is a blessed place. The Birds were about us
on all sides—Skobbys Robins Bullfinches. Crows now &
then flew over our heads as we were warned by the sound of
the beating of the air above. We stayed till the light of day was
going & the little Birds had begun to settle their singing—But
there was a thrush not far off that seemed to sing louder &
clearer than the thrushes had sung when it was quite day. We
came in at 8 o' clock, got tea. Wrote to Coleridge, & I wrote to

Mrs Clarkson part of a letter. We went to bed at 20 minutes past 11 with prayers that Wm might sleep well.

*Saturday May 1st.* Rose not till ½ past 8—a heavenly morning—as soon as Breakfast was over we went into the garden & sowed the scarlet beans about the house. It was a clear sky a heavenly morning. I sowed the flowers William helped me. We then went and sate in the Orchard till dinner-time, it was very hot. William wrote the Celandine. We planned a shed for the sun was too much for us. After dinner we went again to our old resting place in the Hollins under the Rock. We first lay under a holly where we saw nothing but the holly tree & a budding elm mossed with & the sky above our heads. But that holly tree had a beauty about it more than its own, knowing as we did where we were. When the sun had got low enough we went to the Rock shade—Oh the overwhelming beauty of the vale below—greener than green. Two Ravens flew high high in the sky & the sun shone upon their bellys & their wings long after there was none of his light to be seen but a little space on the top of Loughrigg Fell. We went down to tea at 8 o' clock—had lost the poem & returned after tea. The Landscape was fading, sheep & lambs quiet among the Rocks. We walked towards Kings & backwards & forwards. The sky was perfectly Cloudless N.B. is it often so? 3 solitary stars in the middle of the blue vault one or two on the points of the high hills. Wm wrote the Celandine 2nd part tonight. Heard the cuckow today this first of May.

*Sunday 2nd May.* Again a heavenly morning—Letter from Coleridge.

## IV. *4 May 1802 to 16 January 1803*

*Tuesday May 4th.* William had slept pretty well & though he went to bed nervous & jaded in the extreme he rose refreshed. I wrote the Leech Gatherer for him which he had begun the night before & of which he wrote several stanzas in bed this Monday morning. It was very hot, we called at Mr Simpson's door as we passed but did not go in. We rested several times

by the way, read & repeated the Leech gatherer. We were
almost melted before we were at the top of the hill. We saw
Coleridge on the Wytheburn Side of the water, he crossed the
Beck to us. Mr Simpson was fishing there. William & I ate a
Luncheon, then went on towards the Waterfall. It is a glorious
wild solitude under that lofty purple crag. It stood upright by
itself. Its own self & its shadow below, one mass—all else was
sunshine. We went on further. A Bird at the top of the crags
was flying round & round & looked in thinness & transpar-
ency, shape & motion, like a moth. We climbed the hill but
looked in vain for a shade except at the foot of the great
waterfall, & there we did not like to stay on account of the
loose stones above our heads. We came down & rested upon a
moss covered Rock, rising out of the bed of the River. There
we lay ate our dinner & stayed there till about 4 o clock or
later—Wm & C repeated & read verses. I drank a little
Brandy & water & was in Heaven. The Stags horn is very
beautiful & fresh springing upon the fells. Mountain ashes,
green. We drank tea at a farm house. The woman had not a
pleasant countenance, but was civil enough. She had a pretty
Boy a year old whom she suckled. We parted from Coleridge
at Sara's Crag after having looked at the Letters which C
carved in the morning. I kissed them all. Wm deepened the T
with C's penknife. We sate afterwards on the wall, seeing the
sun go down & the reflections in the still water. C looked well
& parted from us chearfully, hopping up upon the Side stones.
On the Rays we met a woman with 2 little girls one in her
arms the other about 4 years old walking by her side, a pretty
little thing, but half starved. She had on a pair of slippers that
had belonged to some gentlemans child, down at the heels, but
it was not easy to keep them on—but, poor thing! young as she
was, she walked carefully with them. Alas too young for such
cares & such travels—The Mother when we accosted her told
us that her Husband had left her & gone off with another
woman & how she 'pursued' them. Then her fury kindled &
her eyes rolled about. She changed again to tears. She was a
Cockermouth woman—30 years of age a child at Cockermouth when I was—I was moved & gave her a shilling, I
believe 6$^{d}$ more than I ought to have given. We had the

Crescent moon with the 'auld moon in her arms'—We rested
often:—always upon the Bridges. Reached home at about 10
o clock. The Lloyds had been here in our absence. We went soon
to bed. I repeated verses to William while he was in bed—he
was soothed & I left him. 'This is the Spot' over & over again.

*Wednesday 5th May 1802.* A very fine morning rather cooler
than yesterday. We planted ¾ths of the Bower. I made bread
—we sate in the Orchard. The Thrush sang all day as he
always sings. I wrote to the Hutchinsons & to Coleridge,
packed off Thalaba. William had kept off work till near
Bedtime when we returned from our walk—then he began
again & went to bed very nervous—we walked in the twilight
& walked till night came on—the moon had the old moon in
her arms but not so plain to be seen as the night before. When
we went to bed it was a Boat without the Circle. I read The
Lover's Complaint to Wm in bed & left him composed.

*6th May Thursday 1802.* A sweet morning we have put the
finishing stroke to our Bower & here we are sitting in the
orchard. It is one o clock. We are sitting upon a seat under
the wall which I found my Brother Building up when I came to
him with his apple—he had intended that it should have been
done before I came. It is a nice cool shady spot. The small
Birds are singing—Lambs bleating, Cuckow calling—The
Thrush sings by Fits, Thomas Ashburner's axe is going
quietly (without passion) in the orchard—Hens are cackling,
Flies humming, the women talking together at their doors—
Plumb & pear trees are in Blossom, apple trees greenish—the
opposite woods green, the crows are cawing. We have heard
Ravens. The Ash Trees are in blossom, Birds flying all about
us. The stitchwort is coming out, there is one budding
Lychnis. The primroses are passing their prime. Celandine
violets & wood sorrel for ever more—little geranium &
pansies on the wall. We walked in the evening to Tail End to
enquire about hurdles for the orchard shed & about Mr Luff's
flower—The flower dead—no hurdles. I went to look at the
falling wood—Wm also, when he had been at Benson's went
with me. They have left a good many small oak trees but we
dare not hope that they are all to remain. The Ladies are come
to Mr Gell's cottage we saw them as we went & their light

when we returned. When we came in we found a Magazine & Review & a letter from Coleridge with verses to Hartley & Sara H. We read the Review &c. The Moon was a perfect Boat a silver Boat when we were out in the Evening. The Birch Tree is all over green in *small* leaf. More light & elegant than when it is full out. It bent to the breezes as if for the love of its own delightful motions. Sloe thorns & Hawthorns in the hedges.

*Friday 7th May*. William had slept uncommonly well so, feeling himself strong, he fell to work at the Leech gatherer— he wrote hard at it till dinner time, then he gave over tired to death—he had finished the poem. I was making Derwents frocks. After dinner we sate in the orchard. It was a thick hazy dull air. The Thrush sang almost continually—the little Birds were more than usually busy with their voices. The sparrows are now full fledged. The nest is so full that they lie upon one another, they sit quietly in their nest with closed mouths. I walked to Rydale after tea which we drank by the kitchen Fire. The Evening very dull—a terrible kind of threatening brightness at sunset above Easedale. The Sloe thorn beautiful in the hedges, & in the wild spots higher up among the hawthorns. No letters. William met me—he had been digging in my absence & cleaning the well. We walked up beyond Lewthwaites a very dull sky, coolish crescent moon now & then. I had a letter brought me from Mrs Clarkson. While we were walking in the orchard I observed the Sorrel leaves opening at about 9 o clock—William went to bed tired with thinking about a poem.

*Saturday Morning May 8th 1802*. We sowed the Scarlet Beans in the orchard I read Henry 5th there—William lay on his back on the seat. 'Wept, For names, sounds paths delights & duties lost'—Taken from a poem upon Cowley's wish to retire to the Plantations, read in the Review. I finished Derwent's frocks—after dinner William added a step to the orchard steps.

*Sunday Morning May 9th 1802*. The air considerably colder today but the sun shone all day—William worked at the Leech gatherer almost incessantly from morning till tea-time. I copied the Leech-gatherer & other poems for Coleridge—I was oppressed & sick at heart for he wearied himself to death. After tea he wrote 2 stanzas in the manner of Thomsons Castle of Indolence—& was tired out. Bad news of Coleridge.

*Monday May 10th.* A fine clear morning but coldish—William is still at work though it is past 10 o clock—he will be tired out I am sure—My heart fails in me—he worked a little at odd things, but after dinner he gave over—an affecting letter from Mary H. We sate in the Orchard before dinner. Old Joyce spent the day. I wrote to Mary H. Mrs Jameson & Miss Simpson called just when William was going to bed at 8 o'clock. I wrote to Coleridge sent off Reviews & poems, went to bed at 12 o'clock William did not sleep till 3 o'clock.

*Tuesday May 11th.* A cool air. William finished the stanzas about C & himself—he did not go out today. Miss Simpson came in to tea which was lucky enough for it interrupted his labours. I walked with her to Rydale—the evening cool—the moon only now & then to be seen—the Lake purple as we went—primroses still in abundance. William did not meet me he completely finished his poems I finished Derwent's frocks. We went to bed at 12 o clock Wm pretty well he looked very well, he complains that he gets cold in his chest.

*Wednesday 12th.* A sunshiny but coldish morning—we walked into Easedale & returned by George Rownson's & the lane. We brought home heckberry blossom, crab blossom—the anemone nemorosa—Marsh Marygold—Speedwell, that beautiful blue one the colour of the blue-stone or glass used in jewellery, with its beautiful pearl-like chives—anemones are in abundance & still the dear dear primroses violets in beds, pansies in abundance, & the little celandine. I pulled a branch of the taller celandine. Butterflies of all colours—I often see some small ones of a pale purple lilac or Emperor's eye colour something of the colour of that large geranium which grows by the lake side. Wm observed the beauty of Geordy Green's house. We see it from our orchard. Wm pulled ivy with beautiful berries—I put it over the chimney piece—sate in the orchard the hour before dinner, coldish. We have now dined. My head aches—William is sleeping in the window. In the Evening we were sitting at the table, writing, when we were rouzed by Coleridge's voice below—he had walked, looked palish but was not much tired. We sate up till one o clock all together then William went to bed & I sate with C in the sitting room (where he slept) till ¼ past 2 o clock. Wrote to MH.

*13th May Thursday 1802.* The day was very cold, with snow showers. Coleridge had intended going in the morning to Keswick but the cold & showers hindered him. We went with him after tea as far as the plantations by the Roadside descending to Wytheburn—he did not look very well when we parted from him.—We sate an hour at Mr Simpsons.

*Friday May 14th 1802.* A very cold morning—hail & snow showers all day. We went to Brothers wood, intending to get plants & to go along the shore of the lake to the foot. We did go a part of the way, but there was no pleasure in stepping along that difficult sauntering Road in this ungenial weather. We turned again & walked backwards & forwards in Brothers' wood. William teased himself with seeking an epithet for the Cuckow. I sate a while upon my last summers seat the mossy stone—William's unemployed beside me, & the space between where Coleridge has so often lain. The oak trees are just putting forth yellow knots of leaves. The ashes with their flowers passing away & leaves coming out. The blue Hyacinth is not quite full blown—Gowans are coming out—marsh marygolds in full glory—the little star plant a star without a flower. We took home a great load of Gowans & planted them in the cold about the orchard. After dinner I worked bread then came & mended stockings beside William he fell asleep. After tea I walked to Rydale for Letters. It was a strange night. The hills were covered over with a slight covering of hail or snow, just so as to give them a hoary winter look with the black Rocks—The woods looked miserable, the coppices green as grass which looked quite unnatural & they seemed half shrivelled up as if they shrunk from the air. O thought I! what a beautiful thing God has made winter to be by stripping the trees & letting us see their shapes & forms. What a freedom does it seem to give to the storms! There were several new flowers out but I had no pleasure in looking at them—I walked as fast as I could back again with my letter from S. H. which I skimmed over at Tommy Fleming's. Met Wm at the top of White Moss we walked a little beyond Olliffs—near 10 when we came in. Wm & Molly had dug the ground & planted potatoes in my absence. We wrote to Coleridge—sent off a letter to Annette, bread & frocks to the C's—Went to bed at ½ past 11, William very nervous—after he was in bed haunted with altering the Rainbow.

*Saturday Morning* [*15th*]. It is now ¼ past 10 & he is not up. Miss Simpson called when I was in bed—I have been in the garden. It looks fresh & neat in spite of the frost. Molly tells me they had thick ice on a jug at their door last night.

*Saturday 15th*. A very cold & cheerless morning. I sate mending stockings all the morning. I read in Shakespeare. William lay very late because he slept ill last night. It snowed this morning just like Christmas. We had a melancholy letter from Coleridge just at Bed-time—.It distressed me very much & I resolved upon going to Keswick the next day.

[*The following is written on the blotting-paper opposite this date:*]

S T Coleridge
Dorothy Wordsworth       William Wordsworth
Mary Hutchinson       Sara Hutchinson
William   Coleridge   Mary
Dorothy   Sara
16th May
1802
John Wordsworth

*Sunday 16th*. William was at work all the morning I did not go to Keswick. A sunny cold frosty day a snow-shower at night. We were a good while in the orchard in the morning.

*Monday 17th May*. William was not well—he went with me to Wytheburn water. He left me in a post chaise. Hail showers snow & cold attacked me. The people were graving peats under Nadel Fell.—A lark & thrush singing near Coleridge's house—Barcrofts there a letter from MH.

*Tuesday 18th May*. Terribly cold. Coleridge not well. Froude called, Wilkinsons called, I not well. C & I walked in the evening in the Garden warmer in the evening wrote to M & S.

*Wednesday 19th May 1802*. A grey morning—not quite so cold. C & I set off at ½ past 9 o clock met William, near the 6 mile

Stone. We sate down by the Road Side, & then went to Wytheburn water, longed to be at the Island sate in the sun, Coleridge's Bowels bad, mine also. We drank tea at John Stanley's—the evening cold & clear a glorious light on Skiddaw. I was tired—brought a cloak down from Mr Simpsons. Packed up Books for Coleridge then got supper & went to bed.

*Thursday 20th May.* A frosty clear morning. I lay in bed late —William got to work. I was somewhat tired. We sate in the Orchard sheltered all the morning. In the evening there was a fine rain. We received a letter from Coleridge, telling us that he wished us not to go to Keswick.

*Friday 21st May.* A very warm gentle morning—a little rain. Wm wrote two sonnets on Buonaparte after I had read Milton's sonnets to him. In the evening he went with Mr Simpson with Borwicks Boat to gather Ling in Bainriggs. I planted about the well—was much heated & I think I caught cold.

*Saturday 22nd May.* A very hot morning, a hot wind as if coming from a sand desert. We met Coleridge, he was sitting under Sara's Rock when we reached him—he turned with us —we sate a long time under the Wall of a sheep-fold, had some interesting melancholy talk about his private affairs. We drank tea at a farm house. The woman was very kind. There was a woman with 3 children travelling from Workington to Manchester. The woman served them liberally. Afterwards she said that she never suffered any to go away without a trifle 'sec as we have'. The woman at whose house we drank tea the last time was rich & senseless—she said 'she never served any but their own poor'—C came home with us. We sate some time in the orchard. Then they came in to supper—mutton chops & potatoes. Letters from S & MH.

*Sunday* [*23rd*]. I sate with C in the orchard all the morning. William was very nervous. I was ill in the afternoon, took laudanum. We walked in Bainriggs after tea, saw the juniper —umbrella shaped.—C went to S & M Points, joined us on White Moss.

*Monday 24th May 1802.* A very hot morning. We were ready to go off with Coleridge, but foolishly sauntered & Miss

Taylor & Miss Stanley called. William & Coleridge & I went afterwards to the top of the Rays. I was ill & left them, lay down at Mrs Simpsons. I had sent off a letter to Mary by C. I wrote again & to C then went to bed. William slept not till 5 o'clock.

*Tuesday 25th.* Very hot—I went to bed after dinner—We walked in the evening. Papers & short note from C—again no sleep for Wm.

*Wednesday 26th.* I was very unwell—went to bed again after dinner. We walked a long time backwards & forwards between Johns Grove & the Lane upon the Turf—a beautiful night, not cloudless, it has never been so since May day.

*Thursday 27th.* I was in bed all day—very ill. William wrote to Rd Cr. & Cook. Wm went after tea into the orchard. I slept in his bed—he slept downstairs. He slept better than before.

*Friday 28th.* I was much better than yesterday, though poorly. Wm tired himself with hammering at a passage. I was out of spirits. After dinner he was better & I grew better. We sate in the orchard. The sky cloudy the air sweet & cool. The young Bullfinches in their party coloured Raiment bustle about among the Blossoms & poize themselves like Wire dancers or tumblers, shaking the twigs & dashing off the Blossoms. There is yet one primrose in the orchard—the stitchwort is fading—the wild columbines are coming into beauty—the vetches are in abundance Blossoming & seeding. That pretty little waxy looking Dial-like yellow flower, the speedwell, & some others whose names I do not yet know. The wild columbines are coming into beauty—some of the gowans fading. In the garden we have lilies & many other flowers. The scarlet Beans are up in crowds. It is now between 8 & nine o'clock. It has rained sweetly for two hours & a half—the air is very mild. The heckberry blossoms are dropping off fast, almost gone—barberries are in beauty—snowballs coming forward—May Roses blossoming.

*Saturday 29th.* I was much better. I made bread & a wee Rhubarb Tart & batter pudding for William. We sate in the orchard after dinner William finished his poem on Going for Mary. I wrote it out—I wrote to Mary H, having received a letter from her in the evening. A sweet day we nailed up the honeysuckles, & hoed the scarlet beans.

*Sunday 30th May 1802.* I wrote to Mrs Clarkson. It was a clear but cold day. The Simpsons called in the Evening. I had been obliged to go to bed before tea & was unwell all day. Gooseberries a present from Peggy Hodgson. I wrote to my Aunt Cookson.

*Monday 31st.* I was much better. We sate out all the day. Mary Jameson dined. I wrote out the poem on 'Our Departure' which he seemed to have finished. In the evening Miss Simpson brought us a letter from MH & a complimentary & critical letter to W from John Wilson of Glasgow Post Paid. I went a little way with Miss S. My Tooth broke today. They will soon be gone. Let that pass I shall be beloved —I want no more.

*Tuesday [1st].* A very sweet day, but a sad want of rain. We went into the Orchard before dinner after I had written to MH. Then on to Mr Olliff's Intakes—we found some torn Birds nests. The Columbine was growing upon the Rocks, here & there a solitary plant—sheltered & shaded by the tufts & Bowers of trees it is a graceful slender creature, a female seeking retirement & growing freest & most graceful where it is most alone. I observed that the more shaded plants were always the tallest—a short note & gooseberries from Coleridge.

*Wednesday 2nd June 1802.* In the morning we observed that the Scarlet Beans were drooping in the leaves in great Numbers owing, we guess to an insect. We sate a while in the orchard— then we went to the old carpenters about the hurdles. Yesterday an old man called, a grey-headed man, above 70 years of age; he said he had been a soldier, that his wife & children had died in Jamaica. He had a Beggars wallet over his shoulders, a coat of shreds & patches altogether of a drab colour—he was tall & though his body was bent he had the look of one used to have been upright. I talked a while to him, & then gave him a piece of cold Bacon & a penny—said he 'You're a fine woman!' I could not help smiling. I suppose he meant 'You're a kind woman'. Afterwards a woman called travelling to Glasgow. After dinner William was very unwell. We went into Frank's field, crawled up the little glen & planned a seat then went to Mr Olliffs Hollins & sate there— found a beautiful shell-like purple fungus in Frank's field.

After tea we walked to Butterlip How & backwards &
forwards there. All the young oak tree leaves are dry as
powder. A cold south wind portending Rain. After we came in
we sate in deep silence at the window—I on a chair & William
with his hand on my shoulder. We were deep in Silence &
Love, a blessed hour. We drew to the fire before bed-time &
ate some Broth for our suppers. I ought to have said that on
Tuesday evening, namely June 1st, we walked upon the Turf
near Johns Grove. It was a lovely night. The clouds of the
western sky reflected a saffron light upon the upper end of the
lake—all was still—We went to look at Rydale. There was an
alpine fire-like red upon the tops of the mountains. This was
gone when we came in view of the Lake. But we saw the Lake
in a new & most beautiful point of view between two little
rocks, & behind a small ridge that had concealed it from us.—
This White Moss a place made for all kinds of beautiful works
of art & nature, woods & valleys, fairy valleys & fairy Tairns,
miniature mountains, alps above alps. Little John Dawson
came past us from the woods with a huge stick over his
shoulder.

*Thursday 3rd June 1802.* A very fine rain. I lay in bed till 10
o'clock. William much better than yesterday—We walked
into Easedale sheltered in a Cow-house. Came home wet—
the Cuckow sang & we watched the little Birds as we sate at
the door of the Cow-house—the oak copses are brown as in
autumn, with the late frosts—scattered over with green Trees,
Birches or hazels—the Ashes are coming into full leaf—some
of them injured. We came home quite wet. We have been
reading the Life & some of the writings of poor Logan since
dinner. 'And everlasting Longings for the lost.' It is an
affecting line. There are many affecting lines & passages in his
poems. William is now sleeping—with the window open lying
on the window Seat. The thrush is singing. There are I do
believe a thousand Buds on the honeysuckle tree all small &
far from blowing save one that is retired behind the twigs close
to the wall & as snug as a Bird's nest. John's Rose tree is very
beautiful blended with the honeysuckle.

On Tuesday Evening when we were among the Rocks we
saw in the woods what seemed to be a man, resting or looking

about him he had a piece of wood near him. William was on before me when we returned, & as I was going up to him, I found that this supposed man was John Dawson. I spoke to him & I suppose he thought I asked him what my Brother had said to him before, for he replied, '*William* asks me how my head is'—Poor fellow!—he says it is worse & worse & he walks as if he were afraid of putting his Body in motion.

Yesterday morning William walked as far as the Swan with Aggy Fisher. She was going to attend upon Goan's dying Infant. She said 'There are many heavier Crosses than the death of an Infant', & went on 'There was a woman in this vale who buried 4 grown-up Children in one year, & I have heard her say when many years were gone by that she had more pleasure in thinking of these 4 than of her living Children, for as Children get up & have families of their own their duty to their parents '*wears out & weakens*'. She could trip lightly by the graves of those who died when they were young—with a light step, as she went to Church on a Sunday.'

*Thursday June 3rd*. We walked while dinner was getting ready up into Mr Kings Hollins. I was weak & made my way down alone, for Wm took a difficult way. After dinner we walked upon the Turf path—a showery afternoon. A very affecting letter came from MH while I was sitting in the window reading Milton's Penseroso to William. I answered this letter before I went to bed.

*Friday June 4th*. It was a very sweet morning there had been much rain in the night. William had slept miserably—but knowing this I lay in bed while he got some sleep but was much disordered, he shaved himself then we went into the orchard—dined late. In the evening we walked on our favorite path. Then we came in & sate in the orchard. The evening was dark & warm—a tranquil night—I left William in the orchard. I read Mother Hubbard's tale before I went to bed.

*Saturday 5th*. A fine showery morning. I made both pies & bread, but we first walked into Easedale, & sate under the oak trees upon the mossy stones. There were one or 2 slight showers. The Gowans were flourishing along the Banks of the stream. The strawberry flower (Geum) hanging over the

Brook—all things soft & green.—In the afternoon William sate in the orchard. I went there, was tired & fell asleep. Mr Simpson drank tea, Mrs Smith called with her daughter. We walked late in the Evening upon our path. We began the letter to John Wilson.

*Sunday 6th June 1802*. A showery morning. We were writing the letter to John Wilson when Ellen came—Molly at Goan's child's funeral. After dinner I walked into John Fisher's Intake with Ellen. She brought us letters from Coleridge, Mrs Clarkson & Sara Hutchinson. William went out in the Evening & sate in the orchard, it was a showery day. In the evening there was one of the heaviest showers I ever remember.

*Monday June 7th*. I wrote to Mary H. this morning, sent the C Indolence poem. Copied the Letter to John Wilson, & wrote to my Brother Richard & Mrs Coleridge. In the evening I walked with Ellen to Butterlip How & to George Mackareth's for the horse—it was a very sweet evening—there was the Cuckow & the little Birds—the copses still injured, but the trees in general looked most soft & beautiful in tufts. William was walking when we came in—he had slept miserably for 2 nights past so we all went to bed soon. I went with Ellen in the morning to Rydale Falls. Letters from Annette, Mary H & Cook.

*Tuesday June 8th*. Ellen & I rode to Windermere. We had a fine sunny day, neither hot nor cold. I mounted the horse at the quarry—we had no difficulties or delays but at the gates. I was enchanted with some of the views. From the High Ray the view is very delightful, rich & festive, water & wood houses groves hedgerows green fields & mountains—white Houses large & small—We passed 2 or 3 nice looking statesmen's houses. Mr Curwen's shrubberies looked pitiful enough under the native Trees. We put up our horses, ate our dinner by the water-side & walked up to the Station. Then we went to the Island, walked round it, & crossed the lake with our horse in the Ferry. The shrubs have been cut away in some parts of the island. I observed to the Boatman that I did not think it improved—he replied—'We think it is for one could hardly see the house before.' It seems to me to be, however, no better than it was. They have made no natural glades, it is merely a lawn with a few miserable young trees standing as if they were half starved. There are no sheep no cattle upon these lawns. It is neither one thing or another—neither *natural* nor wholly cultivated & artificial which it was before, & that great house! Mercy upon us! If it *could* be concealed it would be well for all who are not pained to see the pleasantest of earthly spots deformed by man. But it *cannot* be covered. Even the tallest of our old oak trees would not reach to the top of it. When we went into the boat there were 2 men standing at the landing place. One seemed to be about 60, a man with a jolly red face —he looked as if he might have lived many years in Mr Curwen's house. He wore a blue jacket & Trowsers, as the people who live close by Windermere particularly at the places of chief resort in affectation, I suppose. He looked significantly at our Boatman just as we were rowing off & said 'Thomas mind you take off the directions off that Cask. You know what I mean. It will serve as a blind for them, *you* know. It was a blind business both for you & the coachman & me & all of us. Mind you take off the directions—A wink's as good as a nod with some folks'—& then he turned round looking at his companion with such an air of self-satisfaction & deep insight into unknown things!—I could hardly help laughing outright at him. The Laburnums blossom freely at the Island & in the shrubberies on the shore—they are blighted everywhere else. Roses of various sorts were out. The Brooms were in full glory everywhere 'veins of gold' among the copses. The hawthorns in the valley fading away—beautiful upon the hills. We reached home at 3 o clock. After tea William went out & walked and wrote that poem,

'The sun has long been set' &c—

He first went up to G Mackareths with the horse. Afterwards he walked on our own path & wrote the lines, he called me into the orchard & there repeated them to me—he then stayed there till 11 o clock.

*Wednesday June 9th*. Wm slept ill. A soaking all-day Rain. We should have gone to Mr Simpson's to tea but we walked up after tea. Lloyds called. The hawthorns on the mountain sides like orchards in blossom. Brought Rhubarb down. It rained hard. Ambleside Fair. I wrote to Chris$^r$ & MH.

*Thursday June 10th*. I wrote to Mrs Clarkson & Luff—went with Ellen to Rydale. Coleridge came in with a sack-full of Books &c & a Branch of mountain ash he had been attacked by a Cow—he came over by Grisdale—a furious wind. Mr Simpson drank tea. William very poorly—we went to bed latish. I slept in sitting room.

*Friday June 11th*. A wet day. William had slept very ill. Wm & C walked out—I went to bed after dinner not well. I was tired with making beds cooking &c—Molly being very ill.

*Saturday June 12th*. A rainy morning. C set off before Dinner. We went with him to the Rays but it rained so we went no further—sheltered under a wall—He would be sadly wet for a furious shower came on just when we parted.—We got no dinner, but Gooseberry pie to our tea. I baked both pies & bread, & walked with William first on our own path but it was too wet there, next over the rocks to the Road, & backward & forward, & last of all up to Mr King's. Miss Simpson & Robert had called. Letters from Sara & Annette.

*Sunday June 13th*. A fine morning. Sunshiny & bright, but with rainy clouds. William had slept better—but not well—he has been altering the poem to Mary this morning, he is now washing his feet. I wrote out poems for our journey & I wrote a letter to my Uncle Cookson. Mr Simpson came when we were in the orchard in the morning & brought us a beautiful drawing which he had done. In the evening we walked first on our own path. There we walked a good while—It was a silent night. The stars were out by ones & twos but no cuckow, no little Birds, the air was not warm, & we have observed that since Tuesday 8th when William wrote, 'The sun has long been set', that we have had no Birds singing after the Evening is fairly set in. We walked to our new view of Rydale, but it put on a sullen face. There was an owl hooting in Bainriggs. Its first halloo was so like a human shout that I was surprized when it made its second call, tremulous & lengthened out, to find that the shout had come from an owl. The full moon (not quite full) was among a company of steady island clouds, & the sky bluer about it than the natural sky blue. William observed that the full moon above a dark fir grove is a fine image of the descent of a superior being. There was a shower which drove us into John's grove before we had quitted our favorite path—we walked upon John's path before we went to view Rydale. We went to Bed immediately on our return home.

*Monday June 14th.* I was very unwell—went to bed before I drank my tea—was sick & afterwards almost asleep when Wm brought me a letter from Mary which he read to me sitting by the bed-side—Wm wrote to Mary & Sara about the Leech-gatherer I wrote to both of them in one & to Annette, to Coleridge also. I was better after tea.—I walked with Wm—when I had put up my parcel on our own path— we were driven away by the horses that go on the commons. Then we went to look at Rydale, walked a little in the fir grove, went again to the top of the hill & came home—a mild & sweet night—Wm stayed behind me. I threw him the cloak out of the window the moon overcast, he sate a few minutes in the orchard came in sleepy, & hurried to bed—I carried him his bread & butter.

*Tuesday 15th.* A sweet grey mild morning the birds sing soft & low—William has not slept all night. It wants only 10 minutes of 10 & he is in bed yet. After William rose we went & sate in the orchard till dinner time. We walked a long time in the Evening upon our favorite path—the owls hooted, the night-hawk sang to itself incessantly, but there were no little Birds, no thrushes. I left William writing a few lines about the night-hawk & other images of the evening, & went to seek for letters—none were come.—We walked backwards & forwards a little, after I returned to William, & then up as far as Mr King's. Came in. There was a Basket of Lettuces, a letter from MH about the delay of mine & telling of one she had sent by the other post, one from Wade & one from Sara to C— William did not read them—MH growing fat.

*Wednesday 16th.* We walked towards Rydale for letters—met Frank Baty with the expected one from Mary. We went up into Rydale woods & read it there, we sate near an old wall which fenced a Hazel grove, which Wm said was exactly like the filbert grove at Middleham. It is a beautiful spot, a sloping or rather steep piece of ground, with hazels growing 'tall and erect', in clumps at distances almost seeming regular as if they had been planted. We returned to Dinner. I wrote to Mary after dinner while Wm sate in the orchard. Old Mr Simpson drank tea with us. When Mr S was gone I read my letter to William, speaking to Mary about having a cat. I spoke of the little Birds keeping us company—& William told me that that very morning a Bird had perched upon his leg—he had been lying very still & had watched this little creature, it had come under the Bench where he was sitting & then flew up to his leg, he thoughtlessly stirred himself to look further at it & it flew onto the apple tree above him. It was a little young creature, that had just left its nest, equally unacquainted with man & unaccustomed to struggle against Storms & winds. While it was upon the apple tree the wind blew about the stiff boughs & the Bird seemed bemazed & not strong enough to strive with it. The swallows come to the sitting-room window as if wishing to build but I am afraid they will not have courage for it, but I believe they will build at my room window. They twitter & make a bustle & a little chearful song hanging against the panes of glass, with their soft white bellies close to the glass, & their forked fish-like tails. They swim round & round & again they come.—It was a sweet evening we first walked to the top of the hill to look at Rydale & then to Butterlip How—I do not now see the brownness that was in the coppices. The lower hawthorn blossoms passed away, those on the hills are a faint white. The wild guelder rose is coming out, & the wild roses. I have seen no honeysuckles yet except our own one nestling & a tree of the yellow kind at Mrs Townley's the day I went with Ellen to Windermere. Foxgloves are now frequent, the first I saw was that day with Ellen, & the first ripe strawberries—a letter from Coleridge. I read the first Canto of the fairy Queen to William. William went to bed immediately.

*Thursday 17th.* William had slept well. I took castor oil & lay in bed till 12 o clock. William injured himself with working a little.—When I got up we sate in the orchard, a sweet mild day. Miss Hudson called. I went with her to the top of the hill. When I came home I found William at work, attempting to alter a stanza in the poem on our going for Mary which I convinced him did not need altering—We sate in the house after dinner. In the evening walked on our favorite path, a short letter from Coleridge. William added a little to the Ode he is writing.

*Friday June 18th.* When we were sitting after Breakfast, William about to shave Luff came in. It was a sweet morning he had rode over the Fells—he brought news about Lord Lowther's intention to pay all debts &c & a letter from Mr Clarkson. He saw our garden was astonished at the Scarlet Beans &c &c. When he was gone we wrote to Coleridge M H, & my B$^r$ R$^d$ about the affair. Wm determined to go to Eusemere on Monday. In the afternoon we walked to Rydale with our letters found no letters there. A sweet evening, I had a woful headache & was ill in stomach from agitation of mind —went to bed at nine o'clock but did not sleep till late.

*Saturday 19th.* The Swallows were very busy under my window this morning—I slept pretty well, but William has got no sleep. It is after 11 & he is still in bed—a fine morning— Coleridge when he was last here, told us that for many years there being no quaker meeting held at Keswick, a single old quaker woman used to go regularly alone every Sunday, to attend the meeting-house & there used to sit & perform her worship, alone, in that beautiful place among those fir-trees, in that spacious vale, under the great mountain Skiddaw!!! Poor old Willy—we never pass by his grave close to the churchyard gate without thinking of him & having his figure brought back to our minds. He formerly was an ostler at Hawkshead having spent a little estate. In his old age he was boarded or as they say *let* by the parish. A Boy of the house that hired him was riding one morning pretty briskly beside John Fisher's, 'Hallo! has aught particular happened', said John to the Boy 'Nay naught at aw nobbut auld Willy's dead.' He was going to order the passing bell to be told.—On Thursday morning Miss Hudson of Workington called. She said 'O! I love flowers! I sow flowers in the Parks several miles from home & my mother & I visit them & watch them how they grow.' This may show that Botanists may be often deceived when they find rare flowers growing far from houses.

This was a very ordinary young woman, such as in any town in the North of England one may find a score. I sate up a while after William—he then called me down to him. (I was writing to Mary H.) I read Churchills Rosciad returned again to my writing & did not go to bed till he called to me. The shutters were closed, but I heard the Birds singing. There was our own Thrush shouting with an impatient shout—so it sounded to me. The morning was still, the twittering of the little Birds was very gloomy. The owls had hooted a ¼ of an hour before. Now the cocks were crowing. It was near daylight. I put out my candle & went to bed. In a little time I thought I heard William snoring, so I composed myself to sleep—Charles Lloyd called—'Smiling at my sweet Brother'.

*Sunday 20th.* He had slept better than I could have expected but he was far from well all day; we were in the orchard a great part of the morning. After tea we walked upon our own path for a long time. We talked sweetly together about the disposal of our riches. We lay upon the sloping Turf. Earth & sky were so lovely that they melted our very hearts. The sky to the north was of a chastened yet rich yellow fading into pale blue & streaked & scattered over with steady islands of purple melting away into shades of pink. It made my heart almost feel like a vision to me. We afterwards took our Cloaks & sate in the orchard. Mr & Miss Simpson called. We told them of our expected good fortune. We were astonished & somewhat hurt to see how coldly Mr Simpson received it—Miss S seemed very glad. We went into the house when they left us, & Wm went to bed. I sate up about an hour, he then called me to talk to him—he could not fall asleep. I wrote to Montagu.

*Monday 21st.* William was obliged to be in Bed late, he had slept so miserably. It was a very fine morning, but as we did not leave home till 12 o'clock, it was very hot. I parted from my Beloved in the Green Lane above the Blacksmiths, then went to dinner at Mr Simpsons. We walked afterwards in the garden. Betty Towers & her son & daughter came to tea. The little Lad is 4 years old almost as little a thing as Hartley & as sharp too, they say, but I saw nothing of this, being a stranger, except in his bonny eyes, which had such a sweet brightness in them when any thing was said to him that made him ashamed

& draw his chin into his neck, while he sent his eyes upwards to look at you. His Mother is a delicate woman. She said she thought that both she & her husband were so tender in their health that they must be obliged to sell their Land. Speaking of old Jim Jackson she said 'they might have looked up with the best in Grasmere if they had but been careful.' They began with a clear Estate & had never had but one child, he to be sure is a half-wit—'How did they get through with their money?' 'Why in eating & drinking.' The wife would make tea 4 or 5 times in a day & 'sec folks for sugar!' Then she would have nea Teapot but she would take the water out of a Brass pan on the fire & pour it on to the Tea in a quart pot. This all for herself, for she boiled the tea leaves always for her Husband & their son. I brought plants home, sunflowers, & planted them.

*Tuesday Morning* [*22nd*]. I had my breakfast in bed, being not quite well—I then walked to Rydale, I waited long for the post lying in the field & looking at the distant mountains,—looking & listening to the River. I met the post. Letters from Montagu & R^d—I hurried back, forwarded these to William & wrote to Montagu. When I came home I wrote to my B^r Christopher. I could settle to nothing. Molly washed & glazed the Curtains. I read the 'Midsummers Night's dream' & began 'As You Like It'. Miss Simpson called—Tamar brought me some Berries. I resolved to go to William & for that purpose John Fisher promised to go over the Fells with me. Miss Simpson ate pie, & then left me reading Letters from Mary & Coleridge. The news came that a house was taken for Betsy.

Aggy Fisher was talking with me on Monday morning 21st June about her son. She went on—Old Mary Watson was at Goan's there when the Child died. I had never seen her before since her son was drowned last summer, 'we were all in trouble, & trouble opens folks' hearts'. She began to tell about her daughter that's married to Leonard Holmes, how now that sickness is come upon him they are breaking down & failing in the world. Debts are coming in every day & he can do nothing, & they fret & jar together. One day he came riding over to Grasmere—I wondered what was the matter & I resolved to speak to him when he came back—He was as pale as a ghost

& he did not suffer the horse to gang quicker than a snail could crawl. He had come over in a trick of passion to auld Mary to tell her she might take her own again, her Daughter & the Bairns. Mary replied 'nobly (said Aggy) that she would not part man & wife but that all should come together, & she would keep them while she had anything'. Old Mary went to see them at Ambleside afterwards & he begged her pardon. Aggy observed that they would never have known this sorrow if it had pleased God to take him off suddenly.

I wrote to Mary H. & put up a parcel for Coleridge. The LB arrived. I went to bed at ½ past 11.

*Wednesday June 23rd.* I slept till ½ past 3 o clock—called Molly before 4 & had got myself dressed & breakfasted before 5, but it rained & I went to bed again. It is now 20 minutes past 10, a sunshiny morning—I walked to the top of the hill & sate under a wall near John's Grove facing the sun. I read a scene or 2 in As You Like It. I met Charles Lloyd & old Mr Lloyd was upstairs—Mrs Ll had been to meet me. I wrote a line to Wm by the Lloyds. Coleridge & Leslie came just as I had lain down after dinner. C brought me Wm's letter. He had got well to Eusemere. C & I accompanied Leslie to the Boat House. It was a sullen coldish Evening, no sunshine, but after we had parted from Leslie a light came out suddenly that repaid us for all. It fell only upon one hill, & the island, but it arrayed the grass & trees in gem-like brightness. I cooked C his supper. We sate up till one o clock.

*Thursday June 24th.* I went with C half way up the Rays. It was a cool morning. I dined at Mr Simpsons & helped Aggy Fleming to quilt a petticoat. Miss Simpson came with me after tea round by the White Bridge. I ground paint when I reached home, & was tired. Wm came in just when Molly had left me. It was a mild rainy Evening he was cool & fresh, & smelt sweetly—his clothes were wet. We sate together talking till the first dawning of Day—a happy time—he was well & not much tired. He thought I looked well too.

*Friday June 25th.* Wm had not fallen asleep till after 3 o'clock but he slept tolerably. Miss Simpson came to colour the Rooms. I began with white-washing the ceiling. I worked with them (William was very busy) till dinner time but after dinner I went to bed & fell asleep. When I rose I went just before tea into the Garden, I looked up at my Swallow's nest & it was gone. It had fallen down. Poor little creatures they could not themselves be more distressed than I was I went upstairs to look at the Ruins. They lay in a large heap upon the window ledge; these Swallows had been ten days employed in building this nest, & it seemed to be almost finished—I had watched them early in the morning, in the day many & many a time & in the evenings when it was almost dark I had seen them sitting together side by side in their unfinished nest both morning & night. When they first came about the window they used to hang against the panes, with their white Bellies & their forked tails looking like fish, but then they fluttered & sang their own little twittering song. As soon as the nest was broad enough, a sort of ledge for them they sate both mornings & evenings, but they did not pass the night there. I watched them one morning when William was at Eusemere, for more than an hour. Every now & then there was a feeling motion in their wings a sort of tremulousness & they sang a low song to one another.

[*Tuesday 29th June*.]. . .that they would not call here. I was going to tea. It is an uncertain day, sunshine showers & wind. It is now 8 o'clock I will go & see if my swallows are on their nest. Yes! there they are side by side both looking down into the garden. I have been out on purpose to see their faces. I knew by looking at the window that they were there. Young George Mackareth is come down from London. Molly says 'I did not get him asked if he had got his laal green purse yet.' When he went away he went round to see aw't neighbours & some gave him 6^d, some a shilling, & I have heard his mother say t'laal green purse was never out of his hand. I wrote to M.H. my B^r Chris^er & Miss Griffith then went to bed in the sitting room. C & Wm came in at about ½ past 11—They talked till after 12.

*Wednesday 30 June*. William slept ill, his head terribly bad. We walked part of the way up the Rays with Coleridge, a threatening windy coldish day. We did not go with C far up the Rays but sate down a few minutes together before we parted. I was not very well. I was inclined to go to bed when we reached home, but Wm persuaded me to have tea instead. We met an old man between the Potters shed & Lewthwaites. He wore a rusty but untorn hat, an excellent blue coat, waistcoat & Breeches & good mottled worsted stockings—his beard was very thick & grey of a fortnight's growth, we guessed, it was a regular beard like grey *plush*. His Bundle contained Sheffield wares. William said to him after he had asked him what his business was 'You are a very old man?' 'Aye, I am 83.' I joined in 'Have you any children' Children yes plenty. I have Children & grand-children & great grandchildren. 'I have a great grand daughter a fine Lass 13 years old.' I then said What, they take care of you—he replied half offended Thank God I can take care of myself. He said he had been a servant of the Marquis of Granby—'O he was a good Man he's in heaven—I hope he is.' He then told us how he shot himself at Bath, that he was with him in Germany & travelled with him everywhere, 'he was a famous Boxer, sir' & then he told us a story of his fighting with his Farmer. He used always to call me Hard & Sharp. Then every now & then he broke out, 'He was a good Man! When we were travelling he never asked at the public-houses' as it might be there (pointing to the Swan) what we were to pay but he would put his hand into his pocket & give them what he liked & when he came out of the house he would say 'Now they would have charged me a shilling or 10$^d$ God help them poor creatures!' I asked him again about his Children how many he had. Says he 'I cannot tell you' (I suppose he confounded Children & Grand children together). 'I have one Daughter that keeps a boarding school at Skipton in Craven. She teaches flowering & marking, & another that keeps a Boarding school at Ingleton. I brought up my family under the Marquis.' He was familiar with all parts of Yorkshire. He asked us where we lived, 'At Grasmere.' 'The bonniest Dale in all England!' says the old man. I bought a pair of scissors of him, & we sate together by the Road-side. When we parted I tried to lift his bundle, & it was almost more than I could do. We got tea & I was somewhat better. After tea I wrote to Coleridge & closed up my letter to MH. We went soon to bed. A weight of Children a poor man's blessing.

*Thursday July 1st.* A very rainy Day. We did not go out at all, till evening. I lay down after dinner, but first we sate quietly together by the fire. In the evening we took my cloak & walked first to the top of White Moss, then round by the White Bridge & up again beyond Mr Olliffs. We had a nice walk, & afterwards sate by a nice snug fire & William read Spenser & I read 'As you like it'. The saddle bags came from Keswick with a l[ette]r from M.H. & from C, & Wilkinson's drawings, but no letter from Richard.

*Friday July 2nd.* A very rainy morning there was a gleam of fair weather & we thought of walking into Easedale. Molly began to prepare the Linen for putting out—But it rained worse than ever. In the Evening we walked up to the view of Rydale, & afterwards towards Mr King's. I left William & wrote a short letter to M.H. & to Coleridge & transcribed the alterations in the Leech gatherer.

*Saturday July 3rd.* I breakfasted in bed, being not very well. Aggy Ashburner helped Molly with the Linen. I made veal & Gooseberry pies. It was very cold. Thomas Ashburner went for coals for us. There was snow upon the mountain tops. Letters from MH. & Annette—A's letter sent from G. Hill—written at Blois 23rd.

*Sunday July 4th.* Cold & rain & very dark. I was sick & ill had been made sleepless by letters. I lay in bed till 4 o clock. When I rose I was very far from well but I grew better after tea. William walked out a little I did not. We sate at the window together. It came on a terribly wet night. Wm finished the Leech gatherer today.

*Monday 4 July [5th].* A very sweet morning. William stayed some time in the orchard. I went to him there it was a beautiful morning. I copied out the L[eech] G[atherer] for Coleridge & for us. Wrote to Annette Mrs Clarkson, MH, & Coleridge. It came on a heavy rain & we could not go to Dove Nest as we had intended though we had sent Molly for the horse & it was come. The Roses in the garden are fretted & battered & quite spoiled the honey suckle though in its glory is sadly teazed. The peas are beaten down. The Scarlet Beans want sticking. The garden is overrun with weeds.

*Tuesday 5th July [6th].* It was a very rainy day but in the afternoon it cleared up a little & we set off towards Rydale to go for letters. The Rain met us at the top of the White Moss & it came on very heavily afterwards. It drove past Nab Scar in a substantial shape, as if going Grasmere-wards as fast as it could go. We stopped at Willy Parks & borrowed a plaid. I rested a little while till the Rain seemed passing away & then I went to meet William. I met him near Rydale with a letter from Christopher. We had a pleasant but very rainy walk home. A letter came from Mary in the morning & in the evening one from Coleridge by Fletcher. The swallows have completed their beautiful nest. I baked bread & pies.

*Wednesday 6th* [*7th*]. A very fine day. William had slept ill so he lay in bed till 11 o clock. I wrote to John, ironed the Linen, packed up, lay in the orchard all the afternoon. In the morning Wm nailed up the trees while I was ironing. We lay sweetly in the Orchard the well is beautiful the Orchard full of Foxgloves the honeysuckle beautiful—plenty of roses but they are battered. Wrote to Molly Ritson & Coleridge. Walked on the White Moss—glow-worms—well for them children are in bed when they shine.

*Thursday 7th* [*8th*]. A rainy morning. I paid Thomas Ashburner, & Frank Baty. When I was coming home, a post Chaise passed with a little girl behind in a patched ragged red cloak. The child & cloak—Alice Fells own self. We sate in tranquility together by the fire in the morning, in the afternoon after we had talked a little, Wm fell asleep I read the Winter's Tale. Then I went to bed but did not sleep. The Swallows stole in and out of their nest, & sate there *whiles* quite still, *whiles* they sung low for 2 minutes or more at a time just like a muffled Robin. William was looking at the Pedlar when I got up—he arranged it, & after tea I wrote it out—280 lines. In the meantime the evening being fine he carried his coat to the Tailors & went to George Mackareth's to engage the horse. He came in to me at about ½ past nine pressing me to go out; he had got letters which we were to read out of doors —I was rather unwilling, fearing I could not see to read the letters, but I saw well enough. One was from MH a very tender affecting letter, another from Sara to C, from C to us, & from my B$^r$ R$^d$. The moon was behind. William hurried me out in hopes that I should see her. We walked first to the top of the hill to see Rydale. It was dark & dull but our own vale was very solemn, the shape of helm crag was quite distinct, though black. We walked backwards & forwards on the White Moss path there was a sky-like white brightness on the Lake. The Wyke Cottage Light at the foot of Silver How. Glowworms out, but not so numerous as last night—O beautiful place!—Dear Mary William—The horse is come Friday morning, so I must give over. William is eating his Broth—I must prepare to go—The Swallows I must leave them the well the garden the Roses all—Dear creatures!! they sang last night after I was in bed—seemed to be singing to one another, just before they settled to rest for the night. Well I must go—Farewell.— — —

On Friday morning, July 9th William & I set forward to Keswick on our Road to Gallow Hill—we had a pleasant ride though the day was showery. It rained heavily when Nelly Mackareth took the horse from us, at the Blacksmiths. Coleridge met us at Sara's Rock. He had inquired about us before of Nelly Mackareth, & we had been told by a handsome man, an inhabitant of Wytheburne with whom he had been talking (& who seemed by the Bye much pleased with his companion) that C was waiting for us. We reached Keswick against tea time. We called at Calverts on the Saturday Evening. On Sunday I was poorly & the day was wet, so we could not move from Keswick, but on Monday 11th [12th] July 1802 we went to Eusemere. Coleridge walked with us 6 or 7 miles. He was not well & we had a melancholy parting after having sate together in silence by the Road-side. We turned aside to explore the country near Hutton John, & had a new & delightful walk. The valley which is subject to the decaying Mansion that stands at its head seems to join its testimony to that of the house to the falling away of the family greatness. The hedges are in bad condition, the Land wants draining & is over-run with Brackens, yet there is a something every-where that tells of its former possessors—the trees are left scattered about as if intended to be like a park, & these are very interesting, standing as they do upon the sides of the

steep hills, that slope down to the Bed of the River, a stony
bedded stream that spreads out to a considerable breadth at
the village of Dacre—a little above Dacre we came into the
right road to Mr Clarksons after having walked through
woods & fields never exactly knowing whether we were right
or wrong. We learnt, however, that we had saved half a mile.
We sate down by the River side to rest & saw some swallows
flying about & about under the Bridge, & two little
Schoolboys were loitering among the Scars seeking after their
nests. We reached Mr Clarksons at about 8 o clock after a
sauntering walk, having lingered & loitered & sate down
together that we might be alone. Mr & Mrs C were just come
from Luff's.

We spent Tuesday the 13th of July at Eusemere, & on
Wednesday morning, the 13th [14th], we walked to Emont
Bridge & mounted the Coach between Bird's Nest &
Hartshorn tree. Mr Clarkson's Bitch followed us so far. A
soldier & his young wife wanted to be taken up by the
Coachman but there was no Room. We had a chearful ride
though cold, till we got on to Stanemoor, & then a heavy
shower came on, but we buttoned ourselves up, both together
in the Guard's coat & we liked the hills & the Rain the better
for bringing [us] so close to one another—I never rode more
snugly. At last, however, it grew so very rainy that I was
obliged to go into the Coach at Bowes. Lough of Penrith was
there, & very impertinent—I was right glad to get out again to
my own dear Brother at Greta Bridge, the sun shone
chearfully & a glorious ride we had over Gaterly Moor. Every
Building was bathed in golden light—The trees were more
bright than earthly trees, & we saw round us miles beyond
miles—Darlington Spire, &c &c—We reached Leming Lane
at about 9 o clock, supped comfortably & enjoyed our fire. On
Thursday morning, at a little before 7, being the 14th [15th]
July we got into a post Chaise & went to Thirsk to Breakfast.
We were well treated but when the Landlady understood that
we were going to *walk* off & leave our luggage behind she
threw out some saucy words in our hearing. The day was very
hot & we rested often & long before we reached the foot of the
Ham[b]leton Hills, & while we were climbing them still

oftener. We had a Sandwich in our pockets which we finished when we had climbed part of the hill, & we were almost overpowered with thirst when I heard the trickling of a little stream of water. I was before William & I stopped till he came up to me—We sate a long time by this water, & climbed the hill slowly—I was foot-sore, the Sun shone hot, the little Scotch cattle panted & tossed fretfully about. The view was hazy and we could see nothing from the top of the hill but an indistinct wide-spreading country, full of trees, but the Buildings, towns & houses were lost. We stopped to examine their curious stone, then walked along the flat common, it was now cooler, but I was still foot-sore, & could not walk quick so I left Wm sitting 2 or three times, and when he followed me he took a Sheep for me, & then me for a Sheep. I rested opposite the sign of the Sportsman & was questioned by the Landlady. Arrived very hungry at Ryvaux. Nothing to eat at the Millers, as we expected but, at an exquisitely neat farmhouse we got some boiled milk & bread—this strengthened us, & I went down to look at the Ruins—thrushes were singing, Cattle feeding among green grown hillocks about the Ruins. These hillocks were scattered over with *grovelets* of wild roses & other shrubs, & covered with wild flowers—I could have stayed in this solemn quiet spot till Evening without a thought of moving but William was waiting for me, so in a quarter of an hour I went away. We walked upon Mr Duncombe's terrace & looked down upon the abbey. It stands in a larger valley among a Brotherhood of valleys of different lengths & breadths all woody, & running up into the hills in all directions. We reached Helmsly just at Dusk—we had a beautiful view of the Castle from the top of the hill. Slept at a very nice Inn & were well treated—bright bellows, & floors as smooth as ice. On Friday morning the 16th July we walked to Kirby. Met people coming to Helmsly fair—were misdirected & walked a mile out of our way—met a double horse at Kirby. A beautiful view above Pickering—Sinnington village very beautiful. Met Mary & Sara 7 miles from GH—Sheltered from the Rain beautiful glen, spoiled by the large house— sweet Church & Churchyard arrived at Gallow Hill at 7 o'clock.

*Friday Evening 15th July* [*16th*]. The weather bad, almost all
the time. Sara Tom & I rode up Bedale. Wm Mary Sara & I
went to Scarborough, & we walked in the Abbey pasture, & to
Wykeham & on Monday the 26th we went off with Mary in a
post Chaise. We had an interesting Ride over the Wolds,
though it rained all the way. Single thorn bushes were
scattered about on the Turf, Sheep Sheds here & there, & now
& then a little hut—swelling grounds, & sometimes a single
tree or a Clump of trees. Mary was very sick, & every time we
stopped to open a gate, she felt the motion in her whole body,
indeed I was sick too, & perhaps the smooth gliding of the
Chaise over the Turf made us worse. We passed through one
or two little villages, embosomed in tall trees. After we had
parted from Mary there were gleams of sunshine, but with
showers. We saw Beverly in a heavy rain & yet were much
pleased with the beauty of the town. Saw the Minster a pretty
clean Building but injured very much with Grecian Architecture. The country between Beverly & Hull very rich but
miserably flat—brick houses, windmills, houses again—dull
& endless—Hull a frightful, Dirty, *brick housey* tradesmanlike,
rich, vulgar place—yet the River though the shores are so low
that they can hardly be seen looked beautiful with the evening
lights upon it & Boats moving about—we walked a long
time & returned to our dull day Room, but quiet evening one,
quiet & our own, to supper.

*Tuesday 26th* [*27th*]. Market day streets dirty, very rainy, did
not leave Hull till 4 o clock, & left Barton at about 6—rained
all the way—almost—a beautiful village at the foot of a hill
with trees—a gentleman's house converted into a Lady's
Boarding school. We had a woman in bad health in the Coach,
& took in a Lady & her Daughter—supped at Lincoln. Duck
& peas, & cream cheese—paid 2/–. We left Lincoln on
Wednesday morning 27th July [28th] at six o'clock it rained
heavily & we could see nothing but the antientry of some of
the Buildings as we passed along. The night before, however,
we had seen enough to make us regret this. The minster stands
at the Edge of a hill, overlooking an immense plain. The
country very flat as we went along—the Day mended—We
went to see the outside of the Minster while the passengers

were dining at Peterborough—the West End very grand. The little girl who was a great scholar, & plainly her mothers favorite tho' she had a large family at home had bought The Farmer's Boy. She said it was written by a man without education & was very wonderful.

On Thursday morning, 29th, we arrived in London. Wm left me at the Inn—I went to bed &c &c &c—After various troubles & disasters we left London on Saturday morning at ½ past 5 or 6, the 31st of July (I have forgot which) we mounted the Dover Coach at Charing Cross. It was a beautiful morning. The City, St pauls, with the River & a multitude of little Boats, made a most beautiful sight as we crossed Westminster Bridge. The houses were not overhung by their cloud of smoke & they were spread out endlessly, yet the sun shone so brightly with such a pure light that there was even something like the purity of one of nature's own grand Spectacles. We rode on chearfully now with the Paris Diligence before us, now behind—we walked up the steep hills, beautiful prospects everywhere, till we even reached Dover. At first the rich populous wide spreading woody country about London, then the River Thames, ships sailing, chalk cliffs, trees, little villages. Afterwards Canterbury, situated on a plain, rich & woody, but the City & Cathedral disappointed me. Hop grounds on each side of the road some miles from Canterbury, then we came to a common, the race ground, an elevated plain, villages among trees in the bed of a valley at our right, & rising above this valley, green hills scattered over with wood—neat gentlemen's houses—one white house almost hid with green trees which we longed for & the parsons house as neat a place as could be which would just have suited Coleridge. No doubt we might have found one for Tom Hutchinson & Sara & a good farm too. We halted at a halfway house—fruit carts under the shade of trees, seats for guests, a tempting place to the weary traveller. Still as we went along the country was beautiful, hilly, with cottages lurking under the hills & their little plots of hop ground like vineyards. It was a bad hop-year—a woman on the top of the coach said to me 'it is a sad thing for the poor people for the hop-gathering is the women's harvest, there is employment about

the hops both for women & children'. We saw the Castle of
Dover & the sea beyond 4 or 5 miles before we reached D. We
looked at it through a long vale, the castle being upon an
eminence, as it seemed at the end of this vale which opened to
the Sea. The country now became less fertile but near Dover it
seemed more rich again. Many buildings stand on the flat
fields, sheltered with tall trees. There is one old chapel that
might have been there just in the same state in which it now is,
when this vale was as retired and as little known to travellers,
as our own Cumberland mountain wilds 30 years ago. There
was also a very old Building on the other side of the road
which had a strange effect among the many new ones that are
springing up everywhere. It seemed odd that it could have
kept itself pure in its anciently among so many upstarts. It
was near dark when we reached Dover. We were told that the
packet was about to sail, so we went down to the Custom-
house in half an hour, had our luggage examined &c &c &
then we drank tea, with the honorable Mr Knox & his Tutor.
We arrived at Calais at 4 o'clock on Sunday morning the 31st
of July [1 Aug]. We stayed in the vessel till ½ past 7. Then
Wm went for Letters, at about ½ past 8 or 9. We found out
Annette & C chez Madame Avril dans la Rue de la Tête d'or.
We lodged opposite two Ladies in tolerably decent-sized
rooms but badly furnished, & with large store of bad smells
& dirt in the yard, & all about. The weather was very hot.
We walked by the sea-shore almost every Evening with
Annette & Caroline or Wm & I alone. I had a bad cold &
could not bathe at first but William did. It was a pretty sight
to see as we walked upon the Sands when the tide was low,
perhaps a hundred people bathing about ¼ of a mile distant
from us, and we had delightful walks after the heat of the day
was passed away—seeing far off in the west the Coast of
England like a cloud crested with Dover Castle, which was but
like the summit of the cloud—the Evening star & the glory
of the sky. The Reflections in the water were more beautiful
than the sky itself, purple waves brighter than precious stones
for ever melting away upon the sands. The fort, a wooden
Building, at the Entrance of the harbour at Calais, when the
Evening twilight was coming on, & we could not see anything

of the building but its shape which was far more distinct than in perfect daylight, seemed to be reared upon pillars of Ebony, between which pillars the sea was seen in the most beautiful colours that can be conceived. Nothing in Romance was ever half so beautiful. Now came in view as the Evening star sank down & the colours of the west faded away the two lights of England, lighted up by Englishmen in our Country, to warn vessels of rocks or sands. These we used to see from the Pier when we could see no other distant objects but the Clouds the Sky & the Sea itself. All was dark behind. The town of Calais seemed deserted of the light of heaven, but there was always light, & life, & joy upon the Sea.—One night, though, I shall never forget, the day had been very hot, & William & I walked alone together upon the pier—the sea was gloomy for there was a blackness over all the sky except when it was overspread with lightning which often revealed to us a distant vessel. Near us the waves roared & broke against the pier, & as they broke & as they travelled towards us, they were interfused with greenish fiery light. The more distant sea always black & gloomy. It was, also beautiful on the calm hot nights to see the little Boats row out of harbour with wings of fire & the sail boats with the fiery track which they cut as they went along & which closed up after them with a hundred thousand sparkles balls shootings, & streams of glowworm light. Caroline was delighted.

On Sunday the 29th of August we left Calais at 12 o'clock in the morning & landed at Dover at 1 on Monday the 30th. I was sick all the way. It was very pleasant to me when we were in harbour at Dover to breathe the fresh air, & to look up and see the stars among the Ropes of the vessel. The next day was very hot. We both bathed & sate upon the Dover Cliffs & looked upon France with many a melancholy & tender thought. We could see the shores almost as plain as if it were but an English Lake.—We mounted the coach at ½ past 4 & arrived in London at 6 the 30th August [31st]. It was misty & we could see nothing. We stayed in London till Wednesday the 22nd of September, & arrived at Gallow Hill on Friday 24th September. Mary first met us in the avenue. She looked so fat & well that we were made very happy by the

sight of her—then came Sara, & last of all Joanna. Tom was
forking corn standing upon the corn cart. We dressed
ourselves immediately & got tea—the garden looked gay with
asters & sweet peas—I looked at everything with tranquillity
& happiness but I was ill both on Saturday & Sunday &
continued to be poorly most of the time of our stay. Jack &
George came on Friday Evening 1st October. On Saturday
2nd we rode to Hackness, William Jack George & Sara single,
I behind Tom. On Sunday 3rd Mary & Sara were busy packing.
On Monday 4th October 1802, my Brother William was
married to Mary Hutchinson. I slept a good deal of the night
& rose fresh & well in the morning—at a little after 8 o clock I
saw them go down the avenue towards the Church. William
had parted from me up stairs. I gave him the wedding ring—
with how deep a blessing! I took it from my forefinger where I
had worn it the whole of the night before—he slipped it again
onto my finger and blessed me fervently. When they were
absent my dear little Sara prepared the breakfast. I kept
myself as quiet as I could, but when I saw the two men
running up the walk, coming to tell us it was over, I could
stand it no longer & threw myself on the bed where I lay in
stillness, neither hearing or seeing any thing, till Sara came
upstairs to me & said 'They are coming'. This forced me from
the bed where I lay & I moved I knew not how straight
forward, faster than my strength could carry me till I met my
beloved William & fell upon his bosom. He & John
Hutchinson led me to the house & there I stayed to welcome
my dear Mary. As soon as we had breakfasted we departed. It
rained when we set off. Poor Mary was much agitated when
she parted from her Brothers & Sisters & her home. Nothing
particular occurred till we reached Kirby. We had sunshine &
showers, pleasant talk, love & chearfulness. We were obliged
to stay two hours at K. while the horses were feeding. We
wrote a few lines to Sara & then walked out, the sun shone &
we went to the Church-yard, after we had put a Letter into
the Post office for the York Herald. We sauntered about &
read the Grave-stones. There was one to the memory of 5
Children, who had all died within 5 years, & the longest lived
had only lived 4 years. There was another Stone erected to the

memory of an unfortunate woman (as we supposed, by a stranger). The verses engraved upon it expressed that she had been neglected by her Relations & counselled the Readers of those words to look within & recollect their own frailties. We left Kirby at about ½ past 2. There is not much variety of prospect from K. to Helmsely but the country is very pleasant, being rich & woody, & Helmsely itself stands very sweetly at the foot of the rising grounds of Duncombe Park which is scattered over with tall woods & lifting itself above the common buildings of the Town stands Helmsely Castle, now a Ruin, formerly inhabited by the gay Duke of Buckingham. Every foot of the Road was, of itself interesting to us, for we had travelled along it on foot Wm & I when we went to fetch our dear Mary, & had sate upon the Turf by the roadside more than once. Before we reached Helmsely our Driver told us that he could not take us any further, so we stopped at the same Inn where we had slept before. My heart danced at the sight of its cleanly outside, bright yellow walls, casements overshadowed with jasmine & its low, double gavel-ended front. We were not shewn into the same parlour where Wm & I were, it was a small room with a drawing over the chimney piece which the woman told us had been bought at a sale. Mary & I warmed ourselves at the kitchen fire we then walked into the garden, & looked over a gate up to the old ruin which stands at the top of a mount, & round about it the moats are grown up into soft green cradles, hollows surrounded with green grassy hillocks & these are overshadowed by old trees, chiefly ashes. I prevailed upon William to go up with me to the ruins we left Mary sitting by the kitchen fire. The sun shone, it was warm & very pleasant. One part of the castle seems to be inhabited. There was a man mowing nettles in the open space which had most likely once been the Castle Court. There is one gateway exceedingly beautiful—Children were playing upon the sloping ground. We came home by the Street. After about an hour's delay we set forward again, had an excellent Driver who opened the gates so dexterously that the horses never stopped. Mary was very much delighted with the view of the Castle from the point where we had seen it before. I was pleased to see again the little path which we had walked upon, the gate I had climbed over, & the Road down which we had seen the two little Boys drag a log of wood, & a team of horses struggle under the weight of a great load of timber. We had felt compassion for the poor horses that were under the govern-ance of oppressive & ill-judging drivers, & for the poor Boys who seemed of an age to have been able to have dragged the log of wood merely out of the love of their own activity, but from poverty & bad food they panted for weakness & were obliged to fetch their father from the town to help them. Duncombe House looks well from the Road—a large Build-ing, though I believe only 2 thirds of the original design are completed. We rode down a very steep hill to Ryvaux valley, with woods all round us. We stopped upon the Bridge to look at the Abbey & again when we had crossed it. Dear Mary had never seen a ruined Abbey before except Whitby. We recognized the Cottages, houses, & the little valleys as we went along. We walked up a long hill, the Road carrying us up the cleft or valley with woody hills on each side of us. When we *went* to GH I had walked down this valley alone. Wm followed me. It was not dark evening when we passed the little publick house, but before we had crossed the Hambledon hills & reached the point overlooking Yorkshire it was quite dark. We had not wanted, however, fair prospects before us, as we drove along the flat plain of the high hill, far far off us, in the western sky, we saw shapes of Castles, Ruins among groves, a great, spreading wood, rocks, & single trees, a minster with its tower unusually distinct, minarets in another quarter, & a round Grecian Temple also—the colours of the sky of a bright grey & the forms of a sober grey, with a dome. As we descended the hill there was no distinct view, but of a great space, only near us, we saw the wild & (as the people say) bottomless Tarn in the hollow at the side of the hill. It seemed to be made visible to us only by its own light, for all the hill about us was dark. Before we reached Thirsk we saw a light before us which we at first thought was the moon, then Lime kilns, but when we drove into the market place it proved a large Bonfire with Lads dancing round it, which is a sight I dearly love. The Inn was like an illuminated house—every Room full. We asked the cause, & were told by the Girl that it was 'Mr John Bell's

Birthday, that he had heired his Estate.' The Landlady was very civil. She did not recognise the despised foot-travellers. We rode nicely in the dark, & reached Leming Lane at 11 o'clock. I am always sorry to get out of a Chaise when it is night. The people of the house were going to bed & we were not very well treated though we got a hot supper. We breakfasted the next morning & set off at about ½ past 8 o clock. It was a chearful sunny morning. We soon turned out of Leming Lane & passed a nice village with a beautiful church. We had a few showers, but when we came to the green fields of Wensley, the sun shone upon them all, & the Eure in its many windings glittered as it flowed along under the green slopes of Middleham & Middleham Castle. Mary looked about for her friend Mr Place, & thought she had him sure on the contrary side of the vale from that on which we afterwards found that he lived. We went to a new built house at Leyburn, the same village where Wm & I had dined with George Hutchinson on our Road to Grasmere 2 years & ¾ ago, but not the same house. The Landlady was very civil, giving us cake and wine but the horses being out we were detained at least 2 hours & did not set off till 2 o'clock. We paid for 35 miles, ie to Sedbergh, but the Landlady did not encourage us to hope to get beyond Hawes. A shower came on just after we left the Inn while the Rain beat against the Windows we ate our dinners which M & W heartily enjoyed—I was not quite well. When we passed thro' the village of Wensly my heart was melted away with dear recollections, the Bridge, the little water-spout the steep hill the Church—They are among the most vivid of my own inner visions, for they were the first objects that I saw after we were left to ourselves, & had turned our whole hearts to Grasmere as a home in which we were to rest. The Vale looked most beautiful each way. To the left the bright silver Stream inlaid the flat & very green meadows, winding like a serpent. To the Right we did not see it so far, it was lost among trees & little hills. I could not help observing as we went along how much more *varied* the prospects of Wensly Dale are in the summer time than I could have thought possible in the winter. This seemed to be in great measure owing to the trees being in leaf, & forming groves, &

screens, & thence little openings upon recesses & concealed retreats which in winter only made a part of the one great Vale. The *beauty* of the Summer time here as much excels that of the winter as the variety, owing to the excessive greenness of the fields, & the trees in leaf half concealing, & where they do not conceal, softening the hard bareness of the limey white Roofs. One of our horses seemed to grow a little restive as we went through the first village, a long village on the side of a hill. It grew worse & worse, & at last we durst not go on any longer. We walked a while, & then the Post-Boy was obliged to take the horse out & go back for another. We seated ourselves again snugly in the Post Chaise. The wind struggled about us & rattled the window & gave a gentle motion to the chaise, but we were warm & at our ease within. Our station was at the Top of a hill, opposite Bolton Castle, the Eure flowing beneath. William has since wrote a sonnet on this our imprisonment—Hard was thy Durance Queen compared with ours. Poor Mary! Wm fell asleep, lying upon my breast & I upon Mary. I lay motionless for a long time, but I was at last obliged to move. I became very sick & continued so for some time after the Boy brought the horse to us. Mary had been a little sick but it soon went off.—We had a sweet ride till we came to a public house on the side of a hill where we alighted & walked down to see the waterfalls. The sun was not set, & the woods & fields were spread over with the yellow light of Evening, which made their greenness a thousand times more green. There was too much water in the River for the beauty of the falls, & even the Banks were less interesting than in Winter. Nature had entirely got the better in her struggles against the giants who first cast the mould of these works; for indeed it is a place that did not in winter remind one of God, but one could not help feeling as if there had been the agency of some 'Mortal Instruments' which Nature had been struggling against without making a perfect conquest. There was something so wild & new in this feeling, knowing as we did in the inner man that God alone had laid his hand upon it that I could not help regretting the want of it, besides it is a pleasure to a real lover of Nature to give winter all the glory he can, for summer *will* make its own way, & speak its own praises. We saw the pathway which Wm & I took at the close of Evening, the path leading to the Rabbit Warren where we lost ourselves. The farm with its holly hedges was lost among the green hills & hedgerows in general, but we found it out & were glad to look at it again. When William had left us to seek the waterfalls Mary & I were frightened by a Cow. At our return to the Inn we found new horses & a new Driver, & we went on nicely to Hawes where we arrived before it was quite dark. Mary & I got tea, & William had a partridge & mutton chops & tarts for his supper. Mary sate down with him. We had also a shilling's worth of negus & Mary made me some Broth for all which supper we were only charged 2/–. I could not sit up long. I vomited, & took the Broth & then slept sweetly. We rose at 6 o clock—a rainy morning. We had a good Breakfast & then departed. There was a very pretty view about a mile from Hawes, where we crossed a Bridge, bare, & very green fields with cattle, a glittering stream cottages, a few ill-grown trees, & high hills. The sun shone now. Before we got upon the bare hills there was a hunting lodge on our right exactly like Greta Hill, with fir plantations about it. We were very fortunate in the day, gleams of sunshine passing clouds, that travelled with their shadows below them. Mary was much pleased with Garsdale. It was a dear place to William & me. We noted well the publick-house (Garsdale Hall) where we had baited & drunk our pint of ale, & afterwards the mountain which had been adorned by Jupiter in his glory when we were here before. It was mid-day when we reached Sedbergh, & *market* day. We were in the same Room where we had spent the Evening together in our road to Grasmere. We had a pleasant Ride to Kendal, where we arrived at about 2 o'clock—the day favored us—M & I went to see the house where dear Sara had lived, then went to seek Mr Bousfield's shop but we found him not—he had sold all his goods the Day before. We then went to the Pot woman's & bought 2 jugs & a Dish, & some paper at Pennington's. When we came to the Inn William was almost ready for us. The afternoon was not chearful but it did not rain till we came near Windermere. I am always glad to see Stavely it is a place I dearly love to think of—the first mountain village that I came to with Wm when we first began our pilgrimage together. Here we drank a Bason of milk at a publick house, & here I washed my feet in the Brook & put on a pair of silk stockings by Wm's advice.— Nothing particular occurred till we reached Ing's chapel—the door was open & we went in. It is a neat little place, with a marble floor & marble communion Table with a painting over it of the last supper, & Moses & Aaron on each side. The woman told us that 'they had painted them as near as they could by the dresses as they are described in the Bible', & gay enough they are. The Marble had been sent by Richard Bateman from Leghorn. The woman told us that a Man had been at her house a few days before who told her he had helped to bring it down the Red Sea & she had believed him gladly. It rained very hard when we reached Windermere. We sate in the rain at Wilcocks to change horses, & arrived at Grasmere at about 6 o clock on Wednesday Evening, the 6th of October 1802. Molly was overjoyed to see us,—for my part I cannot describe what I felt, & our dear Mary's feelings would I dare say not be easy to speak of. We went by candle light into the garden & were astonished at the growth of the Brooms, Portugal Laurels, &c &c &—The next day, Thursday, we unpacked the Boxes. On Friday 8th we baked Bread, & Mary & I walked, first upon the Hill side, & then in John's Grove, then in view of Rydale, the first walk that I had taken with my Sister.

*Saturday 9th*. William & I walked to Mr Simpsons.

*Sunday 10th*. Rain all day.

*Monday 11th*. A beautiful day. We walked to the Easedale hills to hunt waterfalls—Wm & Mary left me sitting on a stone on the solitary mountains & went to Easedale Tairn. I grew chilly & followed them. This approach to the Tairn is very beautiful. We expected to have found C at home but he did not come till after dinner—he was well but did not look so.

*Tuesday 12th October 1802*. We walked with C to Rydale.

*Wednesday 13th*. Set forwards with him towards Keswick & he prevailed us to go on. We consented, Mrs C not being at home. The day was delightful. We drank tea at John Stanleys. Wrote to Annette.

*Thursday 14th*. We went in the evening to Calverts. Moonlight. stayed supper.

*Friday 15th*. Walked to L[or]d Wm Gordon's.

*Saturday 16th*. Came home Mary & I, William returned to Coleridge before we reached Nadel Fell. Mary & I had a pleasant walk, the day was very bright, the people busy getting in their corn—reached home at about 5 o clock. I was not quite well but better after tea, we made Cakes &c—

*Sunday 17th*. We had 13 of our neighbours to Tea—Wm came in just as we began tea.

*Monday 18th*. I was not very well. I walked up in the morning to the Simpsons.

*Tuesday 19th*. The Simpsons drank tea & supped. William was much oppressed.

*Wednesday 20th*. We all walked on Butterlip How—it rained.

*Thursday 21st*. I walked with Wm to Rydale.

*Friday 22nd*.

*Saturday 23rd*. Mary was baking. I walked with Wm to see Langdale Rydale & the Foot of Grasmere—we had a heavenly walk, but I came home in the tooth ache—& have since that day been confined up stairs, till now namely Saturday 30th of October 1802. William is gone to Keswick. Mary went with him to the Top of the Rays. She is returned & is now sitting near me by the fire. It is a breathless grey day that leaves the golden woods of Autumn quiet in their own tranquillity, stately & beautiful in their decaying, the lake is a perfect mirror.

*Saturday 30th October*. Wm met Stoddart at the Bridge at the foot of Legberthwaite dale—he returned with him & they surprized us by their arrival at 4 o'clock in the afternoon. Stoddart & W dined. I went to bed, & after tea S read in Chaucer to us.

*Monday 31st October [Sunday]*. John Monkhouse called. Wm & S went to K[eswick]. Mary & I walked to the top of the hill & looked at Rydale. I was much affected when I stood upon the 2nd bar of Sara's Gate. The lake was perfectly still, the Sun shone on Hill & vale, the distant Birch trees looked like large golden Flowers—nothing else in colour was distinct & separate but all the beautiful colours seemed to be melted into one another, & joined together in one mass so that there were no differences though an endless variety when one tried to find it out. The Fields were of one sober yellow brown. After dinner we both lay on the floor. Mary slept. I *could* not for I was thinking of so many things. We sate nicely together after Tea looking over old Letters. Molly was gone up to Mr Simpsons to see Mrs S who was very ill.

*Monday November 1st*. I wrote to Miss Lamb. After dinner Mary walked to Mr Simpson's. Letters from Cook Wrangham Mrs C

*Tuesday 2nd November*. William returned from K—he was not well. Baking Day—Mr BS came in at tea time—Molly sate up with Mrs S. William was not well this evening.

*Wednesday 3rd*. Mr Luff came in to tea.

*Thursday 4th*. I scalded my foot with coffee after having been in bed in the afternoon—I was near fainting, & then bad in my bowels. Mary waited upon me till 2 o'clock, then we went to bed & with applications of vinegar I was lulled to sleep about 4.

*Friday 5th*. I was laid up all day. I wrote to Montagu & Cooke & sent off letters to Miss Lamb & Coleridge.

*Saturday 6th*.

*Sunday 7th*. Fine weather. Letters from Coleridge that he was gone to London—Sara at Penrith. I wrote to Mrs Clarkson. Wm began to translate Ariosto.

*Monday 8th*. A beautiful day. William got to work again at Ariosto, & so continued all the morning, though the day was so delightful that it made my very heart linger to be out of doors, & see & feel the beauty of the Autumn in freedom. The trees on the opposite side of the Lake are of a yellow brown, but there are one or two trees opposite our windows, (an ash tree for instance) quite green, as in spring. The fields are of their winter colour, but the Island is as green as ever it was. Mary has been baking to-day, she is now sitting in the parlour. Wm is writing out his Stanzas from Ariosto. We have a nice fire, the evening is quiet—Poor Coleridge! Sara is at Keswick I hope.—William has been ill in his stomach but he is better tonight—I have read one Canto of Ariosto today.

*24th December 1802, Christmas Eve*. William is now sitting by me at ½ past 10 o'clock. I have been beside him ever since tea running the heel of a stocking, repeating some of his sonnets to him, listening to his own repeating, reading some of Milton's

& the Allegro & Penseroso. It is a quiet keen frost. Mary is in the parlour below attending to the baking of cakes & Jenny Fletcher's pies. Sara is in bed in the tooth ache, & so we are— beloved William is turning over the leaves of Charlotte Smith's sonnets, but he keeps his hand to his poor chest pushing aside his breastplate. Mary is well & I am well, & Molly is as blithe as last year at this time. Coleridge came this morning with Wedgwood. We all turned out of Wm's bedroom one by one to meet him—he looked well. We had to tell him of the Birth of his little Girl, born yesterday morning at 6 o clock. W went with them to Wytheburn in the Chaise, & M & I met Wm on the Rays. It was not an unpleasant morning to the feelings—far from it—the sun shone now & then, & there was no wind, but all things looked chearless & distinct, no meltings of sky into mountains—the mountains like stone-work wrought up with huge hammers.—Last Sunday was as mild a day as I ever remember—We all set off together to walk. I went to Rydale & Wm returned with me. M & S went round the Lakes. There were flowers of various kinds the topmost bell of a fox-glove, geraniums, daisies—a buttercup in the water (but this I saw two or three days before) small yellow flowers (I do not know their name) in the turf a large bunch of strawberry blossoms. Wm sate a while with me, then went to meet M. & S.—Last Saturday I dined at Mr Simpsons also a beautiful mild day. Monday was a frosty day, & it has been frost ever since. On Saturday I dined with Mrs Simpson. It is today Christmas-day Saturday 25th December 1802. I am 31 years of age.—It is a dull frosty day.

Again I have neglected to write my Journal—New Years Day is passed Old Christmas day & I have recorded nothing. —It is today January 11th Tuesday.—On Christmas Day I dressed myself ready to go to Keswick in a returned chaise, but did not go. On Thursday 30th December I went to K. Wm rode before me to the foot of the hill nearest Keswick. There we parted close to a little water course, which was then noisy with water, but on my return a dry channel. We ate some potted Beef on Horseback, & sweet cake. We stopped our horse close to the ledge opposite a tuft of primroses three flowers in full blossom & a Bud, they reared themselves up among the green moss. We debated long whether we should pluck & at last left them to live out their day, which I was right glad of at my return the Sunday following for there they remained uninjured either by cold or wet—I stayed at K. over New Year's Day, & returned on Sunday the 2nd January. Wm Mackareth fetched me. (M & S walked as far as John Stanley's.) Wm was alarmed at my long delay & came to within 3 miles of Keswick, he mounted before me. It had been a sweet mild day & was a pleasant Evening. C stayed with us till Tuesday January 4th. W. & I walked up to George M's to endeavour to get the horse, then walked with him to Ambleside. We parted with him at the turning of the Lane, he going on horseback to the top of Kirkstone. On Thursday 6th, C. returned, & on Friday the 7th he and Sara went to Keswick. W accompanied them to the foot of Wytheburn—I to Mrs Simpson's & dined & called on Aggy Fleming sick in bed. It was a gentle day, & when Wm & I returned home just before sunset, it was a heavenly evening. A soft sky was among the hills, & a summer sunshine above, & blending with this sky, for it was more like sky than clouds. The turf looked warm & soft.

*Saturday January 9th* [*8th*]. Wm & I walked to Rydale—no letters—still as mild as Spring, a beautiful moonlight evening & a quiet night but before morning the wind rose & it became dreadfully cold. We were not well on Sunday Mary & I.

*Sunday January 9th.* Mary lay long in bed, & did not walk. Wm & I walked in Brothers Wood. I was *astonished* with the beauty of the place, for I had never been there since my return home—never since before I went away in June!! Wrote to Miss Lamb.

*Monday January 10th.* I lay in bed to have a Drench of sleep till one o'clock. Worked all Day petticoats—Mrs C's wrists. Ran Wm's woollen stockings for he put them on today for the first time. We walked to Rydale, & brought letters from Sara, Annette & Peggy—furiously cold.

*Tuesday January 11th.* A very cold day. Wm promised me he would rise as soon as I had carried him his Breakfast but he lay in bed till between 12 & one. We talked of walking, but the blackness of the Cold made us slow to put forward & we did

not walk at all. Mary read the Prologue to Chaucer's tales to
me, in the morning William was working at his poem to C.
Letter from Keswick & from Taylor on Wm's marriage. C
poorly, in bad spirits—Canaries. Before tea I sate 2 hours in
the parlour—read part of The Knights Tale with exquisite
delight. Since Tea Mary has been down stairs copying out
Italian poems for Stuart—Wm has been working beside me,
& here ends this imperfect summary. I will take a nice Calais
Book & *will* for the future write regularly &, if I can legibly, so
much for this my resolution on Tuesday night, January 11th
1803. Now I am going to take Tapioca for my supper, & Mary
an Egg, William some cold mutton, his poor Chest is tired.

*Wednesday 12th.* Very cold, & cold all the week.

*Sunday the 16th.* Intensely cold. Wm had a fancy for some
ginger-bread I put on Molly's Cloak & my Spenser, & we
walked towards Matthew Newtons—I went into the house—
the blind Man & his Wife & Sister were sitting by the fire, all
dressed very clean in their Sunday's Clothes, the sister
reading. They took their little stock of gingerbread out of the
cubboard & I bought 6 pennyworth. They were so grateful
when I paid them for it that I could not find in my heart to tell
them we were going to make Gingerbread ourselves. I had
asked them if they had no thick 'No' answered Matthew 'there
was none on Friday but we'll *endeavour* to get some.' The next
Day the woman came just when we were baking & we bought
2 pennyworth—

*Monda[y]*

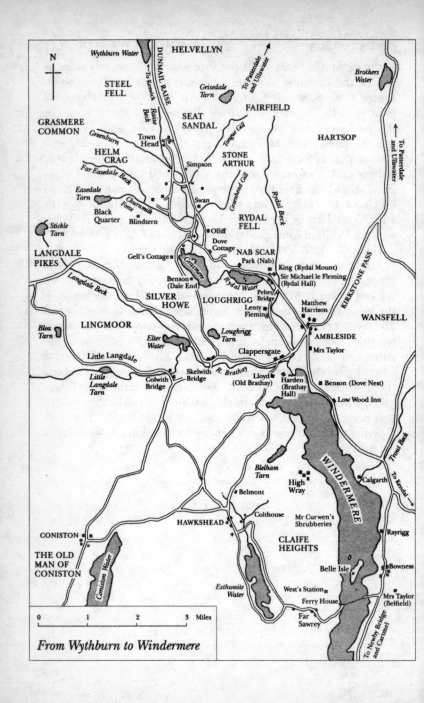

*From Wythburn to Windermere*

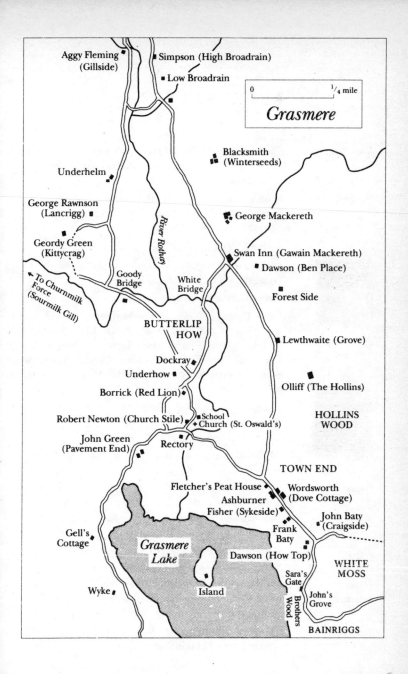

Aggy Fleming
(Gillside)

Simpson (High Broadrain)

Low Broadrain

Grasmere

0                    ¼ mile

Blacksmith
(Winterseeds)

Underhelm

George Rawson
(Lancrigg)

George Mackereth

Geordy Green
(Kittycrag)

Swan Inn (Gawain Mackereth)

Dawson (Ben Place)

To Churnmilk
Force
(Sourmilk Gill)

Goody
Bridge

White
Bridge

Forest Side

River Rothay

BUTTERLIP
HOW

Lewthwaite (Grove)

Dockray

Underhow

Olliff (The Hollins)

Borrick (Red Lion)

HOLLINS
WOOD

Robert Newton (Church Stile)

School
Church (St. Oswald's)

John Green
(Pavement End)

Rectory

TOWN END

Fletcher's Peat House

Wordsworth
(Dove Cottage)

Ashburner
Fisher (Sykeside)

John Baty
(Craigside)

Frank
Baty

Gell's
Cottage

Grasmere
Lake

Dawson (How Top)

Sara's
Gate

WHITE
MOSS

Wyke

Island

John's
Grove

Brothers Wood

BAINRIGGS

# ABBREVIATIONS

Anderson
: *The Works of the British Poets with Prefaces, Biographical and Critical*, edited by Robert Anderson, 13 vols. (London, 1795).

*Benjamin*
: Wordsworth, *Benjamin the Waggoner*, ed. Paul F. Betz, Cornell Wordsworth Series (Ithaca, NY, 1981).

C
: Samuel Taylor Coleridge

*CL*
: *Collected Letters of Samuel Taylor Coleridge*, ed. E. L. Griggs, 6 vols. (Oxford, 1956–71).

D
: Dorothy Wordsworth

DC
: Dove Cottage. Note: in the Ws' time the cottage was simply the cottage at Town End. Stopford Brooke used the name Dove Cottage (from its old inn name, The Dove and Olive) in 1890 when the newly formed Trust was negotiating for purchase of the house.

*EY*
: *Letters of William and Dorothy Wordsworth*, ed. E. de Selincourt; *The Early Years, 1787–1805*, rev. Chester L. Shaver (Oxford, 1967).

Gill
: *William Wordsworth*, ed. Stephen Gill, Oxford Authors (Oxford, 1984).

*Guide*
: William Green, *The Tourist's New Guide, containing a Description of the Lakes, Mountains, and Scenery, in Cumberland, Westmorland, and Lancashire*, 2 vols. (Kendal, 1819).

Harper
: George McLean Harper, *William Wordsworth*, 2 vols. (New York, 1960).

*Home at Grasmere*
: Wordsworth, *Home at Grasmere*, ed. Beth Darlington, Cornell Wordsworth Series (Ithaca, NY, 1977).

*Journals*
: Dorothy Wordsworth, *Journals*, ed. E. de Selincourt, 2 vols. (Macmillan, 1941).

| | |
|---|---|
| *LB* | *Lyrical Ballads*, 1st edn. (1 vol.) (1798); 2nd edn. (2 vols.) (1800); 3rd edn. (2 vols.) (1802). |
| *LY* | *Letters of William and Dorothy Wordsworth*, ed. E. de Selincourt; *The Later Years, 1821–50*, re-edited Alan G. Hill, 4 vols. (Oxford, 1978–88). |
| *LJW* | *The Letters of John Wordsworth*, ed. Carl H. Ketcham, Cornell (Ithaca, NY, 1969). |
| Marrs | *The Letters of Charles and Mary Anne Lamb*, ed. Edwin W. Marrs, jun. 3 vols. (Ithaca, NY, 1975–8). |
| Masson | *The Collected Writings of Thomas De Quincey*, ed. David Masson, 14 vols. (London, 1896). |
| *Memoirs* | Christopher Wordsworth, *Memoirs of William Wordsworth*, 2 vols. (London, 1851). |
| MH, MW | Mary Hutchinson, after 4 October 1802 Mary Wordsworth. |
| Moorman | *Journals of Dorothy Wordsworth*, ed. Mary Moorman, 2nd edn. (Oxford, 1971). |
| *MP* | The *Morning Post*, editor Daniel Stuart. |
| *MY* | *The Letters of William and Dorothy Wordsworth*, ed. E. de Selincourt; *The Middle Years, 1806–11*, rev. Mary Moorman (Oxford, 1969); *1812–1820*, rev. Mary Moorman and Alan G. Hill (Oxford, 1970). |
| *Notebooks* | *The Notebooks of Samuel Taylor Coleridge*, ed. Kathleen Coburn, 6 vols. (New York, 1957– continuing). |
| *Poems in Two Volumes* | Wordsworth, *Poems in Two Volumes and other poems*, ed. Jared Curtis, Cornell Wordsworth Series (Ithaca, NY, 1983). |
| *Prose* | *The Prose Works of William Wordsworth*, ed. W. J. B. Owen and Jane Worthington Smyser, 3 vols. (Oxford, 1974). |
| *PW* | Wordsworth, *Poetical Works*, ed. E. de Selincourt and Helen Darbishire, 5 vols. (Oxford, 1940–9). |
| *Tuft of Primroses* | Wordsworth, *The Tuft of Primroses*, ed. Joseph F. Kishel, Cornell Wordsworth Series (Ithaca, NY, 1986). |
| W | William Wordsworth |

West               [Thomas West], *A Guide to the Lakes in Cumberland, Westmorland and Lancashire*, 2nd edn. (Kendal, 1780)

WL                 The Wordsworth Library, Grasmere.

# NOTES

This, the first of the four notebooks containing the Grasmere Journal, is à book of less than 4″ × 6″, its boards covered in mottled brown paper. On the first page are the words 'May—1800. Wm & John set off into Yorkshire', and with this plain fact, after two or three preliminary 'amens' to test the sharpened end of her quill pen, D launched into her great Journal. She drew a full line across the page after each entry.

It had not been a completely empty notebook when D picked it up in May; she had first used it in the German winter of 1798–9 when she and W stayed in Goslar. We know this from the jottings and sums on both inside covers: these are lists of clothes that range from shirts, nightcaps, and handkerchiefs to the more expensive fur items that were needed in that cold winter, see 14 Mar. 1802 n.; there is also a list of groceries—bread, milk, sugar, rum. There are prices in German currency against the items, and scattered conversion sums: 16*d.* to the mark, D tells us in her Hamburg Journal. There are random phrases of German and English, written and re-written in a small .elaborate hand; D was clearly practising the formal 18th-c. German script. The phrase 'with Peter' is in this tiny script (W had been 'employed in hewing down Peter Bell', *EY*, p. 256); so is the unlikely word, 'industry', and the repeatedly written name, 'Madama Deppermann'; this lady was the 'good kind of a respectable woman . . . a widow with 5 children and keeps a linen draper's shop' (*EY*, p. 245) with whom the Ws lodged at 107 Breitstrasse in Goslar. There is a list of clothes without prices—as though of garments to be packed; D, having no maid, takes an apron as well as a gown. Whatever else the notebook contained of that time in Goslar is lost, because 6 pages have been cut out at the front and 5 at the back, and some of these, as the remains indicate, contained lists and accounts. D had next used the notebook, from the back, on their return from Germany, when, from the early summer of 1799, she and W stayed with their friends the Hutchinsons at Sockburn in Co. Durham. She copied out 4 epitaphs: 2 from a *Life* of Benjamin Franklin (1st edn.,

1793), one from Hutchinson's *History of Durham* (1794), and one taken from the Churchyard at Marske, Yorkshire (30 miles from Sockburn). Alongside the first epitaph (the first 5 pages having gone), and filling up small spaces amongst the heterogeneous items on the back cover, are two tiny drawings of a church, one complete with churchyard and tombstones. After the epitaphs D has written out 5 verses for the 'Complaint of the Forsaken Indian Woman', verses not however used for the 2nd edn. of *LB* (1800) (see *PW* ii. 475–6). These verses meet the Dec. end of the Grasmere Journal as it comes from the front of the book.

*14 May 1800* *John* John W (1772–1805), W and D's younger brother; at sea from leaving Hawkshead Grammar School at Christmas 1787 and with the East India Company from 1790. He lived at DC Jan.–Sept. 1800, before becoming Captain of the *Earl of Abergavenny*. D had not seen him for nearly 8 years; W saw him briefly between voyages in 1795 and again in early Nov. 1799 for 5 days when John joined him and C in their Lake District exploration. Now the brothers were walking through Yorkshire to Gallow Hill, near Scarborough, the farm newly acquired by their old Penrith friends, the Hutchinsons. They stayed with Tom, Mary, and Joanna and were back in Grasmere on 7 June. 'He loved our cottage', wrote D later, 'he helped us to furnish it, and to make the gardens' (*EY*, pp. 559–60).

*Low-wood* D walked about 5 miles with her brothers, not quite as far as the Low Wood inn on Lake Windermere.

*margin of the lake* D first wrote 'foot of the lake'.

*ranunculus* Globe flower (*Trollius Europeus*). On 3 June D uses the local name, 'Lockety Goldings', a corruption of the alternative name that Withering (16 May 1800 n.) gives, 'Locker-gowlans'.

*Rabbit-toothed white flower* Stitchwort (*Stellaria holostea*).

*heckberry* Bird-cherry or wild cherry (*Prunus padus*).

*by Clappersgate* Literally by and not into the hamlet of Clappersgate; D avoided Ambleside on her return, taking the road that winds under Loughrigg Fell to Pelter Bridge at Rydal.

*fine houses* D shared with W the view that modern gentlemen's houses could be intrusive. Yet one of these houses, an old farm-house that had become 'fine', was the High House, known after 1803 as Rydal Mount, where the Ws themselves were to live from 1813 until their deaths.

*the Bridge*    Pelter Bridge over the Rothay, reconstructed as a double-arched bridge in 1799.

*Sir Michaels*    Rydal Hall, newly fronted in classical style, seat of Sir Michael le Fleming (1748–1806).

*Pleasure*    The earlier Alfoxden Journal, Jan.–May 1798, had clearly given W pleasure: he had written out its first 4 sentences and substantially used one of D's night-sky descriptions in his poem 'A Night Piece'. Many phrases show that he shared D's perceptions and knew her writing. But we cannot know how frequently W actually read the Grasmere Journal. When he asked D to 'set down the story of Barbara Wilkinsons Turtle Dove' (30 Jan. 1802), did he read it? Or was it simply preserved in case he might need it? Perhaps in the same way, on 10 June 1800, D set down the account of the tall beggar woman, probably after telling W about her as they both walked to Ambleside, and almost two years later read it to W after he had begun the poem (13 Mar. 1802). W's reading or listening to passages was probably sporadic: he never, for instance, filled in the words of the inscription that he had seen on a decayed house in Borrowdale, though D left space in the Journal for at least 12 words (12 Sept. 1800). Yet his pleasure in D's instinct for preservation, in her openness, and in her creative vision, whenever he came across it in writing, must have been, as D knew, real.

*grave stone*    The word 'grave' is inserted above the line as a gloss to 'stone', just as, in the next line, 'the right' is an insertion to explain an original 'it'.

*16 May 1800    Mr Gells*    William Gell (1777–1836), just graduated from Cambridge, built a single-storey cottage *c.*1798 across the lake from Town End where the Ws were to live. James Plumptre, a university friend, called in July 1799 when Gell was away and noticed the four small rooms, in one of which was an organ. This cottage, later enlarged, became Silver Howe House. Gell made only occasional visits, and W and D had general use of his boat. He made drawings of the site of Troy during a 5-day stay in Asia Minor in 1801, and became Sir William Gell at the age of 26. 'I leave topography to classic Gell', wrote Byron in *English Bards and Scotch Reviewers* (1809), revising this to 'rapid

Gell' when he discovered that Gell had spent only a day at Troy itself. Gell was later Chamberlain to Queen Caroline and lived much of his time, and died, in Italy.

*a book of botany*   In Mar. 1801 W wrote to the publishers of *LB*, Longman and Rees, 'Mr C. and I conjointly are in your debt for two Copies of Withering's Botany and two botanical microscopes' (*EY*, p. 321). It was £1. 12*s.* for each set of William Withering, *An Arrangement of British Plants according to the latest Improvements of the Linnean System and an Introduction to the Study of Botany*, 3rd edn., 4 vols. (Birmingham, 1796). See 28 May 1802 n.

*shadows under*   'upon' crossed out.

*stepping stones*   D, completing her circuit of the lake, walked on from Mr Gell's but could not cross at the foot of Grasmere, where the lake narrows into the River Rothay. She went on to the stepping stones at White Moss and crossed before the river enters Rydal Water. In 1800 there was no bridge between Church Bridge north of Grasmere lake and Pelter Bridge south of Rydal.

*Aggy*   Agnes Fisher (buried 23 Apr. 1804), with her husband John and his sister Molly, lived in the small 17th-c. 'statesman's' dwelling, Sykeside, across the road from DC and a little to the south (its barn became the first Wordsworth Museum in 1936). She had probably lived there since 1785 when John's father, Robert, died. Before her marriage in 1774 she had been a Mackereth, and this explains D's and W's early and easy acquaintance with such useful village residents as Aggy's brothers, George and Gawain Mackereth, respectively parish clerk and innkeeper of the Swan. Aggy's frustration can be gauged from W's tribute to her 'eloquent discourse' and 'keen desire of knowledge', and from D's comment that the house 'in Aggy's life time was the dirtiest in Grasmere' (*Excursion*, VI. 675–777 and *EY*, p. 480).

*Mary Hutchinson*   MH (1770–1859), eldest daughter of John H, a tobacco merchant of Penrith with roots in Co. Durham, and Mary Monkhouse, daughter of the Penrith postmaster who had a small country estate at nearby Sebergham. As a small child she was at the same Penrith Dame School as W. At 8 she went to live for 4 years with her Hutchinson grandparents at Bishopton, Co. Durham. She was scarcely back in Penrith when her mother died after the birth of the tenth child, and her father died 2 years later. Her aunt Elizabeth Monkhouse took charge. At 16 she became a friend of D, recently come from Halifax to grandparents in Penrith, and of W in school holidays. She married W, 4 Oct. 1802.

*Matthew Jobson's lost a cow*   Matthew Jopson by 1795, when the burial of a daughter is registered, was innkeeper of The Cherry Tree, the Wythburn hostelry now famous through W's poem *Benjamin the Waggoner*. He was there in 1803 when his son William died, but when his wife Jane was buried in 1807 he was at the nearby Horse Head or Nag's Head. He must have been still there in 1834 when Southey's daughters in a Jan. snowstorm had to abandon their post-chaise on Dunmail Raise and go 'crawling and clinging to walls and stones' for 4 miles, wrote D, 'till they reached Matthew Jobson's' (*LY* ii. 680).

*17 May 1800   T. Ashburner*   Thomas Ashburner (b. 1754) was a widower in 1791 with 5 young daughters, and that same year he married Peggy (Margaret Lancaster), a local girl. He lived at Below Sike, a cottage almost opposite DC but slightly to the north, and supplied the Ws with 'coals' from Keswick. He had been forced to sell his patrimonial land; see 24 Nov. 1801, and W's poem 'Repentance'.

*coals*   This meant charcoal when W was a boy at Hawkshead, but here it probably refers to sea-coal picked up from the coast around Whitehaven where the extensive Lowther mines, both working and deserted, meant that coal was washed ashore. There was a good transport road between Whitehaven and Keswick. The Ws also burnt local peat (8 Feb. 1802, and see 16 June 1800) and wood (23 Feb. 1802).

*The Skobby*   The chaffinch.

*19[18] May 1800   Miss Simpson*   Elizabeth Jane Sympson, younger daughter of the Revd Joseph Sympson of High Broadraine, Grasmere, vicar of the small church at Wythburn. Elizabeth, then aged 36, in Dec. 1803, did, said D (*EY*, p. 430), 'a very foolish thing'; she married the son of the Ambleside-based artist Julius Caesar Ibbetson, a young man, 'little more than half her age', and by the next autumn she was dead of consumption and her baby daughter died shortly afterwards.

*Mr Benson's*   John Benson of Tail End, now Dale End, on the other side of the lake, was W's landlord, and he had probably owned the house at Town End when it was an inn, The Dove and Olive Branch. Its last surviving licence was issued in 1793. When W saw it in Nov. 1799 it was 'a small house at Grasmere empty which perhaps we may take' (*EY*, p. 272). James Losh, during his Sept. 1800 visit, noted that the Ws 'pay only £5 a year rent and 6s for taxes' (Losh Diary, MS, Tullie House, Carlisle), but W, years later, told Miss Fenwick that he paid 'as a married man . . . £8 per annum rent' (*PW* v. 457). (Alfoxden House where D and W had lived, 1797–8, had been £23 for the year.)

*Mrs Taylors* A fine new house on the road out of Ambleside towards Windermere (now the old road) then known as The Cottage (now Iveing Cottage, the YWCA house), one of those 'works of art' which 'give an air of consequence to the country' (West, 70, Pennington's fn.). Mrs Taylor, a widow since 1784, had previously lived at Abbot Hall, Kendal.

*Coleridge* C (1772–1834) had left DC on 4 May; he had been staying there, for the first time, for almost a month.

*Cottle* Joseph Cottle (1770–1853), bookseller, publisher, and minor poet of Bristol; generous in publishing C's early poetry, and *LB* in 1798—although he soon sold the copyright to Longmans. After C's death in 1834 he published in 1837 his lively *Early Recollections* of C and his friends.

*are forced to sell* John Fisher, registered on his marriage to Aggy in 1774 as 'Cordwainer', and described by C as a 'Shoemaker—a fine enthusiastic noble minded Creature' (*CL* ii. 973), was essentially a small '(e)statesman': he had an 'apprentice' (1 June 1800) and was registered at his death in 1820 as 'yeoman'. He saw only too accurately that such small properties as Sykeside could not long be economic. In 1800 there were 36 hereditary statesmen in the parish of Grasmere; in 1885 only 1. The Ashburners had already sold their land. W regretted this trend (see 'Michael', 1800, and the *Guide to the Lakes*, first written in 1810). Sykeside, however, continued to be a very small working farm. After Aggy's death John Fisher kept 'but one cow, just enough for Molly to manage' (*EY*, p. 480).

*19 May 1800  Molly* Mary Fisher (1741–1808), Molly, or old Molly, as D came increasingly to call her, John Fisher's sister. It was she who lit fires for a fortnight before the Ws arrived at DC in

Dec. 1799 and who would never forget D standing there 'in t'laal striped gown and tlaal straw Bonnet' (*EY*, p. 661). For 2*s*. a week she came across to clean, light fires, wash dishes, prepare vegetables, do the weekly small clothes wash, and the 5-weekly 'great wash' (D helping with the ironing). C characterized her as 'Wordsworth's old Molly with her washing Tub' (*CL* ii. 768), 'a drollery belonging to the Cottage' (*EY*, p. 476). But when Aggy Fisher died in May 1804 and Molly was 'promoted to the high office of her Brother's Housekeeper' (*EY*, p. 471), the Ws were relieved at her so naturally ceasing to work for them; the growing household needed a younger servant. Hazlitt in 1819 remembered 'our laughing [in the summer of 1803] a good deal at W's old Molly, who had never heard of the French Revolution, ten years after it happened. Oh worse than Gothic ignorance!' ('On the Character of the Country People', *The Examiner*, July 1819, Hazlitt, *Works*, ed. P. P. Howe, vol. 17, p. 68).

*the Black quarter*   The name given by the Ws when they were new to Grasmere, to Easedale, the north-western arm of the valley. They 'named' rocks and hills; W wrote Poems on the Naming of Places; and the valley soon 'belonged' to them.

*24 May 1800   Douglass*   Charles Douglas (1772–1806), barrister of Jamaica. W knew him at Cambridge and in Jan. 1796 lent him £200 (out of the Calvert bequest). Half of this was passed on to Montagu, who signed with Douglas a joint promissory note for £200 payable to W in Jan. 1797. Montagu did not promptly pay his share; Douglas paid £10 in May 1799 and the rest, £104. 17*s*. (to include interest), at this time, May 1800.

*nailed up the beds*   A reference to either (*a*): the fixing-up or moving of camp or trestle beds. Certainly in 1800 in the downstairs 'lodging-room' (this was D's bedroom until early summer 1802 when it became W's, and on W's marriage in Oct. 1802 it was W's and Mary's room) there was 'only a camp bed', but one 'large enough for two people to sleep in'; the house had one upstairs 'lodging-room with two single beds' (for W and John); there was 'a sort of lumber room ' in which a camp bed could be put up for a guest; and in the 'small low unceiled room' which D 'papered with newspapers' was 'a small bed without curtains' (*EY*, pp. 295–6)—by 1805 D was sleeping here, and sharing the tiny room with baby John; or (*b*): the replacing of bed hangings after the recent washing and ironing. Lower and upper hangings were frequently nailed in pleats onto the wooden bed-frame. See 31 May 1800 when D was 'putting up vallances' and 5 Sept. 1800 when she was 'putting up' the white bed.

*worked in the garden*   D records this frequently in this first spring; she was, after all, not simply adding to a garden but making a new one from space formerly fronting an inn. She told Jane Marshall in Sept., 'we have . . . a small orchard and a smaller *garden* which as it is the work of our own hands we regard with pride and partiality. This garden we enclosed from the road and pulled down a fence which formerly divided it from the orchard' (*EY*, p. 295). So, the new fence of upright slates sheltered the small garden along the front and to the north of the house. It was here that D worked so hard and, as the orchard to the south and back of the house was not now separate from the new garden, many wild, and some garden, plants and flowers were planted 'on the Borders' (30 May) of the paths perhaps, or of the patches of onions, peas, carrots, turnips, french beans. Thus the front garden gradually mingled with the orchard, its vegetables, and its fruit trees.

25 *May 1800   my Brother Christopher*   At this stage Christopher (1774–1846) was a Fellow of Trinity College, Cambridge, and private tutor of Charles Manners-Sutton, whose father, the Bishop of Norwich, was to become Archbishop of Canterbury in 1805. Christopher became his domestic chaplain. Other preferments followed, finally St Mary's, Lambeth. Then, from 1820–41, Christopher was Master of Trinity College, Cambridge. After the death of his wife Priscilla Lloyd in 1815 Christopher and his three sons were more frequent visitors at Rydal Mount, and W and D stayed with him in Cambridge and London.

*Charles Lloyd*   Charles Lloyd (1775–1839) of the Birmingham Quaker banking family. He first got to know the Lakes in 1795 when he stayed with the Quaker farmer Thomas Wilkinson at Yanwath, near Penrith. He published poetry at Carlisle in 1795. Lloyd then met C and paid him £80 in order to live with him for a time as a pupil/companion. In 1797 Cottle published *Poems* by Coleridge, Lamb, and Lloyd; C, under the signature Nehemiah Higginbottom, published in *MP* a satire of Lloyd's poems, and in 1798 Lloyd drew what was an unkind portrait of C in his novel, *Edmund Oliver*. Lloyd married Sophia Pemberton and came in late autumn 1800 to live in Ambleside; from 1802 he was at Old Brathay, Clappersgate. The Lloyds and the Ws visited in a friendly way for about a year but then a coolness developed: 'Miss W I much like', wrote Charles Lloyd to Manning, 26 Jan. 1801, 'but her Brother is not a man after my own heart—I always feel myself depressed in his society.' Charles Lloyd's sister Priscilla (who married Christopher W) was, as D said, the 'one chain . . . but she shall only drag us to Brathay about once a year' (14 June 1802, *EY*, p. 362).

*26 May 1800   after 12*   William Green recollected (*Guide* i. 402) that 'Mr. Sympson was a most cheerful and entertaining companion, and frequently walked after he was eighty to Ambleside and back in the same day. He died suddenly on the 27th June, 1807, aged 92.' And D describes him in Sept. 1800 as going 'a fishing to the Tarns on the hill-tops with my Brothers and he is as active as many men of 50' (*EY*, p. 299).

*JH*   Joanna Hutchinson (1780–1843), youngest of the Hutchinson sisters; D's travelling companion in Scotland in 1822 and the Isle of Man in 1828. Like D and her own sister Sara, Joanna remained unmarried and lived largely with a married brother (or sister) and family.

*'When pleasant thoughts &c'*—   From W's 'Lines written in Early Spring', composed Apr. 1798 at Alfoxden,

> I heard a thousand blended notes,
> While in a grove I sate reclined
> In that sweet mood when pleasant thoughts
> Bring sad thoughts to the mind.

*27 May 1800   Mr Partridges*   Edward Partridge was owner, with a Mr Cooper, of the linsey or linen mill at the bottom of Stock Ghyll in Ambleside. He gave employment 'in the worst of times to a numerous body of mechanics' and 'comforts gratuitously in all needful cases' (*Guide* i. 154). He built several houses at Waterhead, Ambleside, 'very rich in views' (ibid., 380). But it was probably his own old family home, Covey Cottage (now Gale Bank), 'a charming place', says Green, that D and W went to see later in the summer (22 Aug. 1800).

*28 May 1800   I planted*   Janet Dockray lived in either Underhow or Dockray, small family farmsteads near the Red Lion and the

Easedale road. The lilies that she gives D here grow well: see 28 May 1802. Her kindness continued: in Feb. 1802 she took the Ws 'a present of Eggs & milk', and D laments the death of 'old Jenny Dockwray' in 1807 after she and the Ws have returned from their winter at Coleorton (*MY* i. 158).

*helm crag*  A much painted hill, not high but dramatic, and from the craggy rocks on its summit, sometimes known as the Lion and the Lamb: 'the Lion is a prodigious stone, and the Lamb, which is near it, is not a small one', wrote Green (*Guide* i. 417).

*30 May 1800  Mr Ollifs*  John Olive lived in the new house, a 'trim box' D called it (*EY*, p. 638), later known as The Hollins (until recently a hotel). It is half-way between DC and the Swan, and it was possibly John Olive who was the man 'fra London' who bought the Ashburners' land (see 24 Nov. 1801). The Olives sold up and left in spring 1802 after the death of their second child, an infant daughter. 'Most things' at the sale 'sold beyond their worth' (*EY*, p. 351–2); the house was bought by Thomas King, and D ceased to call.

*12 papers*  All editors of the Journal, except Moorman (1971), prefer to read D's figures as 12 rather than 2. Copies of *MP* were sent to C, as a valued contributor, by the editor, Daniel Stuart (1776–1846), and they were still coming to DC for him (he had been there 6 April–4 May). On 15 July C wrote to Stuart asking for papers to be sent in future to Greta Hall, Keswick, his new residence, and he added the comment, substantiated by D's Journal, 'The newspapers come very irregularly indeed' (*CL* i. 604). After that date D less frequently notes the arrival of papers; some came for W who contributed occasional poems.

*John sodded the wall*  John Fisher. The wall was the recently built supporting wall for the new platform or small terrace in the garden (orchard) behind the house.

*31 May 1800  Grundy*  Probably the A. Grundy of the early 19th-c. Kendal firm A. Grundy and Sons, Carpet Manufacturers, Kendal.

*the Blind man's*  Matthew Newton, 'the honest itinerant bread-merchant', who 'lost his eyes, by an unfortunate blast' at the White Moss Slate Quarry between Grasmere and Rydal, now a car-park, but then 'a grand subject for the pencil', according to Green (*Guide* i. 392). Matthew Newton had been blind for some 20 years when D came to Grasmere, and was about 70 years old. He lived with his wife and sister and died in 1816. See the final entry for the Journal, 16 Jan. 1803, where D records buying gingerbread from him.

*Brathay Bridge*   At Clappersgate; probably again the circular walk under Loughrigg and back via Ambleside.

*Tommy*   The Revd Joseph Sympson's grandson (1789–1827), son of his eldest daughter Mary and her first husband, a builder, Thomas Jameson, very shortly to die, see 23 June. By 1808, through the encouragement of John Harden of Brathay Hall, Tommy was an aspiring artist in London.

*2 June 1800   Mrs Nicholson*   Agnes Nicholson, postmistress at Ambleside (d. 1862, aged 83). In 1850 she recalled how her husband Joseph, the first postmaster, would get up late at night and let Mr and Miss W into the parlour or kitchen where they would have the 'letter out of the box . . . and sit up reading and changing till they had made it quite to their minds' (Harper ii. 316).

*3 June 1800   R[ichar]d*   Richard W (1768–1816), the Ws' eldest brother, the lawyer, who managed, not always smoothly, their financial affairs.

*4 June 1800   Mr Jackson*   D had first written 'Coleridge'; this is deleted. William Jackson (1748–1809) was a retired Keswick carrier, later to take his place in literature as the employer of the unfortunate Benjamin, hero of W's *Benjamin*. He was also brother-in-law to W's landlord, John Benson, and D was clearly writing to him on C's account, since Jackson, over several years, had been building a double house at Keswick (its central portion seems already to have had a use as Peter Crosthwaite's Observatory); it was to become Greta Hall. C moved there in July. From Sept. 1803 Southey and his family occupied the other half of the by then almost completed house. Mr Jackson retained a small back portion for his own use.

*5 June 1800   the Blacksmith's*   The blacksmith, John Watson, lived at Winterseeds on the old pack-horse track (possibly even Roman) through Grasmere valley east of the present road. The small building that was Watson's smithy is still by Winterseeds. He married a servant girl, Sarah Wilson, in 1788, repaired the church bells periodically, attended to the clock, made the splendid handle and hinges of the church door in 1821, and at his death in 1852 left £100 to Grasmere school. When he became old he had a smithy set up by the main road at Tongue Gill.

*6 June 1800   my aunt Cookson*   Wife of D's uncle William, her mother's brother. D had liked aunt Cookson from her girlhood days at her grandmother's in Penrith, and had hoped that uncle William would marry Miss Dorothy Cowper, daughter of the vicar of St Andrew's, Penrith. He married her in Oct. 1788, and gave D some happy 6 or 7 years with him and his young family, mainly at Forncett Rectory, Norfolk, and for a time, in autumn 1792, at Windsor, where William Cookson had been made a Canon, and became tutor to the royal children.

*Matthew Harrisons*   Matthew Harrison (1753–1824), the splendidly efficient steward, under George Knott, of the Newlands Co. Ironworks; after Knott's death in 1784, its sole manager; after 1812, when he bought out the Knotts, its major director under the new name Harrison, Ainslie and Co. Matthew Harrison's house, later known as Bellevue, was in the upper part of Ambleside, not far above the new house that he was building, or shortly to build, Greenbank: this, from 1827, was to be the home of D's second cousin, another Dorothy W, daughter of Robinson W of Whitehaven, when she married Matthew's son, Benson Harrison. It is now the Charlotte Mason College of Education.

*Jack Hutchinson*   John Hutchinson (1768–1831), eldest brother of MH, W's future wife. He was a farmer and ham-factor of Stockton-on-Tees, friendly to the Ws and well-disposed towards poets.

*Montagu*   Basil Montagu (1770–1851), 2nd (natural) son of John Montagu, 4th Earl of Sandwich, by his mistress the singer Martha Ray—she was shot dead when Montagu was 9 by the Revd John Hackman (whose proposal of marriage Martha Ray had rejected). Montagu was acknowledged by his father but he married without approval in 1791 and earned some subsistence by taking pupils at Cambridge: he had been fifth wrangler in 1790. His wife died in childbirth in 1793, and Montagu, with a friend's help, went to read for the Bar in London. He met W in 1795: 'I consider my having met Wm. Wordsworth the most fortunate event of my life' (MS, WL). It is not only that W lent

Montagu money; he took the young child Basil away from the unsuitable life of London chambers and he and D looked after the boy at Racedown and Alfoxden.

*near home*   This phrase replaces a crossed-out 'home'.

*Cock fighting*   The Grasmere cock-pit, at Church Stile, as in so many English villages and towns, was near the church, the inn, and the school (cf. the traditional cockpenny given by schoolboys to their master—the W boys paid 'Cockpenys' at Hawkshead). The sport was not made illegal until 1849, and then on grounds of rowdiness, drunkenness, and gambling rather than of cruelty.

*Mr Borricks opening*   Of the new Red Lion inn. George Borwick was the first innkeeper. Robert Newton's house round the corner at Church Stile had previously been the inn (also officially the Red Lion, but usually referred to as Robert Newton's). George Borwick, originally of Borwick Ground, Hawkshead, had been at Hawkshead Grammar School; he donated 10s. 6d. to the New Library of the school in 1789. When he married Agnes Walker in Hawkshead in 1796 he was described as 'Gentleman' (and D refers to him as *Mr* Borwick). Agnes Walker died within a year of coming to Grasmere in 1800, and was buried at Hawkshead in March 1801. In Nov. 1802 Mr Borwick married a Grasmere girl, Agnes Penny, had a son William the following year, and was living at Moss-side, a house close by the new inn (and still there). But he did not stay long at the Red Lion. On the afternoon of 6 Mar. 1804 D and Mary were 'at Borrwick's Sale. He is broken up and the house is taken by the people of the Nag's Head of Wytheburn' (*EY*, p. 449).

*9 June 1800   evidently Tourists*   It was rare for a landau to go by and worthy of remark that a coronetted landau passed. But the tourists were beginning to arrive in numbers: the first guide book, Thomas West's, had appeared more than 20 years earlier. Coming down the hill in a high landau, it would be possible to see the Ws sitting on their newly sodded wall behind the house. By 1805 tourists were no novelty to D; the Ws' 'quiet enjoyment of home' was in spring and early summer, while the 'end of summer and the autumn' was 'the season of bustle for we are directly in the highway of the Tourists' (*EY*, p. 621).

*R Newtons* Robert Newton, after ceasing to be innkeeper, remained at the same house, now known as Church Stile. D had stayed at his inn for 1 night in 1794 as she walked through Grasmere with W on their way to Windy Brow, Keswick. It was already of some note. Joseph Budworth in the first published walking tour of the Lake District, *A Fortnight's Ramble in the Lakes*, 1792, sang the praises of Mrs Newton's preserved gooseberries with rich cream and went on to reproduce the entire menu for dinner for two people at ten-pence a head:

> Roast pike, stuffed,
> A boiled fowl,
> Veal-cutlets and ham,
> Beans and bacon,
> Cabbage,
> Pease and potatoes,
> Anchovy sauce,
> Parsley and butter,
> Plain butter,
> Butter and cheese,
> Wheat bread and oat cake,
> Three cups of preserved gooseberries,
> with a bowl of rich cream in the centre.

W stayed there again, with C, in Nov. 1799. Robert Newton continued to let rooms; the Clarksons rented a small house, perhaps hitherto part of the inn, for 3 months in 1805 for 14*s*. per week including 'a garden with plenty of gooseberries' (*EY*, p. 575).

*Lathe* Dialect for 'barn'.

*Mayor of Kendal* Thomas Holme Maude (1770–1849), banker, eldest son of a Kendal merchant and banker; a contemporary of W's at Hawkshead, even, for some months in 1786, a boarder along with W at Ann Tyson's; also at W's college, St John's, Cambridge.

*10 June 1800* a very tall woman This description of the beggar woman and her boys was written 2 weeks after D encountered them; then she had merely recorded, 'walked to Ambleside with letters'. Her full description was written on the day of her first walk to Ambleside with W since the encounter and is probably a result of telling him about the beggars as they walked. Almost 2 years later W wrote his poem 'Beggars' (13 Mar. 1802 n.), and he told Miss Fenwick in 1842 that the beggars were 'Met, and described to me by my Sister, near the quarry at the head of Rydal Lake, a place still a chosen resort of vagrants travelling with their families' (*PW* ii. 508). He had clearly responded strongly to D's story of children who were both beautiful and corrupt (his phrase in 1808 was 'moral depravity', quoted by H. Crabb Robinson, see Gill, p. 702). D's description is particularly scrupulous: she inserted 'before me' to define where precisely she saw the two boys; replaced the pronoun 'her' with 'the woman who had called at the door'; crossed out 'at Ambleside' where the boys 'sauntered so long' and replaced it with the phrase 'in their road'; and inserted the phrases 'through Ambleside' and 'in the street' to define precisely where she met the mother on her return.

*11 June 1800   returned to dinner*   D first wrote this after the first sentence, then crossed it out as she recalled that there were 2 excursions onto the water.

*13 June 1800   trolling*   Trailing a baited line behind a boat. It was usual for lines to be as long as 50 yards.

*16 June 1800   the Gale*   Sweet gale or bog myrtle, very common; boiled in autumn it was used for dyeing wool yellow. The Ws, like all country people, used vegetable dyes.

*not more than 5*   D will remember this child and his going to beg a measure of meal. See 12 Feb. 1802 for her association of him with the little boy she had looked after, Basil Montagu, and her sadness at his worsening plight.

*Mr Ibbetsons*   Julius Caesar Ibbetson (1759–1817), a Yorkshireman; assistant to a picture-dealer in London and then a landscape painter; he escaped from his London debts and deaths (of 8 children and wife), and came in 1798 to live at Clappersgate, Ambleside. He painted scenes and inn-signs and in June 1801 married a local girl, 18-year-old Bella Thompson. In that year he painted a happy picture in oils of Grasmere with the longhorn cattle that D was afraid of, milkmaids, spilt milk, and the white church shining below Helm Crag. But the Ws did not continue to call after walks and to take tea. In 1802 the Ibbetsons moved to Troutbeck and in July 1804 D told Lady Beaumont that she believed Ibbetson proud and high-spirited:

'I know nothing ill of him except that he is addicted to drinking violently, by fits, and I have been told that his conversation in the company of women is unbecoming and indecent. We have seen nothing of him for at least three years.' (*EY*, pp. 494–5.)

*17 June 1800    the new window*    Probably in the 'newspaper room', the 'small low unceiled room, which I have papered with news-papers' (see 24 May 1800 n.). Certainly, a window in the front of this 'out-jutting' (*EY*, p. 622), along with the new garden fence, is much in evidence in the Ws' drawing of the house by Amos Green (d. 1807). There is no window there now, but there is a projecting overhang (or sill) where a window must have been, and this must have been low in the room, which itself was, as D indicates, not only 'unceiled' but 'low'. At some point after the Ws' time at DC the outjutting must have been built up (compare its roof-line in the Green drawing with the present levels), the room raised, its roof ceiled, the present window on the south wall installed, and the 'new window' of 1800 removed.

*18 June 1800    the lower waterfall at Rydale*    Noted since the mid-17th c. when Sir Daniel Fleming of Rydal Hall either built or repaired a little summer-house, called by him a grotto, directly opposite the Lower Falls. From this small room with its square window, the Falls with the pool below, and the bridge, stream, and wood above, could be seen framed as in a picture. After Mason described this view in his edition of the *Works* of Thomas Gray in 1775 (reprinted in editions of West's *Guide*, from the 2nd edn., 1780) many artists and seekers of the picturesque came to Rydal. W's own calculatedly picturesque description of the Falls appears in his early *Evening Walk* (1793), ll. 71–84. In 1810 in *Select Views* (his *Guide* of 1822) he merely commented that the Falls 'are pointed out to everyone' (*Prose* ii. 162).

*19 June 1800    Wytheburn water*    Also known as Thirlmere and as Leathes Water (from the Leathes family who owned much of it and lived at Dale Park on its eastern shore). Its western shore, wrote Green, 'is irregular, and formed into many beautiful bays' with 'a singular Alpine bridge connecting two far out-stretching promontories' (*Guide* i. 422). Towards the end of the century the hamlet of Wythburn, its bridge, road, and beautiful bays, was flooded, and Wythburn Water, with a dam at its north end, was opened in 1894 as Thirlmere, the reservoir for Manchester.

*over Grasmere water*  D had first written 'over Wytheburn water'.

*20 June 1800   implements of trade*  D had first written 'household goods'; but it was the implements of trade that would prevent the parish from helping. Cf. W's 'The Last of the Flock'.

*21 June 1800   Young Mr S.*  Bartholomew Sympson (1757–1831), son of the Revd Joseph Sympson, 'an interesting man', said D, 'about 40, manages his Father's glebe land, reads a little and spends much time in fishing' (*EY*, p. 299).

*23 June 1800   the old road from Rydale*  D and John carried the jug of tea up the hill, past Dawson's at How Top, up again, leaving the main Rydal road and going along the 'coffin' path past White Moss Tarn; they then must have turned immediately right to go down the steep hill towards Rydal, and would meet W in that 'ancient road' to Grasmere—as Black's *Guide* of 1840 called it. This is still a path and it leaves the main road at White Moss Quarry.

*25 June 1800   till the 23 [24th] July*  After recording the flowers and foxgloves of Wednesday, D wrote nothing for a time and then left a deeper than usual space below her last line of writing as she began her scanty summary of the 3½ week visit of the Cs. From letters to the printers we know that C, D, and W spent a lot of time preparing text for the 2nd edn. *LB*; and from C's Notebooks we learn of excursions to Dungeon Ghyll and Watendlath, of his noticing Ladies reading Gilpin's *Observations . . . on the Picturesque*, 'while passing by the very places instead of looking at the places' (*Notebooks* i. 760), and that, like W, he had been impressed by the man 'in peasant's garb' idly fishing during hay-time: 'Come near—thin, pale, can scarce speak— or throw out his fishing-rod' (ibid., 761, and W's poem 'A narrow girdle of rough stones', see 10 Oct. 1800 n.). By 24 July the Cs had left for Greta Hall and on the following day D resumed her Journal.

*We made a great fire*  C describes this bonfire of 20 July: 'Mountains &c seen thro' the smoke of our wild fire, made of fir apples—Alder bush outmost twigs [s]mouldering in [flare *deleted*] sparks green ling—column of Smoke—the twigs & boughs heav'd up by the smoke—' (*Notebooks* i. 758: 'Ling' is the local word for heather: to burn it green, in July, would produce a lot of smoke). And note C's letter of 25 July to Davy describing the Island picnic and the 'glorious Bonfire' of fir-apples with the 'ruddy laughing faces in the twilight' of 'us that danced round it' (*CL* i. 612).

*25 July 1800   our Somersetshire goods*   D and W had left Alfoxden for Germany in the summer of 1798. Presumably the Cs brought up things they had left behind at Nether Stowey.

*26 July 1800   with washing myself*   'all over' has been crossed out here.

*27 July 1800   Mr Knight's Landscape*   Richard Payne Knight (1750–1824), collector of coins and bronzes, scholar, and, in his *Landscape: a Didactic Poem in Three Books* (1794), advocate of landscapes where time and nature brought a controlled fullness and variety, such as the paintings of Claude or Salvator depict. Knight opposed the picturesque if it was contrived and reconstructed, and he disliked such bare 'improved' landscapes as Capability Brown advocated.

*28 July 1800   Mr Davy*   Humphry Davy (1778–1829); C had met him in Bristol in 1799; a young Cornishman who had been apprenticed to a surgeon and had also published verses; a chemist working on gases at Thomas Beddoes's Bristol Pneumatic Institute, he agreed to see *LB* 1800 through the press. Davy soon left Bristol for the Royal Institution in London. He came twice to Grasmere and shared, perhaps more passionately than in poetry, W's interest in fishing. He was knighted in 1812 and has retained a popular fame for his invention of the miner's safety lamp in 1815–16.

*30 July 1800   Rays gap*   Dunmail Raise, the highest point of the pass between Grasmere and Thirlmere.

*10 o clock*   The preceding two sentences are written and crossed through at the end of Tuesday's entry after the word 'weary', but they clearly belong to Wednesday since D has begun to copy them after Wednesday's 'headach': 'The Evening &c see above'. D's confusion is another indication that she by no means always kept her Journal daily.

*31 July 1800   the Anthology*   The *Annual Anthology* 1800, the second, and last, of two anthologies of modern verse edited by Robert Southey. His friends contributed, and Southey wrote many poems himself. This volume contained several poems by C;

some had appeared in *MP*, but this was the first time W and D would see C's great poem 'This Lime Tree Bower' in print.

*1 Aug. 1800    The Brothers*    i.e. text for the new *LB*. 'The Brothers', a 'beautiful Poem', in C's phrase (*CL* i. 611), was written in Grasmere in early 1800, and it concerns the history of two brothers of Ennerdale, the Bowmans, a shepherd and a mariner. By 10 Apr. C (D had not begun her Journal) indicated that W had 'Pastorals' for the new volume.

*Mary Point*    A 'heath-clad Rock' in Bainriggs Wood at the foot of Grasmere, named after MH; an 'eminence' close by was named after Sara. W in 1845 recalled the 'twin Peaks' and the sisters in their youth in 'Forth from a jutting ridge'. Sara was then dead and the road of 1831 separated the crags from the lake.

*'The Whirlblast &c'*    'A whirl-blast from behind the hill', composed 18 March 1798 when D had written in her Alfoxden Journal 'sheltered under the hollies, during a hail-shower. The withered leaves danced with the hailstones. William wrote a description of the storm.'

*2 Aug. 1800    Lewthwaite's cottage*    George Lewthwaite of Grove Cottage, a house still by the roadside between Town End and the Swan. His wife Anne died in childbed at Grove Cottage in May 1797. D had the young Hannah L (bapt. from Rydal 20 May 1794) to help with the Ws' first baby, John (b. June 1803), and again with John and the new baby Dora in 1805 when MW was away. W used the name of Hannah's beautiful older sister Barbara for the child character of his short pastoral poem, 'The Pet Lamb', 1800; Barbara's vanity about this was something W regretted.

*4 Aug. 1800    honeysuckles &c &c*    D was attaching the plants to the house. The dry-stone walls of DC were (and are) covered by roughcast, a mixture of lime and gravel, which was then white-washed. This was customary; it was thought to help in weather-proofing and it gave houses a finish different from nearby barns or farm-buildings, left dark in local slate. By Sept. the house was 'covered all over with green leaves and scarlet flowers, for we have trained scarlet beans upon threads' (*EY*, p. 295). By 1809 De Quincey described the house as 'embossed—nay . . . smothered in roses . . . with as much jessamine and honeysuckle as could find room to flourish' (Masson, ii. 361).

*walk*   'go' was first written and crossed out here.

*8 Aug. 1800   Wattenlath*   A tarn and hamlet in the fells between Thirlmere and Derwentwater.

*9 Aug. 1800   Windy Brow woods*   D had known these woods in 1794 when she had lived for a few weeks with W in the farmhouse belonging to his old school friend William Calvert and his brother Raisley. After their deaths Windy Brow was bought in the early 1830s by Anthony Spedding of Mirehouse; recently its association with the Calverts has been renewed, the farmhouse becoming a central building for the Calvert Trust for the Disabled.

*10 Aug. 1800   to church*   D notes the Cs' churchgoing. See 13 Aug. 1800 n. for further evidence of C's piety and 20 March 1802.

*11 Aug. 1800   Walked*   After the word 'Walked', 'with Mrs C' is crossed out.

*12 Aug. 1800   the Cockins*   The 3 Miss Cockins lived with elderly parents in Keswick. The mother and one daughter, Hannah, died in 1801. They were among the 'principal inhabitants' of Keswick listed in the *Universal British Directory* of 1790.

*13 Aug. 1800   Windy Brow seat*   In 1794 W had written 'Inscription for a Seat by the Pathway side ascending to Windy Brow', a rhyming poem. Later, perhaps at Racedown, W extended the poem and recast it in blank verse. Now, 6 years after their stay at Windy Brow, W and D, and perhaps C, remake the natural seat. The poem too is again remade, probably by C, for there is an Oct. entry in his Notebook referring to the Windy Brow seat and poem: 'Sopha of Sods . . . Lattrig . . . stooping from sublime Thoughts to reckon how many Lines the poem would make' (*Notebooks* i. 830). It made 41 lines and now ended piously, with Heaven and the 'seat Not built by hands'. Published in *MP* on 21 Oct. 1800 under the signature 'Ventifrons' (Windy Brow).

*14 Aug. 1800   the Speddings*   Friends of D from 1794, with John Spedding an exact contemporary of W at Hawkshead; his younger brothers were also fellow-pupils. At Windy Brow in 1794 D had 'received the kindest civilities from Mrs Spedding of Armathwaite' (*EY*, p. 117), and had stayed with W at Armathwaite Hall, Bassenthwaite, for 3 days. The Miss Speddings were Mary, the eldest, and Margaret (later Mrs Froude; 18 May 1802 n.). In 1800 the Ws would call on the

Speddings, not at Armathwaite Hall (sold in 1796 when the family moved to Bath for health reasons), but at Governor's House in Keswick (opposite the George Hotel). The family returned north after Mrs Spedding's death in 1797, and the new Mrs Spedding with whom W was 'a good deal pleased' in 1800 (*EY*, p. 299) was John Spedding's wife, Sarah Gibson of Newcastle. In 1802 the Speddings moved to Mirehouse on Bassenthwaite.

*15 Aug. 1800 Silver hill* Water End (more generally known as Derwent Bay House) and Silver Hill were houses and contiguous estates belonging to Lord William Gordon on the west side of Derwentwater. They were particularly secluded since Lord William Gordon had had a road built well behind them and away from the lake shore.

*17 Aug. 1800 the 7 Sisters* 'The Seven Sisters or The Solitude of Binnorie', a tale of male pursuit and female flight and death, an adaptation of a German poem by Frederica Brun, in a rapid rhyming metre suggested by a poem of Mrs Robinson's; so uncharacteristic of W that he did not include it in *LB* 1800. Published unsigned, probably to help C out, in *MP*, 14 Oct. 1800. At Walter Scott's request it was included in W's *Poems* (1807).

*21 Aug. 1800 Wallenstein* 'I could have written a far better play myself in half the time', wrote C to Wedgwood, 21 Apr. 1800, as he finished his translation of these 'prolix Plays of Schiller'. But Schiller was fashionable and Longmans had his 3 plays about the Thirty Years War General, Wallenstein, in manuscript; C translated 2 (pub. 1800), and conceded in Sept. 1800 that *Wallenstein* was 'quite a model for it's judicious management of the *Sequence* of Scenes' (*CL* i. 621).

*23 Aug. 1800 Peter Bell* Composed 1798, 'Peter Bell' was probably read to both John and D. John was appreciative, since D copied out the first part for him for his voyage of May 1801 and he asked for more. Much revised, it was published in 1819. 'To Joanna', a Poem on the Naming of Places, was recently written, (about echoes among the mountains rather than Joanna Hutchinson, who did not visit until 1803). And see p. xxi.

*24 Aug. 1800 Mr Twining called* Probably Richard Twining (1749–1824), described as 'a considerable tea-dealer in London' in a note in the Encyclopaedia temporarily possessed by W (31 Jan. 1802). He and his half-brother Thomas were old friends of the Ws' uncle, the Revd William Cookson. The Ws at some point took Mr Twining's advice in the Encyclopaedia note (under 'Tea') not to buy cheap tea at, say, 4¼d. or even 9d. per lb. (often adulterated with sheep's dung) but to purchase 'from persons of character'. There was a heavy tax on tea and it could cost up to £1 per lb. (see 21 June 1802 for the excessively disastrous consequences of drinking tea). In the early DC years John might send an occasional, 'Box of Tea' (*EY*, p. 385); later the Ws bought from Richard Twining and from his son Richard. Their bill from Mr Twining for tea bought between Oct. 1808 and Aug. 1809 was £29. 12s. (*MY* i. 403), and in 1813 D ordered '40 lb of Souchong Tea at 7/– 1 lb Pekoe Tea and 1 lb of the best black tea to be sent to Mr Cookson . . . by the Kendal Waggon (*MY* ii. 94). After 1819 the tea was regularly sent to Kendal by canal. The Ws' own used tea leaves were dried and given away.

*Mrs Rawson* Elizabeth Threlkeld (1745–1837), daughter of Elizabeth Cookson (sister of D's Cookson grandfather) and the Revd Samuel Threlkeld, who became Unitarian minister at Halifax. With the help of her brother William Threlkeld she gave D a loving home after the Ws' mother's death in March 1778 when D was 6. She was adding 1 more motherless child to those she had brought up: 5 orphans of her own sister Mrs Ferguson. D lived in Halifax for 9 years. In 1791 Elizabeth Threlkeld married a Halifax merchant, William Rawson.

*27 Aug. 1800 In the morning . . . John Baty passed us* These sentences added in a cramped hand; 'John Baty' has hitherto been misread as 'Mr. Palmer' (see 13 Sept. 1800). John Bateman 'of Crag Top, Grasmere' was buried on 9 June 1804. Crag Top was up the hill from DC, where the present Craigside (probably built on the old site) is now. Gordon W, the poet's grandson, identified a Bateman house, probably Frank's (John's son), as at right angles to the road and nearer DC.

*28 Aug. 1800 by Rydale* 'We walked in the wood' crossed out.

*29 Aug. 1800 Inscription—that about the path* Probably 'When to the attractions of the busy world'. In this poem the poet comes upon a path 'winding on with such an easy line' through the crowded fir trees and realizes that it had been made by his brother John. The path becomes a symbol linking poet and sailor. The Firgrove became 'John's Grove' for the Ws, and the 'favourite haunt of us all'. It is almost opposite the Wishing Gate beyond How Top on the old Rydal road, and it had then, according to W's poem, 'a single beech tree'. The following year, in 1801, the firs were cut down (John W would have liked to give the 'monster' who cut them 'a tight flogging' in his ship (*LJW*, p. 104) ). The Firgrove is now mainly a beech wood.

*30 Aug. 1800 Anthony Harrison* Son of Anthony Harrison, surgeon, of Penrith, and a contemporary of W at Hawkshead: he and his brother John each donated 10*s.* 6*d.* to the New School Library in 1792. A Penrith lawyer who published *Poetical Recreations*, 2 vols. (1806); in 1808 he helped proof-read *The Friend* for C.

*George Mackareth's* George Mackereth (1752–1832) lived at Knott Houses, the fine old farm-house near the Swan. He was parish clerk from 1785 at the death of his father, also parish clerk.

*31 Aug. 1800 Miss Thrale's hatred* A difficult phrase to read: Knight (1897) omitted it from his edition of the Journals, de Selincourt (1941) and Helen Darbishire (1958) offered 'Miss Thrale's [?]', Mary Moorman (1971) decided on 'Mrs Thrale's [?matter]'; 'Miss Thrale's' is not in doubt and the noun is almost certainly 'hatred'. 'Queeney', Mrs Thrale's eldest daughter, is not prominent in Boswell's *Life of Johnson*, which D had been reading only the previous day and was still reading on 14 Sept. But the conversation of W, C, and D was not confined; it ranged over at least 3 topics and could quite easily have moved from Boswell's *Life* to the problems surrounding Mrs Thrale's re-marriage to Gabriel Piozzi, her daughters' music master. Mrs Thrale's infatuation with the Italian and Catholic tutor was universally decried, famously by Dr Johnson but also by the 5 daughters, particularly the eldest, Miss Thrale, who persisted in scorn and coldness towards her mother. Mrs Thrale was the subject of cartoons and gossip. Nevertheless her marriage took place in 1784, and in itself was happy. C very recently may have come upon discussions of the Thrale family problems in a back number (1788) of the *European Magazine*: he quotes from a 1791 issue during this same Aug. (*Notebooks* i. 775).

*Losh's opinion . . . the first of poets* James Losh (1763–1833), a northerner and radical whom W met in London in 1795. In 1800 he was a lawyer in Newcastle upon Tyne, but his family home was Woodside near Carlisle. A democrat who nearly lost his head in Paris, a reformer and Unitarian, Losh was in Bath from 1795 to 1797 because of ill health, and he lent or sent many books and contemporary pamphlets to W at Racedown and Alfoxden. It says not a lot for Losh's taste in poetry that he was known to think Southey the first of poets. He was shortly to be set right about this: on 5 Sept., he had tea with C in Keswick—and C indicated that he, C, considered W 'the first Poet now living' (Losh Diary, MS, Tullie House, Carlisle)—and on the same day Losh and his wife called at DC. W was out walking, but next morning went with D to breakfast with the Loshes in Ambleside. Losh was convinced; in the following year, Aug. 1801, he wrote in his Diary, 'I still retain my opinion that Wordsworth will be one day a great poet.'

*1 Sept. 1800   the Firgrove*   See 29 Aug. 1800 n.

*2 Sept. 1800   Stickel Tarn*   Stickle Tarn on the Langdales below the precipice of Pavey Ark.

   *little Sally*   Sara Ashburner (bapt. 7 Feb. 1790). In 1804 she helped the Ws with their 6-month-old baby John when they were temporarily without a servant. In 1807 she was in service with a Mr Ferrier of Heriot Row, Edinburgh; in 1809 she married Charles Stuart of Windermere, and D next writes of her on 16 June 1811: 'You remember Sally Ashburner? She was buried last Saturday but one—we followed her to her grave. Her husband attended almost heartbroken, she died in a galloping consumption at the age of 21 and has left one daughter, a pretty delicate creature, likely enough soon to be laid by the side of her Mother' (*MY* i. 495).

   *much beer sold*   D's comment on the 'very few people and very few stalls' becomes a virtue of the Grasmere fair in W's account of it at the beginning of Book VIII of *The Prelude*.

*3 Sept. 1800   John Dawsons*   The farm, now known as How Top, at the top of the hill beyond DC on the old road to Rydal. The funeral was of Susan Shacklock, a pauper, mother of 'a baseborn daughter' Betty, born 1768, buried 1796, a pauper.

   *The priest*   Edward Rowlandson, curate of Grasmere for more than 40 years. He died in 1811 aged 77. The rector, John

Craik, was absentee and insane. The general doubt about Mr Rowlandson's sobriety was justified. 'Two vices used to struggle in him for mastery,' said W, 'avarice and the love of strong drink: but avarice, as is common in like cases, always got the better of its opponent; for, though he was often intoxicated, it was never, I believe, at his own expense.' (*PW* iv. 434.)

*4 Sept. 1800   Mrs Clarkson*   Catherine Clarkson (1772–1856), wife of Thomas Clarkson (1760–1846) who, from 1785, had worked alongside Wilberforce for the abolition of the slave trade. Clarkson resigned his ministry and travelled about the ports from Liverpool to Portsmouth collecting evidence from ships' crews. When his health broke down in 1794, he built a house, Eusemere, on Ullswater. W called there with C during the walking tour of late 1799, but D did not meet the Clarksons until the visit this week. She reported immediately to her old Halifax friend, Jane Marshall, 'Mr Clarkson is the man who took so much pains about the slave trade, he has a farm at Ulswater and has built a house. Mrs. C. is a pleasant woman' (*EY*, pp. 300–1). This 'pleasant woman' became a close friend, but had to leave Eusemere for her old home at Bury St Edmunds in the summer of 1803 for health reasons. Shortly afterwards Eusemere was sold to the Earl of Lonsdale and the Clarksons ultimately lived at Playford Hall near Ipswich. It is from D's letters to Catherine Clarkson that we learn most about the everyday family life of the Ws.

*5 Sept. 1800   Mrs Losh*   Cecilia, daughter of the Revd Roger Baldwin of Aldingham, near Ulverston; her brother John was 2 years junior to W at St John's College, Cambridge.

*9 Sept. 1800   Mr Marshall*   John Marshall (1765–1845), linen and wool manufacturer of Leeds; in 1795 he married D's early Halifax friend, Jane Pollard. From 1810 the Marshalls rented Halsteads at Watermillock, Ullswater, as their summer home and in 1824 they bought the Patterdale Hall Estate from John Mounsey.

*10 Sept. 1800   wrote to Mrs Marshall*   A long letter (*EY*, pp. 293–301) with details about the house, Grasmere, and the Ws' way of life; and some extra details about Mr M's visit, e.g. that 'I was left at home to make pies and dumplings' while the men began their walk round the two lakes. Mr M stayed at the Red Lion before leaving with John and W to visit C, riding through

Borrowdale to Buttermere (with John only), returning to Keswick and possibly going on to the Clarksons at Ullswater. Jane Marshall by now had 3 children.

*Mr Bousfield*   Probably 'Robert Bowsfield, linen draper', of Kendal (*Universal Directory*, 1790). Mr Bousfield moved on 5 Oct. 1802 (see D's account of 6 Oct.) and is perhaps connected with William Bousfield whose business premises behind the New Inn on Soutergate (High Street) are noted in 1819.

*12 Sept. 1800   inscription*   Space for 10 or 12 words has been left, but the Inscription has not been supplied. This suggests that W was not regularly reading or discussing the Journal (see 14 May 1800 n.).

*13 Sept. 1800   his preface*   The famous essay on the language and subject-matter of poetry, its origins and purpose, which prefaced *LB* 1800 (2nd edn.).

*Jones & Mr Palmer*   Both Jones and Mr Palmer were contemporaries of W at St John's College, Cambridge. In 1790 Robert Jones (1769–1835) had been W's companion on the long vacation walk through Revolutionary France and across the Alps. W's *Descriptive Sketches of the Alps*, 1793, is dedicated to him, and at intervals throughout their lives W and Jones visited: in Grasmere and Rydal, at Jones's family home at Plas-yn-Llan, Denbighshire, and at his Oxfordshire parsonage at Souldern. Now Jones continued a few days with Palmer and then returned to stay at DC for a week. After his departure on 26 Sept. W wrote 'A Character', and indicated that Jones lay behind the 'odd . . . kind happy creature' of the poem. John Palmer (1769–1840) was born at Whitehaven, and was probably on his way to visit his widowed mother, now Mrs Elizabeth Greenhow. He was senior wrangler, and a Fellow of St John's, Cambridge; President, 1815–19; Professor of Arabic, 1804–19; and curate of Brinkley in Cambridgeshire (for the absentee vicar, Reginald Brathwaite of Hawkshead).

*Mrs Clarkson*   The text is clear but the expression is awkward. It is possible (see D's letter to Jane Marshall, *EY*, pp. 293–301) that W, ill himself and his horse lame, had returned on Mr Marshall's horse, which now had to be sent back to Mr M, presumably staying with the Clarksons at Eusemere. All editors have repunctuated, and preferred the reading, 'John came home

from Mr Marshall. Sent back word to Mrs Clarkson': only de
Selincourt indicated the manuscript reading 'backward'.

*21 Sept. 1800   Tom Myers & Father*   Father was widowed Thomas
Myers (1735–1826), of Brow, a farm near Barton, Penrith,
husband of D's aunt Anne W (died 1787), and Vicar of
Lazonby. Thomas Myers (1764–1835), the son, was assisted in
his career by his mother's cousin, John Robinson of Appleby,
the influential MP for Harwich; at 17, like John W, he joined the
East India Company and in 1796 became Accountant-General
of Bengal. There was a plan in 1795 for D to look after a natural
daughter of her cousin Tom, a child of 3 or 4, born in India.
Had the child come she would have been a companion for little
Basil Montagu at Racedown. Nothing more is heard of this
proposal (see *EY*, p. 147). Thomas Myers returned from India
in 1798 and married, in Jan. 1802, Lady Mary Nevill, John
Robinson's grand-daughter and his own second cousin once
removed. On John Robinson's death at the end of that year he
too became MP for Harwich.

*27 Sept. 1800   Abergavennys arrival*   The *Earl of Abergavenny*, the
East India ship of which John W was to become Captain in Jan.
1801 in succession to his much older cousin, also John W (1754–
1819), son of Uncle Richard of Whitehaven. The ship was called
the *Earl of Abergavenny* through W's father's cousin, John
Robinson, who partly owned it and whose daughter Mary
married Henry Nevill in Oct. 1781; in 1785 Henry Nevill
became 2nd Earl of Abergavenny.

*28 Sept. 1800   Mr & Miss Smith*   Elizabeth Smith (1776–1806) and
her father Colonel George Smith. D, more than 20 years after
Elizabeth Smith's death, spoke to a friend, Miss Laing, of 'the
learned and accomplished Miss Elizabeth Smith, who died
young at Coniston, and was buried at Hawkshead. I think you
must have heard and read of Miss Smith. Mrs Bowdler
published a short account of her life, and early and lamented
death, with some of her letters and translations from the
German—and a few other compositions' (*LY* i. 571). Elizabeth
Smith was mainly a self-taught scholar, not only in European
languages but in Oriental and Hebrew. In 1800 the Smiths were
at Patterdale but in 1801 the wandering military family settled
at Coniston and Elizabeth spent much of her last illness in a tent
overlooking the 'whole charming view of the lake, the church,

and scattered village of Coniston' (*Guide* i. 80–8). Her parents called their new house Tent Lodge.

*29 Sept. 1800   in sight of Ulswater*   John never came again to Grasmere. He left to prepare for his first voyage as Captain of the East Indiaman, The *Earl of Abergavenny*. The ship did not leave Portsmouth for China until mid-May 1801, and docked back into Gravesend, London, in Sept. 1802. D and W were themselves in London at that time after their visit to Annette Vallon in France, and they spent some days with John. It was their last time together. Between May 1803 and Aug. 1804 John W made another voyage to China, and was again setting out, in early 1805, this time for Bengal as well as for China, when on 5 Feb. the ship struck rocks off Portland and Captain W was among the 232 people to be drowned. So the parting 'in sight of Ulswater' was of profound importance to D and W. It was at Grisedale Tarn, the lonely tarn high up on the pass under Helvellyn between Grasmere and Patterdale where John had on occasion gone alone, sometimes for solitude, sometimes to fish. 'We were in view of the head of Ulswater,' wrote D to Lady Beaumont in June 1805 after the first shock of John's death, 'and stood till we could see him no longer, watching him as he *hurried* down the stony mountain. Oh! my dear Friend, you will not wonder that we love that place' (*EY*, pp. 598–9). For W's elegiac verses describing the place and the parting, 'I only looked for pain and grief', written 1805 but not published till 1842, see Gill, p. 308.

*2 Oct. 1800   Churnmilk force*   The waterfall on the descent from Easedale Tarn to Grasmere, now known as Sour Milk Ghyll.

*3 Oct. 1800   learning to mark*   See 30 June 1802, where the old man's daughter teaches 'flowering & marking'—the embroidering of identification signs on linen.

*Amos Cottle's*   Amos Cottle (1768–1800), elder brother of Joseph, the bookseller and publisher. In Dec. 1797 W was given his translation from the Icelandic (or more probably from a Latin version) of the *Edda of Saemund* and he wrote to Amos's brother, Joseph, about the 'considerable pleasure' it gave him despite the 'many inaccuracies which ought to have been avoided' (*EY*, p. 196).

*S Lowthian*   Sally Lowthian. D's father's account book (WL) shows that a Nurse was hired in the Cockermouth house from

Christmas 1771: D was born that Christmas Day. The nurse, Sally Lowthian, is not mentioned by name until the final payment of 3 guineas (for a half year) at Martinmas 1778.

*an old man almost double*    D writes this detailed description a week after she and W met the old leech-gatherer. They had gone with Jones (and C) north on 26 Sept. and met the old man when they were almost back, 'a few hundred yards from my cottage', W told Miss Fenwick in 1842 (*PW* ii. 510). The meeting, and D's account of it (a consequence of talking about the Preface?), lies behind W's poem 'The Leech-gatherer', written 18 months later (see 4 May 1802), revised and published in 1807 as 'Resolution and Independence'. D's narrative ends with the old man's actual words—a quotation not hitherto noted.

*to gather leeches*    Leeches were in demand for blood-letting right through the 19th c. (and they still have some specialist use); country people would apply the leeches themselves. Ellen (6 June 1802 n.) 'had', wrote D in May 1804 'a couple of Leeches in a Bottle with which she was going to bleed herself' (*EY*, p. 474).

*4 Oct. 1800*    Lambs play.    The tragedy, *John Woodvil*, as it came to be called when it was published in early 1802—at Lamb's own expense. Begun in late 1798, it was sent to friends and to John Kemble at the Drury Lane Theatre; it was lost, rewritten, and rejected. D's criticism was right, and Lamb later admitted that his language 'imperceptibly took a tinge' of his '*first love*', the Jacobean playwrights (Dedicatory letter to C, *Works* i (1818) ).

*Essays for the newspaper*    Essays and letters on the subject of Farmers and Monopolists appear in the *MP* about this time, some by C, and some by his tanner and farmer friend from Somerset, Thomas Poole. C had been an intermittent contributor of political essays (usually printed anonymously as leaders and for which he was paid 4 or 5 guineas each), and of verses (a guinea) since his first introduction to Daniel Stuart in late 1797. In 1803 Stuart sold the *MP*, but his other paper, the *Courier*, continued to provide C with regular money. C's last letter, on 'Children in the Cotton Factories', appeared in March 1818.

*His youngest child*    Derwent, the Cs' 3rd son, less than 3 weeks old (b. 14 Sept. 1800); their 2nd son, Berkeley, had died the previous year, aged 8 months.

*2nd part of Christabel*   The first part of 'Christabel', delicate, moonlit, and ballad-like, had been written in Somerset in spring 1798. The new second part had a specific Lake District setting, and the poem, until the decision of 6 Oct., was intended for *LB* 1800. Finally published, through Byron's encouragement, in 1816, it was still unfinished.

*5 Oct. 1800  were employed*   D's first account was 'Wm was . . .'; she then crossed out 'was' and acknowledged her own share in the work.

*Silver How in both lakes*   The same observation was made by C: 'Silver How casts its shadow in two Lakes—Rydale & Grasmere' (*Notebooks*, i. 769).

*7 Oct. 1800  Mary*   Mr Sympson's grand-daughter Mary Jameson (bapt. 7 Aug. 1791), Tommy's younger sister. She continued to live in Ambleside after her father's death: her mother took lodgers and in 1804 married William Ross, surgeon of Ambleside.

*8 Oct. 1800  The Beggar*   Now that 'Christabel' was not going to fill up (or over-fill) the alloted space in the new *LB*—already partially in type—W was obliged both to write more, and to re-furbish old poems. 'The Old Cumberland Beggar', begun possibly as early as the Racedown days of autumn 1795 as 'Description of a Beggar', was expanded now to explore W's belief that individual acts of charity are of value to the giver as well as to the receiver.

*9 Oct. 1800  at Flemings*   Thomas Fleming (d. 1815, aged 95) lived in what was possibly still an inn, the Hare and Hounds at Rydal, next door to what is now Rydal Lodge. The inn sign was taken down at about this time to avoid the possibility of soldiers being quartered on the house at 9*d.* a head. Lady Diana Fleming of Rydal Hall (no relation) refused to have the sign replaced and the inn ceased to be. The Flemings were an old yeoman family.

*Ball at Rydale*   Perhaps the ball was for Anne Frederica, only child of Sir Michael le and Lady Diana Fleming. Anne Frederica, however, appears not to have inherited her father's love of society: Boswell recalls that 'fashionable baronet's preference for the smell of a flambeau at the playhouse' to 'the fragrance of a May evening in the country' (*Life of Johnson*, ch. 17). His daughter, after trying London and marriage to her cousin Sir Daniel Fleming in 1807, returned alone and lived quietly with her mother at Rydal Hall. There were no more balls: Lady Anne Frederica built a chapel at Rydal in 1824, partly that she might avoid services at Grasmere conducted by her husband's brother, the Rector Richard Fleming.

*10 Oct. 1800  tramper's*  Gypsies could be called trampers, and were quite distinct from pedlars such as the Cockermouth traveller and her husband.

*read Southey's letters  Letters Written during a Short Residence in Spain and Portugal*, 1797, 2nd edn. 1799. See 14 Oct. Joseph Cottle had offered, before Southey went to Spain and Portugal at the end of 1795, to publish any description he might bring back. Southey was in Portugal again for a second, longer visit for most of 1800; he was not to become a neighbour of the Ws until his move to Greta Hall, Sept. 1803.

*Point Rash judgment*  See 25 June 1800 n. W writes about an episode of some 2½ months earlier, and gives it a Sept. setting.

*11 Oct. 1800  in search of a Sheepfold*  For some 2 months from this date, W thinks about and composes 'Michael', the final poem in *LB* 1800, and the replacement for 'Christabel'. He and D went to find the actual sheepfold, 'on which so much of the poem turns' (Fenwick Note, *PW* ii. 478). The ruins of it were, and perhaps still are, by Greenhead Ghyll. W had known about the unfinished Grasmere sheepfold from his boyhood, because Ann Tyson, his Hawkshead 'Dame', had worked as a girl for a family of Grasmere origin, the Knotts, then living in Rydal (at the house W was himself to live in, Rydal Mount). It was Ann Tyson who told him the story of the Grasmere shepherd.

*may be swept away*  A sheep swept away from a little green island in the middle of a stream and a boy almost swept away are the subject of a passage written during this autumn and intended for 'Michael'. In it a shepherd father rescues his son. Though it is in the same plain style as 'Michael' and though, as in D's entry, it belongs to that same world of real shepherds, it was not finally part of the poem. It temporarily found a place in *The Prelude* (VIII. 222–311) in 1804.

*15 Oct. 1800  at the sheep-fold*  Not the place, nor the poem 'Michael' as we know it, but an earlier treatment of the subject in stanza and rhyme, at which W seemed to labour without much success. Finally (see 9 Nov.) he burnt the greater part of what he had written, and went on to compose, finishing on 9 Dec., the great blank verse pastoral, 'Michael'.

*16 Oct. 1800 Miss Nicholson* Caroline Nicholson, eldest daughter of Samuel Nicholson, wholesale haberdasher of Cateaton Street, London. D and W knew the Nicholsons through the Threlkelds and Fergusons of Halifax, whose connection with the London Nicholsons was one of both business and friendship. They stayed with the Nicholsons at the end of Dec. 1797 when W took his play, *The Borderers*, to the manager at Covent Garden and awaited a decision. At the end of Sept. 1802 when W and D were in London, D regretted not seeing Caroline 'whom I should have liked dearly to see and whom I love and respect very much' (*EY*, p. 378). Despite this, D seems to have drifted into silence as regards Miss Nicholson and they appear not to have met again.

*Mr Griffith* Robert Eaglesfield Griffith (1756–1833), a cousin of D's mother Ann Cookson. His father was a Whitehaven merchant, and he seems to have worked as a commercial traveller for a Manchester cotton house. He had clearly been kind to D when she was miserable in Penrith with her grandmother in 1787 and was missing her Halifax friends; she would have been 'delighted' to go with him to Newcastle upon Tyne to stay with his sisters (*EY*, p. 12). In 1793, again wanting to go to Halifax, she thought of her 'good friend Mr Griffith' as taking her 'along with him' (*EY*, p. 95). Married in Philadelphia in 1797, Mr Griffith became a prosperous shipping merchant, sent D and W 'a barrel of the best american flour, which has been most acceptable to us' and £10 in 1801 (*EY*, p. 337), and received from them a copy of *LB* 1800.

*17 Oct. 1800 The swan hunt* Killing swans was permitted, 'though it was accounted felony to steal their eggs', remarks Thomas Bewick in *British Birds*, 1797. Cygnets were fattened for the table and 'sold very high, commonly for a guinea each', but the swan itself was 'accounted a coarse kind of food'. W in *Home at Grasmere* regrets the disappearance from the lake of 'a lonely pair / Of milk-white Swans' and fears that 'for the sake of those he loves at home', 'the Shepherd' 'may have seized the deadly tube' (ll. 322 ff.).

*Biggs* Nathaniel Biggs, the active partner for Biggs and Cottle, Printers, St Augustine's Back, Bristol; Cottle retained a financial interest in this business; see also 15 March 1802 n.

Copy for *LB* 1800 was frequently sent from Grasmere to Biggs at this time.

   *a very fine mild evening*   '. . . morning' crossed out.

   *Parkes*   Nab Cottage, Rydal, home of William Park (1741–1825), uncle of the Hawkshead schoolboy Tom Park with whom W as a boy used to go fishing. The house finally left the Park family in 1832 when William Park's grand-daughter Margaret Simpson and her husband Thomas De Quincey had to sell it. It was with the new farmers at The Nab, William and Eleanor Richardson, that Hartley C lodged at the end of his life. He died there in 1849.

   *Coleridge had done nothing for the LB*   D makes the same comment on 22 Oct. On 30 Oct. C wrote in his notebook,

He knew not what to do—something, he felt, must be done—he rose, drew his writing-desk suddenly before him—sate down, took the pen—& found that he knew not what to do. (*Notebooks* i. 834)

*19 Oct. 1800   the two points*   Promontories on Rydal.

*22 Oct. 1800   Stoddart*   John Stoddart (1773–1856), knighted 1826; journalist, editor, King's Advocate at Malta, brother-in-law of Hazlitt, and, in 1801, author of *Remarks on the Local Scenery and Manners of Scotland*. Walking with his friend James Moncrieff from Edinburgh to London in the spring of 1800 he had called at Grasmere to see W—whom he had known in the early republican London days, e.g. at Godwin's house—and had found C at DC. This Oct. call was his second visit north in 1800; he had every inducement to revisit Scotland, partly to prepare his *Remarks*, partly to woo his future wife, Isabella Moncrieff of Tulliebole Castle. For a second time he found C at DC, and went to stay with him for a week at Keswick, before returning for a few days with W and D.

   *Christabel*   Stoddart, who had what W called 'a very wicked memory' (Samuel Rogers, *Table Talk*, 1887, p. 209), later recited 'Christabel' to Walter Scott who caught something of C's ideas and rhythms, and published in 1805 his own long ballad poem, *The Lay of the Last Minstrel*. It 'shews how cautious Poets ought to be in lending their manuscripts, or even *reading* them to Authors' wrote D in Oct. 1805 (*EY*, p. 633).

*25 Oct. 1800   Rogers, Miss Seward, Cowper &c.*   The most popular of the elder contemporary poets. The banker and art collector Samuel Rogers (1763–1855) published his *Pleasures of Memory* in 1792, and D had known the poem since Aug. 1795 when it had been given to her, along with Akenside's *Pleasures of Imagination*, by William Rawson of Halifax. Its conventional 'tumbling tide of dread Lodore' and 'cliffs, that scaled the sky' measure the advance in realism of W's new matter-of-fact landscape description in 'Michael'.

*Miss Seward*    Anna Seward (1747–1809), the 'Swan of Lichfield'. Her most recent volume of sonnets, with such titles as 'An Evening in November, which had been stormy, gradually clearing up, in a mountainous country', perfectly embodied the late 18th-c. sensibility for landscape and atmosphere.

*Cowper*    William Cowper (1731–1800), son of a clergyman; a lawyer and scholar, a man to whom religion was wonder, and torture, and the only writer, wrote W 'with the exception of Burns, of recent verse, that sticks to my memory (I mean which I get by heart)' (*MY* ii. 179).

*27 Oct. 1800    Not fine*    The word 'fine' unaccountably is deleted.

*wife's glass*    Doubtless one of the popular Claude Lorraine or Gray glasses: these essentially were slightly convex, darkened pocket mirrors, often with coloured filters, that could convey a concentrated and picturesque image of the landscape.

*28 Oct. 1800    the whole vale*    Here D began to record the next day: 'Wednesday 30th A cold & rainy m' but crossed this out and added more to Tuesday's entry, 'In the evening . . .'.

*31 Oct. 1800    moonshine*    This single word, which drops at the bottom of a page into the central fold of the note-book, has been previously thought to be 'moon shone'.

*1 Nov. 1800    Don Quixote*    Probably to borrow the book from W. The Lloyds were still in temporary lodgings in Ambleside; not till the end of Nov. were they in their own house, 'our goods have been so long in coming' (Lloyd to Manning, 10 Dec. 1800, *The Lloyd–Manning Letters*, p. 56). W kept all his life the *Don Quixote* (in Smollett's translation) that his father had bought from Anthony Soulby, bookseller of Penrith, the text he probably read as a boy (*Memoir* i. 10). Along with two other editions it is in the Rydal Mount Library list.

*3 Nov. 1800   still talking*   The incessant talking was to some purpose. C at Keswick and W at Grasmere must have taught Stoddart to read the *LB* sympathetically; in a letter of late Feb. 1801 W demonstrates, albeit with comic exaggeration, how much Stoddart was in need of instruction: his reaction to 'The Idiot Boy' for example—'thrown into a *fit* almost with disgust, cannot *possibly* read it' (*EY*, p. 320). Despite this basic reaction, and as a result of talking, Stoddart's flattering review appeared in *The British Critic*, Feb. 1801, and in his *Remarks on . . . Scotland*, 1801, Stoddart made several admiring references to W's poetry. His zeal indeed was in danger of being counter-productive.

*4 Nov. 1800   the Tarn*   Grisedale Tarn.

*7 Nov. 1800   Amelia*   D presumably completes *Amelia* as no other reading is mentioned until she turns to *Tom Jones* on 25 Nov. Fielding's *Works* had been among her 'pretty little collection of Books from my Brothers' (*EY*, p. 8) since 1787.

*The poor woman . . . warm that day*   This sentence is an inserted afterthought: the concluding line had been drawn under the 'quite brown' copses. D then forgetfully began and dated the day's entry again.

*still unwell*   Two words, apparently '& melancholy', are crossed out here.

*8 Nov. 1800   Monk Lewis*   Matthew Gregory Lewis (1775–1818), at the age of 20 famous for his sensational novel *Ambrosio or the Monk*, 1795. When he was 23 his play *The Castle Spectre* was a success, while W's play, *The Borderers*, was rejected, and W attributed this rejection to 'the deprav'd State of the Stage at present' (*EY*, p. 197). Monk Lewis was writing and collecting stories and poems for, first, *Tales of Terror*, 1799 and 1801, and second, *Tales of Wonder*, 1801. Scott and Southey both contributed; possibly Lewis was writing to W for a contribution.

*9 Nov. 1800   burnt the sheep fold*   See above 15 Oct. n.

*11 Nov. 1800   salving sheep*   In her short Journal of an Excursion on the banks of Ullswater of Nov. 1805 D commented on the Martindale farmer 'who was sitting at the door salving sheep'. W, revising this Journal for his *Guide*, expanded D's phrase: the farmer at his door had 'sheep collected round him one of which he was smearing with tar for protection against the winter cold' (*Prose* ii. 247 and 372).

*14 Nov. 1800  Molly Ashburner*  Mary (bapt. 30 March 1788), fourth daughter of Thomas Ashburner.

*19 Nov. 1800  Mr Denton's*  Isaac Denton, vicar 1786–1820 of Crosthwaite Church, Keswick. His family had owned Warnell Hall, Sebergham, Cumberland, but the estate was sold in 1774 to Sir James Lowther. C, relishing the absurdity, heard him preach to his country congregation about 'the inordinate vice of ambition' and the 'shocking' dangers of being a courtier (*MY* i. 94).

*20 Nov. 1800  Mr Jackson & Mr Peach*  Mr Jackson, builder and owner of Greta Hall, lived in the back portion of the house, and this was large enough for a Keswick friend, Mr Peach, to live there for well over a year. He had moved out by Jan. 1802 when C wrote to Sara Hutchinson, 'Peach has left Greta Hall, & with him went his china men, & beasts, & unpetticoated Beauties— & of course, the Bull-dog, that so long had been Hartley's Bedfellow' (*CL* ii. 780). The Chinese pictures that D saw on 22 Nov. 1800 were clearly part of this collection. Mr Peach must not be confused with that flamboyant summer resident of the island house Colonel William Peachey.

*23 Nov. 1800  Mr Gawthorpe*  Robert Gawthorpe (1754–1844), 101–5 Soutergate, Kendal, a prosperous woollen and linsey manu-facturer: one of his partners (Christopher Wilson) was to buy Abbot Hall in 1801.

*24 Nov. 1800  took Laudanum*  Dr Johnson's 'soporifick tincture': a preparation of opium simmered into a syrup with fortified wine, spices, and either quince or orange juice. D could have taken either of two local patent 'Tinctures of Opium': the Lancaster Blackdrop or the Kendal. These, regarded as common pain-killers, were available in grocers' shops. The Genuine Quaker's Black Drop at Kendal was 1s. 6d. a bottle. After 1833, the beginning of her long illness, D was prescribed opium more regularly. In Dec. 1835 the treatment was withdrawn, and Mary W wrote to Jane Marshall of 'our poor Invalid . . . quite without her treacherous support' (*LY* iii. 140).

*26 Nov. 1800  home,—*  This word is clear but it has been consist-ently misread as 'dinner'. There are frequent examples of 'before' meaning 'ahead'—see 27, 30 Nov., 23 Dec. 1801, 1 Mar. 1802. Sara and D walked on ahead because W was 'highly poetical', no doubt 'mumbling to hissel' along t'roads', as W's Rydal neighbour would later express it (H. D. Rawnsley, *Reminiscences of W among the Peasantry of Westmoreland*, 1968, p. 32).

*27 Nov. 1800   Tom Hutchinson*   Tom Hutchinson (1773–1849) had recently taken a farm at Gallow Hill near Scarborough. His sisters Mary, Sara, and Joanna, when they were not staying with John at Stockton, George at Middleham, or the Ws in Grasmere, kept house for him. Mary married W from Gallow Hill. In spring 1804 Tom came to farm at Park House near Penrith, 'Mr Hazel's Farm, formerly occupied by Johnny Armstrong, that white house on the hill above Dalemain' (*EY*, p. 417); D and Sara 'worked diligently all day . . . fitting up beds, curtains, &c &c &c' (*EY*, p. 476), but Tom was not 'entirely satisfied with his Farm', despite its association with the famous freebooter of the Borders. He did not settle till 1809 when he took a farm at Hindwell in Radnorshire. In 1812 he married his cousin Mary Monkhouse and had 5 children.

*before dinner.*   After this 'Miss Simpson drank tea' has been written and crossed out. It belongs to the following day.

*1 Dec. 1800   Mr King's*   Rydal Mount (14 May 1800 n.). In 1800 it was in the tenancy of Thomas King (1772–1831), a Leicestershire farmer of means recently come north with his wife in compliance with her plan to separate him from his former love, Hannah Goude. But Mr King secretly established Hannah in Patterdale and by her had two children. In 1802 he bought and moved to the Olliffs' house in Grasmere, the Hollens, and began to offend the Ws by surrounding the house with 'fir and Larch plantations, that look like a blotch or scar' wrote D in 1805 (*EY*, p. 638), and by building what the Ws deemed an unsightly barn. In 1813 he left Grasmere for Patterdale; Mrs King went to Kendal.

An example of an entry clearly written later: D had begun to write that the delightful walk was 'round R[ydale]'; remembering, she crossed this out and gave the precise route. The final phrase about Baking day is recollected even later and inserted comically between 'delightful' on one page and 'walk' on the next.

*3 Dec. 1800   MH*   D wrote 'Pork from Mr Simpson' here, crossed it out, and made a note of the gift in the following day's entry.

*4 Dec. 1800   the old man*   Coniston Old Man, a mountain.

*8 Dec. 1800   Miss Griffith*   Robert Griffith had 3 older sisters: Grace, the eldest (d. 1796), Ann (1742–1804), and Elizabeth (1747–1812) of Northumberland Place, Newcastle upon Tyne. They helped out their income by letting rooms. John W had stayed briefly in May 1792; D was with them for 3 or 4 months from Dec. 1794, 'very happy in the company of our good friends the Miss Griffiths who are very cheerful pleasant companions and excellent women' (*EY*, p. 140); and W stayed some weeks, Jan.–Feb. 1795. Interestingly, it was from Newcastle at the end of her visit to the Miss Griffiths that D so significantly renewed the Ws' relationship with 'my friends the Hutchinsons, my sole companions at Penrith . . . they are settled at Sockburn—six miles from Darlington'. She apparently had promised to see them 'whenever I came to Newcastle' (*EY*, p. 141–2).

*9 Dec. 1800   I*   Written over 'We'; *his poem* i.e. 'Michael'.

*10 Dec. 1800   John Stanley's*   John Stanley was landlord of the King's Head at Thirlspot on the way to Keswick.


## The Second Notebook: Grasmere Journal, 10 October 1801–14 February 1802 (DC MS 25)

The first notebook ends in mid-sentence. There must have been another containing entries from 22 Dec. 1800 to 9 Oct. 1801. This book has not been found. The second Grasmere Journal runs from 10 Oct. 1801 to 14 Feb. 1802. It is written in a small book bound in blue marbled board, again just under 4″ wide and 6″ deep. D first used it to record her journey to and stay in Hamburg from 14 Sept.–1 Oct. 1798. At the other end of the book, inside the cover and on the second and third pages, are D's sums and expenses connected with the Ws' journey by coach to Yarmouth, and by packet to Hamburg; and on the first page at this end, as though trying out a freshly made nib, the word *amen* is written out again and again, and there are two phrases, 'God be with Wm. Wordsworth' and 'God save Dorothy Wordsworth'. In 1800 W used the book at this rough end for drafts of 'The Brothers' and 'Emma's Dell', and here, many pages are cut out. The Grasmere Journal follows the drafts and fills the pages until, on 14 Feb. 1802, it reaches the Hamburg account of 1798.

The first pages at the rough end have an additional Journal

interest. In the margin, and in the space below the 'amens', and moving on to the second page is a list of jotted items:

Penshurst—Pedlar—Mary H.—Grasmere & Keswick—Sara's waistcoats—Fable of the Dogs—Cows—Lambs Londoner—Lucy Aikins poems—Mr Graham—Mrs Clarkson health—My German —our Riches—Miss Simpson—The poor woman who was drowned —Williams health—medicines—The garden—Wm working there —quietness from Company—Letting our house—keeping it— Books that we are to carry—L. degrades himself—narrow minded Bigotry—unfortunate quotation—Letter from Sara—Montagu— Dr Dodd—Rubbing tables.

Five extra items are added in pencil: 'Mrs Clarkson   Mary H   Mr G—   Lives P   Dr Dodd'. Some of these items have their explanation in the Journal itself during early 1802. Others require a note:

(1)   *Fable of the Dogs*: A reference perhaps to Burns' 'The Twa Dogs', from which W quotes (8 June 1802 n.) or to Lessing's Fable 'Die Hunde' ('The Dogs', 6 Feb. 1802 n.).

(2)   *Lambs Londoner*: A short essay, one of Lamb's first, in praise of London (published in *MP*, 1 Feb. 1802), in which Lamb declares his love of crowds, Fleet Street, and Drury Lane Theatre. His 3-week stay in the Lake District during Aug. 1802 was to shake his loyalty a little, but not damage it permanently: 'after all, Fleet Street & the Strand are better places to live in for good & all than among Skiddaw', he declared to his friend Manning, 24 Sept. 1802 (Marrs, ii. 70). D and W must have seen the essay in the newspaper and recalled Lamb's letter to W of a year previous when he first wrote passionately about the wonder of London (Marrs, i. 267).

(3)   *Lucy Aikins poems*: Lucy Aikin (1781–1864), daughter of John Aikin, doctor, man of letters, Unitarian; niece of Mrs Barbauld; her first considerable work in verse, *Epistles on Women*, did not appear till 1810, but she was contributing to magazines by 1799.

(4)   *Letting our house—keeping it*: A reference probably to the plan of 1802 to live in France (see 8 Feb. 1802 and n.).

(5)   *Dr Dodd*: Dr William Dodd (1729–77), a popular preacher; poet, editor of *The Beauties of Shakespeare*, 1752; from 1763 chaplain to the King, theological writer, author of a commentary on the Bible. He moved in high society, got into debt, and forged a bond of over £4,000 in Lord Chesterfield's name. Lord Chesterfield, a former pupil of Dr Dodd, appeared against him, and despite a petition for

mercy to the King signed by 23,000 people, and despite letters written on Dodd's behalf by Dr Johnson, Dr Dodd was executed in June 1777. His life and fate must have been part of the adult gossip of the Ws' childhood: there were numerous accounts of the trial, his Prison Thoughts, his Dying Words; the *Gentleman's Magazine* ran a series of articles. D would have come across Dr Dodd in her reading of Boswell in autumn 1800: 'Lives P' (Johnson's *Lives of the Poets?*) is written in pencil next to her second 'Dr Dodd' jotting. The name Dr Dodd remained potent in the W circle: in Aug. 1802 when C and his children were shouting and listening for echoes in the mountains they found that 'Joanna' was a good echoing word (23 Aug. 1800 n.), '& then' wrote C to Sara Hutchinson, 'not to forget an old Friend, I made them all say Dr Dodd &c—' (*CL* ii. 844).

*10 Oct. 1801 Sara's seat* Sara was not there to help build her seat on White Moss Common but she had laid the first stone of it 'so long back as Thursday March 26th 1801'. It remained unbuilt until 'Saturday noon, Oct. 10 1801—when between the hours of 12 and 2, William Wordsworth & his sister—with S.T. Coleridge built it'. C noted this in the copy of Matthisson's *Gedichte* that was in his pocket (see George Whalley, *Coleridge and Sara Hutchinson and the Asra Poems*, Toronto, 1955, p. 123).

*13 Oct. 1801 wet day* The words 'Wednesday 14th omitted. Thursday' are written here and in part crossed out.

*15 Oct. 1801 Mr Luffs* Charles Luff, commissioned in 1803 Captain of the Patterdale (or Wedgwood) Loyal Mountaineers (financed by Tom Wedgwood), and his wife Letitia were in lodgings in Ambleside. This was for social reasons; their own cottage was in Patterdale. The Ws got to know them as friends of the Clarksons. In 1812 they emigrated to Mauritius where Luff died in 1815. Mrs Luff lived finally with Lady Farquhar at Dale Lodge, Grasmere.

*23 Oct. 1801 Mr Curwen's nursery* John Christian (1756–1828), becoming John Christian Curwen in 1782 on his marriage to Isabella Curwen of Workington Hall, Cumberland, and Belle Isle, Windermere; MP for Carlisle; owned and planted much of the western shore of Windermere: the lands about the Ferry from 1786, almost all of Claife Heights by 1798, and the higher land by the 'Station' from 1800 (8 June 1802 n.). He planted 30,000 larches and many exotic shrubs (to W's dismay), but also, 'got a Medal for dibbling this with Acorns 1798' (note on estate map). He wrote about agricultural reform and established this nursery garden. It was however D's normal practice to transplant into the garden from the wild.

*25 Oct. 1801  Legberthwaite*  A hamlet beyond the north-eastern end of Thirlmere towards Keswick. North of the bridge that once divided the old Leathes Water and on the old high road at its highest point, one could see, in Thomas West's words, 'the narrow green vale of Legberthwaite, divided into small enclosures, peopled with a few cots, and nobly terminated by the romantic castle-like rock of St. John' (p. 83). W thought that the traveller should go specially 'for the sake of that View' (*Prose* ii. 273).

*expecting Mary*  MH was at Greta Hall from Friday morning, 23rd. (*Notebooks*, i. 999).

*26 Oct. 1800  They*  presumably Tom Hutchinson and W.

*9 Nov. 1801  sate in C's room a while*  MH's arrival at DC only 3 days previously on 6 Nov. is unnoted in the Journal as we have it: a page has been torn out containing entries from 5 Nov. to the start of 9 Nov. MH and the Ws accompanied C to Greta Hall for his last night there before his London winter. Their sense of being *'at home'* was, sadly, no doubt due to Mrs C's absence with the children at the Clarksons at Eusemere, where C was to join them before leaving the north. Mrs Coleridge's 'radical fault', wrote D, was 'want of sensibility and what can such a woman be to Coleridge?' (*EY*, p. 331). The words 'left us' remain on the stub at 5 Nov., and 'Coleridge came' and 'Walked with Coleridge to Keswick' for 6 and 9 Nov. are fortunately included in the selection from D's Journal printed in her nephew Christopher's *Memoirs of Wordsworth* (1851), i. 177.

*10 Nov. 1801  Aquafortis*  Popular name for nitric acid, a corrosive and solvent.

*15 Nov. 1801  Heifer crags*  Probably Calf Crags at the end of Far Easedale valley.

*Bishop Hall*  Joseph Hall (1574–1656), Bishop of Exeter 1627, and of Norwich 1641; deprived of his see in the Commonwealth 1643. W and D were undoubtedly reading Hall's early Satires in Anderson, ii. The first satires are on the art of poetry and there is praise of the 'eternal legends' of 'Renowned Spenser', whom W reads next day from the same volume.

*16 Nov. 1801   little John Dawson*   Little John Dawson of How Top
(bapt. 3 Mar. 1799) seems too young for either D's lecture or his
accusation of Jenny Baty. Jenny defends herself against the
charge, but, significantly, ill-treatment of a parish apprentice
by 'one of our near Neighbours' is discussed at some length by D
in her manuscript appeal for the orphan children of the Greens
in 1808. The boy in this case came 'from a distant place' and so
the Parish officers did not monitor his treatment. D describes
the boy's nursing his mistress's numerous children, his slavish
condition, the lack of religious instruction, the 'almost savage
ignorance with bold vice', despite the traces of natural sense and
good temper. The boy was 16 in 1808, and thus would be 7 or 8
when D lectured a boy for lying and for charging Jenny Baty
with beating him. If this was that same boy (and the name John
Dawson is common and could be entirely unconnected with the
little child at How Top), then perhaps he was not lying, and was
ultimately vindicated by D herself in the Green story. D
observes him again on 20 Feb. and 1 June 1802.

*18 Nov. 1801   Wm wrote some lines upon it*   Probably a draft of

> yon gracious Church,
> That has a look so full of peace and hope
> And love—benignant Mother of the Vale,
> How fair amid her brood of Cottages!
> (*Home at Grasmere*, ll. 524–7)

*Saras   Gate*   Sara   Hutchinson   'had'   an   Eminence
(1 Aug. 1800 n.), a seat (10 Oct. 1801), a Rock (28 Dec. 1801),
and here a gate. Strictly speaking she had had the gate, more
generally known as the Wishing Gate, since her visit of March
1801. W wrote to MH about it in Apr., 'You will recollect that
there is a gate just across the road, directly opposite the firgrove,
this gate was always a favorite station of ours; we love it far
more now on Sara's account. You know that it commands a
beautiful prospect; Sara carved her cypher upon one of its bars
and we call it her gate. We will find out another place for your
cypher' (*EY*, p. 332–3). See 31 Oct. 1802 when D is again at
Sara's Gate with Mary, now W's wife.

*20 Nov. 1801   I wrote . . . morning*   This first sentence is crossed
out. 'I wrote' was originally 'We wrote'.

*21 Nov. 1801   the Swan*   The word 'Blacks' is crossed out in front of

'Swan'. D corrects herself to indicate that W and MH did not walk as far as the Blacksmith's at Tongue Gill.

24 *Nov. 1801    John Greens house*    Pavement End, near the head of the lake, the Greens' house for several generations. John Green (1758–1839), a butcher, lived with his old father and some 6 or 7 sons. W describes the family in *The Excursion* VII. 635–94, and tells how the late arriving and much adored daughter died as a small girl, and how the family coped with this sudden turn from joy to grief.

*I found*    The italicized 'I' is written over 'We'.

*'alas! the gratitude of men has &c'*    The last 2 lines of W's 'Simon Lee' (*LB* 1798),

> Alas! the gratitude of men
> Has oftner left me mourning.

*sold his land*    W perhaps takes a hint from D here and in his poem 'Repentance' (see 24 Mar. 1802) makes the wife the speaker of the grief that followed the selling of the land,

> But now we are strangers, go early or late;
> O Thomas! like one over-burthen'd with sin,
> Sometimes when I lift up the latch of a gate,
> I look at the fields and I cannot go in.

> (ll. 13–16 (earliest version), *Poems in Two Volumes*, p. 573)

*she may last*    She 'lasted' till 1816.

*a poem of Daniell upon Learning*    Samuel Daniel (1562–1619), after Spenser Poet Laureate to the Queen. Mary read 'Musophilus, containing a General Defence of Learning' (Anderson, iv).

*the Stone man*    Stone Arthur, 'the loneliest place we have among the clouds', W calls it in his 1800 Poem on the Naming of Places, 'There is an Eminence'. MH and Sara had been 'given' rocky hillocks near the lake; this was W's. D had made it his, had said, 'this lonesome Peak shall bear my Name'.

27 *Nov. 1801    the Cock*    The Black Cock, one of the smaller inns at Ambleside. A Thomas Keen was landlord there in 1791.

*Judge Chambray*    Sir Alan Chambré (1739–1823) of Hallhead Hall near Kendal, Recorder of Lancaster from 1796, and a judge from 1800. From 1788–1801 he owned and lived in Abbot Hall, Kendal.

*the stepping stones*  It is still possible to cross the Rothay by these stones south of Pelter Bridge.

*her aunt*  See 29 Dec. 1801 n.

*29 Nov. 1801  George Olliff*  The Olliffs' young son, bapt. 19 Oct. 1798.

*2 Dec. 1801  Phœbus & the Crow*  Chaucer's 'Manciple's Tale' (Anderson, i). W's modern verse translations from Chaucer were finished in 1802 but he did not choose to publish until 1839, and then withdrew this tale in deference to 'the judgments of others'. Miss Fenwick and Quillinan took, he thought, 'a rather narrow view' of the narrator's moral attitude to both truth and women (*PW* iv. 471).

*4 Dec. 1801  George Dyer*  George Dyer (1755–1841), like Lamb and C a one-time pupil at Christ's Hospital. With 'a head uniformly wrong & a heart uniformly right' (Lamb to C, 14 Aug. 1800, Marrs, i. 226), Dyer's notions of criticism, poetry, dress, social behaviour, provided Lamb with constant amusement as he wrote about him in letters and essays. This letter is lost. Dyer had also been a friend of W's headmaster, William Taylor (d. 1786).

*6 Dec. 1801  Wilcocks door*  William Wilcock was innkeeper of the Salutation Inn, Ambleside. He had stabling for the post-horses (see 6 Oct. 1802) and in 1813, along with John Ianson of Keswick and 4 innkeepers, he became part-owner of the Good Intent and Volunteer stage coaches that regularly plied the Kendal–Whitehaven and Penrith–Keswick roads.

*7 Dec. 1801  'Liverpool complaint'*  Miss Barcroft's 'complaint' may well have been associated with the weather that stopped her visiting her neighbours. Her family seem not to have been natives of the Wythburn–Castlerigg area of Keswick (on the Grasmere side) in which, in 1802 a Mr Barecroft, according to Land Tax returns, was tenant-occupier of an estate owned by John (or Jonathan) Banks; there is no Barcroft mentioned in the previous Land Tax returns of 1794, and it seems likely, from Miss Barcroft's 'complaint' that the family came from Liverpool. This town, though 'very healthful' through a 'natural purity of the air' and the 'constant circulation' of the beneficial 'aromatic effluvia of tar and pitch', was nevertheless subject to 'sudden and frequent variations in temperature' and was 'more than usually sharp and keen'. It could therefore, according to William Moss a local surgeon, be 'unfavourable' to 'those persons who are subject to coughs, asthmas, and other affections of the breast and lungs' (*The Liverpool Guide*, 1797, pp. 132–3; see also Moss's *Familiar Medical Survey of Liverpool*, 1784).

*Cotton mills*   Green (*Guide*, ii. 11) mentions only 1 cotton mill in Keswick, at the Forge on the Greta below the Windy Brow woods, but at least a dozen woollen manufactories. The population of Keswick in 1801 was 1350.

*The God of Love*   'The Cuckoo and the Nightingale', attributed (wrongly) to Chaucer (Anderson, i). W, walking to Yarrow in 1814 with James Hogg, was joined for some of the way by the then elderly Dr Anderson: 'I was much pleased to meet with him and to acknowledge my obligation to his collection, which had been my brother John's companion on more than one voyage to India, and which he gave me before his departure from Grasmere, never to return. Through these Volumes I became first familiar with Chaucer, and so little money had I then to spare for books, that, in all probability, but for this same work, I should have known little of Drayton, Daniel, and other distinguished poets of the Elizabethan age, and their immediate successors, till a much later period of my life' (Fenwick Note, *PW* iii. 450–1). W's tribute to Anderson is just and John did indeed send him his set of Anderson (13 vols., now in WL), but not until more than a year after D and W's 1801 reading of Chaucer, Spenser, Daniel, etc. John, in May 1801 and ready to sail, had 'got Anderson's poets', though was 'at a loss where to begin' and asked W's advice; 18 months later, back in England, he packed the books up for Grasmere in Dec. 1802. In 1801 and 1802, therefore, W must have had another set of Anderson, and this must have come from Greta Hall. C had acquired a set in 1796, and in at least 4 of these volumes, and particularly against the poetry of Chaucer, there are pencilled comments by W. 'The Cuckoo and the Nightingale' was not withdrawn, as was 'The Manciple's Tale', from Thomas Powell's section in R. H. Horne's *The Poems of Geoffrey Chaucer, Modernized*, 1841; it was revised after 1839, on W's realizing that Anderson's text of the medieval poem was in some places corrupt.

*8 Dec. 1801   Tuesday 8th November*   D's hurried reporting is clear from a crossed out Monday in front of Tuesday, her calling Dec.

November and her writing 'he' instead of 'I'; it was of course she who was in bed while W walked with MH.

*Bruce's Lochleven & Life* Michael Bruce (1746–67), a country boy from Kinross-shire, a weaver's son who was given the English poets to read by a nearby man of taste, Mr Arnot. Arnot farmed on the banks of Lochleven and Bruce's poem of that name has a mild, melancholy, and derivative charm:

> Thus sung the youth, amid unfertile wilds
> And nameless deserts, unpoetic ground!

Bruce wrote an elegy for himself:

> Now spring returns: but not to me returns
> The vernal joy my better years have known

He died of consumption aged 21. D read the poems and the memoir in Anderson, xi.

*9 Dec. 1801   Palamon & Arcite* Chaucer's 'Knight's Tale'; or just possibly Dryden's version, 'Palamon and Arcite', both in Anderson. In 1805 W discusses Dryden's version at some length (*EY*, p. 641).

*George Rawnson's* George Rowlandson lived at Under Lancrigg in the small farmhouse enlarged in 1841, with W's advice, for the widowed Mrs Fletcher and her family; the present Lancrigg.

*10 Dec. 1801   Aggy Fleming's* Gillside, below Helm Crag. Aggy had married John Fleming, slater from Ulverston, in 1788; he died in 1798 when the youngest child was a year old. A son William died in July 1805, and Aggy Fleming, still a widow, died in Jan. 1808.

*after mosses.* The sentence following, 'I began a letter to John', is written and crossed out.

*12 Dec. 1801   Met Townley with his dogs* Jonathan Townley (1774–1848), a younger contemporary of W at Hawkshead. He was a Cambridge friend of James Plumptre, who stayed with him and his mother in Ambleside in 1796 (and wrote a satire, *The Lakers*, as a result of his visit). D noticed Mrs Townley's yellow honeysuckle in June 1802. In Jan. 1804 'Charles Son of The Revd. Jonathan Townley at Ambleside' was registered for burial at Grasmere. Townley was finally Vicar of Steeple Bumstead, Essex.

*14 Dec. 1801   Mary fell & hurt her wrist*   This sentence is an added insertion. Mice must have been a problem; they would eat the tallow candles (made of mutton fat) if these were not kept in a metal candle box. See 16 June 1802 where MH, perhaps remembering this unfortunate excursion to buy mousetraps, has clearly wondered about the possibility of keeping a cat.

*18 Dec. 1801   wrote to Coleridge for money*   D's letter apparently did not reach C, and so W, on 21 Dec., wrote to Stuart at the *MP* for the £10 he needed: Stuart was to consider C his debtor; alternatively, W would send contributions for the newspaper (see 27 Jan. 1802). At the same time W wrote to C to inform him of this, and this second letter was directed not to London but to Somerset. Next day (see 22 Dec.) the Ws wondered about borrowing the money from Luff.

*21 Dec. 1801   wearisome*   Originally 'terrible'.

   *clapped*   Flattened and smoothed the clothes, more probably with the hand than with a flat-iron; northern usage.

   *from France*   From now until the summer visit of 1802 there is a flurry of letters to and from France. None of these survives. Only 3 letters from W's early love relationship are known, and these are from Annette: one late, in 1834, and the other two from the early 1790s. These last were published in 1922 some 6 years after the relationship came to light. They were in archives at Blois, confiscated by French authorities during the war of 1793 onwards. A political situation was to intervene a second time to delay letters and a visit. D and W were hoping to attend the marriage in 1815 of W and Annette's daughter Caroline, but Napoleon—'the wretch', said D—and his troops entered Paris. In 1820, however, at the end of their tour of the Continent, they spent, with Mary, some days in Paris and once again saw Annette and Caroline (now with two small daughters).

   *while he was reading*   An instance of D's absence of mind: she first wrote 'while they were riding'.

   *Fletcher's peat house*   John Fletcher was a regular carrier on the road through Grasmere to Keswick. His peat house at Town End was rented from John Benson, W's landlord (annual land tax in 1808 3½d.), as was his coach-house (tax 4s. 2d.). He lived in a house of his own at Townhead, the other end of the valley, and the Ws, before the present arrangement, had to walk

up there with letters and parcels (*EY*, p. 334). In 1805 the Ws'
new servant, Molly's replacement, was sleeping across the road
at Fletcher's house (*EY*, p. 596).

*22 Dec. 1801   Wm composed*   Originally 'Wm wrote'.

*Sir Hugh Palmer*   D returned to insert the captain's name and
the number of years on the man-of-war; she changed
'followed' to 'joined in' and 'served' to 'have been . . . at sea'.

*overtook*   At first 'met': D's regard for truth.

*path to the necessary*   Before spring 1804 when the staircase
door was made into the back garden, the Ws could only reach
the 'necessary' by walking from the front door along the side of
the house, past and round their own low peat-house (they had
the roof raised in 1805 so that it could provide another
sleeping-place) and there, backing onto the peat-house, was
(and still is) the 'necessary'.

*used to drinking*   The word 'somewhat' has been inserted and
the word 'whiskey' crossed out.

*the Stone seat*   Probably Sara's seat, built on 10 Oct. 1801.

*Queen of Patterdale*   The Mounseys of Patterdale Hall had
been known locally as the Kings of Patterdale, and their house
as the Palace of Patterdale. The present 'Palace' was a new
house, built in 1796, 'an offensive object,' said D (*EY*, p. 637).
Peggy Ashburner's story concerned the previous queen, John
Mounsey's mother. His father, the 'King' before him, also John
Mounsey (1701–93), was a local tyrant, a notorious miser and,
according to Budworth, 'only *in his amours* has he been
(sometimes) over-reached. These are more funny to hear than
it would be decent to relate' (*A Fortnight's Ramble*, 3rd edn.
(1810), 123). The legend of the Mounseys, as D demonstrates,
quoting Peggy Ashburner, outlived their time. A 1791 engraving
of Mrs Mounsey, 'sketched from nature', smoking a clay pipe
and holding a jug and bottle, was still being issued in 1794.
There was no such interest in the current Mr and Mrs
Mounsey. Their son, however, after his father's death in 1820,
sold the Patterdale estate to the Marshalls of Leeds in 1824, and
there were no more Kings of Patterdale.

*23 Dec. 1801   very ill*   'The Ruined Cottage', written at Alfoxden
1797–8, is a story in blank verse of Margaret and her sinking
into depression and death after her husband, out of work, has

sold himself into the army in order to give her a little money. She waits in vain and in anguish for his return, and the garden and cottage, like her, fall into decay; the tale is told by a Pedlar to a Poet. W never published the poem in this early version. See 30 Jan. 1802 n.

*24 Dec. 1801   my old journal*   This sentence and 'Thoughts of last year' are inserted after the day's entry has been ruled off. The next day was D's 30th birthday. The 'old journal' is the notebook that is lost.

*26 Dec. 1801   Tom Dawsons*   Tom Dawson lived at Ben Place, behind the Swan; his grandchild was probably the girl who brought the letter from Eusemere on 10 Feb. 1802, and had by then some employment with Mrs Clarkson.

*27 Dec. 1801   3rd part of Wm's poem*   Probably the beginning of Book III of *The Prelude*, where W moves away from his schooldays to his Cambridge experience. Nothing else is written for this poem until 1803. It was known in the W circle as 'the poem to Coleridge' (see last sentence, inserted, of 26 Dec.): W's friend and fellow-poet is addressed throughout as one who can most sympathetically understand his meditation on the growth and powers of his own mind. MW gave it the title *The Prelude* on its publication after W's death in 1850 in its final, much revised form.

*28 Dec. 1801   Sara's Rock*   By the roadside about a mile beyond Wythburn Chapel towards Keswick, and midway between DC and Greta Hall. On 4 May 1802 D calls it 'Sara's Crag', but by then it is no longer only Sara's; all their initials are there: WW, MH, DW, STC, JW, SH, and it has become the Rock of Names. C was perhaps the most zealous initial-carver: 'April 20, 1802 Tuesday Evening, ½ after 7 / Cut out my name & Dorothy's over the S.H. at Sara's Rock—' (*Notebooks* i. 1163). Shortly afterwards, on 4 May, W deepened the T of C's initials. The Rock was marked by 'hands of those I love the best', wrote W about this time, hoping that it would, its 'record duly keep / Long after [we] are laid asleep' (*Benjamin*, ll. 82–4). But the Rock could not withstand the Manchester Water Authority. In the late 1880s the water level of Thirlmere was raised, the old road blasted, and the Rock with it, to make way for a higher road and to find rubble for the dam. Fragments of the Rock of Names were gathered up by Canon H. D. Rawnsley, cemented into a small pyramid of stone, and placed above the new road. In 1984 there were new fears for the safety of the initials and they were fixed into natural slate in their original configuration (as early photographs make clear) and embedded into a rock-face behind the W Museum at Grasmere.

*Spenser*  Usually spelt 'Spencer'—a close fitting bodice or jacket. D wrote 'hedge' first, then wrote 'Bank'.

*Wilkinson*  Joshua Lucock Wilkinson, of the Cockermouth Lucock family who had built in 1745 the fine house by the river in Cockermouth where W and D were born; a solicitor sharing chambers with their brother Richard at Staple Inn, London, he was in the north to settle the affairs of his mother who had died at Lorton Hall, near Cockermouth, on 1 Dec. 1801.

*Johnston*  Possibly John Hope Johnstone (1765–1843), son of James, 3rd Earl of Hopetoun, who claimed, through a deceased grand-uncle, the Marquisate of Annandale. This title, however, fell into disuse. Johnstone became the 4th Earl in 1816. Interestingly, a few months after he met W in Keswick it was thought that his brother too was in the area. But this was the imposter John Hatfield, who, as the Honourable Colonel Alexander Augustus Hope, courted a rich young lady, and then married (bigamously) Mary Robinson, the Beauty of Buttermere. It is not surprising that Johnstone reported seeing *LB* at court: William Cookson, W's uncle, was, after all, a Canon of Windsor and had been tutor to the royal children.

*Mrs Harcourt*  Major-General William Harcourt, 1743–1830 (in 1809 3rd Earl Harcourt) and Mrs Harcourt were in the intimate royal circle. William Harcourt became Deputy Lieutenant of Windsor Castle, and lived at St Leonard's Hill, 'one of the most beautiful places near Windsor', said Dorothy when she went there in 1792 (*EY*, p. 85).

29 *Dec. 1801*  *Martindale*  D of course means Matterdale; Martindale is on the other side of Ullswater and she walks towards it on New Year's Day. Now she and W walk through Matterdale south of the Keswick–Penrith road on their way to the Clarksons at Eusemere.

*Mr Walker*  Brother to the Revd Robert Walker of Pennington, near Ulverston, Furness. His children were soon to inherit the wealth, for he died in 1802 (the son William, a Whitehaven merchant, died in 1819—attacked by a Spanish gunboat as he was returning from buying ornamental trees in Italy; the daughter, in 1824, married the Captain of the rescuing ship. He was James Robertson–Walker, later High Sheriff of Cumberland). The sickly sister was Isabel Walker, whose death at Under Lancrigg, Grasmere, is recorded in June 1808. The family kept property in Grasmere, in the Goody Bridge area, until at least the 1830s.

*Mary fell many a time*   Difficult though the walk was, it was safer than the shorter route over Grisedale by which W and D chose to return on 23 Jan.

*in Dunmallet*   A hill at the foot of Ullswater, known to W and D from Thomas Gray's Journal of 1769:

Approached Dunmallet, a fine pointed hill, covered with wood, planted by old Mr. Hasell . . . who lives always at home [Dalemain], and delights in planting.

*parted from Mary*   Mary went on to Penrith to stay till 17 Jan. with her aunt, Miss Elizabeth Monkhouse (1750–1828), daughter of John Monkhouse, postmaster of Penrith. Mary had lived with her mother's sister between the ages of 15 and 18 and she kept in touch with her throughout her life: Elizabeth Monkhouse stayed at DC in 1804, at Allan Bank in 1808 and 1811, and as she got older she spent long periods, and indeed died, at Rydal Mount.

*2 Jan. 1802   Dalemain*   The estate and home, between Ullswater and Penrith, of Edward Hasell (1765–1825). The Hasells owned the deer and the hunting rights in Martindale.

*3 Jan. 1802   to Sockbridge*   W and D's grandfather Richard W (1690–1760), when he first arrived from Yorkshire, bought a farm at Sockbridge, between Eusemere and Penrith, in the parish of Barton. This now belonged to their eldest brother Richard, and sometime during this month's stay at Eusemere, W and D called at the farmer's, 'and had the pleasure of hearing a very good character of the Man' (*EY*, p. 344).

*Thomas Wilkinson*   Thomas Wilkinson (1751–1836), Quaker, petitioner against the slave trade; active on Clarkson's behalf in 1795 in getting Eusemere built; of the Grotto, a 40–acre farm at Yanwath, near Penrith. He was, wrote W in Oct. 1805, 'an amiable inoffensive man; and a little of a Poet too; who has amused himself upon his own small estate upon the Emont in twining pathways along the banks of the River, making little Cells and bowers with inscriptions of his own writing, all very pretty as not spreading far' (*EY*, p. 626). By 1802 W had known him about a year; in 1805 a phrase of his suggested W's 'Solitary Reaper'; in 1806 he acted for W in the purchase of Broadhow, a small estate under Place Fell in Patterdale; and in 1806 W wrote his tribute, 'To the Spade of a Friend' (*PW* iv. 75).

*as at Sockburn*   Thomas Hutchinson's farmhouse on the Tees in Co. Durham, where M and Sara H had lived in the 1790s. D and W made it in effect their home on their return from Goslar in May 1799 until the move to Grasmere in Dec. The Hutchinsons themselves moved in 1800, George to Bishop Middleham, Co. Durham, and Tom to Gallow Hill, near Scarborough.

*22 Jan. 1802*   *among the trees & slips of lawn*   Before writing this D wrote and crossed out 'on the opposite side of the . . .'.

*23 Jan. 1802*   *a heap of stones . . . remembered*   Originally 'that heap of stones which we so well remembered'.

*fresh & clean*   Relief that they were home is understandable. In 1808 George and Sarah Green, who knew the hills better probably than W, were to be lost, and to perish in a snowstorm going from Langdale to Grasmere; and see 8 Feb. 1802— Willy Park's tale of three men lost coming, like the Ws, over Grisedale.

*20£*   This was Christopher's annual allowance to D. John gave her a similar sum, and Richard in June 1802 was prepared to do the same, so that W, with an income of about £70 p.a., would be able to afford marriage (Mary had only some £400 of her own), and D, with £60 p.a., could be financially independent, though continuing to live with W. These arrangements were made unnecessary when the Lowther debt was paid (see 18 June 1802 n.).

*the descriptive Sketches*   After their adventure W and D intensify their sense of comfort by reading of the dangerous and the sublime in W's own early poem of 1793, *Descriptive Sketches of the Alps*, where 'bewildering mists' and snow do indeed close around a solitary traveller. Lake Como in the same poem is, like Grasmere, a paradise valley of 'open beauties' and of 'lone retreats'.

*26 Jan. 1802 (½ past 1 o'clock)* Despite a morning devoted to writing D goes back to the Clarkson stories: the 'Suffolk' word 'clemmed' becomes now a 'Cheshire' word, and the Irish murderer, his knife and stick and the Postboy are added.

*beyond the Wyke*   Wyke Cottage, home of James Dawson, on the west side of the lake, about half-way between Gell's cottage (Silverhowe house) and John Benson's (Tail End). A Mr Greenwood was shortly to build a new house, the Wyke, near it.

*sate*   After the word 'sate' the words 'nicely together & talked by the fire—went to bed' are deleted. D clearly and immediately recollected that these describe the events of the following evening, Wednesday 27 Jan.

*so made himself ill*   W was working a good deal on his 1798 composition, 'The Pedlar'; D would not be surprised at his illness. She had written to MH about his poor digestion in April 1801, '—he is always very ill when he tries to alter an old poem —but new composition does not hurt him so much. I hope he will soon be able to work without hurting himself' (*EY*, p. 332).

*Wm wrote to Annette*   Just before and during the brief peace formalized by the Treaty of Amiens 1802, it was possible for the first time for 10 years to feel certain that letters reached their destination, and it was possible to visit France. W, with D, decided to see Annette before his marriage to MH. The need to marry Annette was gone in the enforced 10 years' absence of war; but Caroline, daughter of Annette and W, born after he left France in 1792, was 10 years old, and it was needful to see her and her mother. Marie-Anne, or Annette, Vallon (1766–1841), daughter of a surgeon at Blois, and still living there, had longed for marriage at first, as apparently had W. But the week after W published *Evening Walk* and *Descriptive Sketches* (Jan. 1793) in the hope of making money, war was declared and he was compelled to remain in England. Meanwhile Madame Williams, or the Veuve Williams, as Annette called herself, was a staunch Royalist and Catholic; she worked heroically to effect the escape of aristocrats threatened with the guillotine. On Caroline's marriage in 1816 W settled on her £30 p.a., commuting this to a capital sum of £400 in 1835.

*27 Jan. 1802  copied out sonnets for him*   Two of the three poems D copied were sonnets: 'If grief dismiss me not to them that rest', translated from Petrarch during W's Cambridge days some 10 years earlier, and 'Calm is all nature as a resting wheel', written 1786 while W was still at school; they appeared unsigned, *MP*, 2 and 13 Feb. 1802. The third poem, of 3 stanzas, 'To a Beautiful Young Lady who had been harshly spoken of on account of her fondness for taking long walks in the country', the only recent composition, appeared 12 Feb. Clearly, W was doing something towards fulfilling his £10 obligation to Stuart of 18 Dec. 1801.

*sonnets for him.* The words following, 'we walked to Rydale', are crossed out here.

*Mr Patrick* Sara's letter does not exist, but details already imagined in W's portrait of the Pedlar were 'clothed in reality, and fresh ones suggested, by what she reported of this man's tenderness of heart, his strong and pure imagination, and his solid attainments in literature, chiefly religious whether in prose or verse' (Fenwick Note, *PW* v. 374). Sara H, motherless at 8 and an orphan at 10, went to live in Kendal with her mother's cousin Margaret Robison, whose family had a century-old hardware business in Penrith. Margaret Robison had married James Patrick, linendraper of Kendal. Patrick was a Scotsman who, before becoming a pedlar and then draper, had herded cattle on Perthshire hills. W's Pedlar now does likewise. MW later defined Patrick as the 'intellectual Pedlar', and added that though Sara went to school in Kendal, 'the most important part of her education was gathered from the stores of that good man's mind' (ibid.). James Patrick's own daughter had died in 1767 'of the small pox by innoculation'. He died in March 1787 and Sara had at most only 4 years of knowing him.

*come over Grisdale* D had first written 'walk'.

*at Penrith* Postage charges were generally paid by the receiver of letters, not the sender (but see 31 May 1802 where the young John Wilson, then a stranger to W, sends his letter Post Paid). And they were expensive—as D's calculation of the cost for 2 months seems to suggest. Charges varied, depending upon the weight of a letter, the number of sheets of paper (ascertained by holding it in front of a candle) and the distance travelled. There clearly were country letter carriers delivering and collecting from the receiving offices, such as the trudging postman of 8 Feb. 1802, but probably there was an extra charge for this service. This would explain D's frequent walking to and from Rydal and Ambleside for post, and her slipping letters for Keswick under Fletcher's door.

*wasted his mind in the Magazines*   D did not extend the same criticism to herself (8 May 1802). 'Wasted' is a strong expression. It must be remembered that 'The Ancient Mariner', and thus *LB*, had sprung out of W's and C's intention to write for the new *Monthly Magazine* in Sept. 1797, and that reviews of their work, however hostile, in such magazines as the *Monthly Review*, the *Analytical*, the *Critical*, did much to promote sales. The *British Critic*'s review of *LB* 1800 came out of conversations with the poets themselves (3 Nov. 1800). The practice of quoting long extracts from books under review kept readers in touch with contemporary writing. There was much to recommend the magazines as occasional reading.

*Ianson*   Previously misread as [?Samson]. William Ianson of Keswick, married 1766, or his son William, born 1768. He may have been the tenant-caretaker of the Calverts' house at Windy Brow (as C. Shaver suggests, *EY*, p. 114) when D stayed there in spring 1794, and with whose family she was delighted: 'honest, worthy, uncorrupted people' (*EY*, p. 117). In 1799 Richard W wrote to a Mr Ianson of Keswick for a list of the books that W had left behind at Windy Brow, hoping to find among them 2 of his own volumes of Blackstone's *Commentaries* (*EY*, p. 674). The Iansons were clearly invaluable: when C in Dec. 1802 was bringing Tom Wedgwood up to Greta Hall for a short stay, he suggested to Mrs C that Mrs Ianson would 'probably accommodate you with a Fowl or two' (*CL* ii. 899). In 1802 William Ianson may have been nearer to Greta Hall; he was then, according to land tax returns, occupying the property of a Mr Gatescale, and Matthew Stables was in Mr Calvert's property (presumably Windy Brow).

*28 Jan. 1802   when he was a Boy*   The new epitaph has not been identified. The one that W wrote as a boy must be,

> HERE MARGARET lies, who liv'd a Patriarch's days;
> In youth so fair, so heavenly fair, that death
> Mistook her for an Angel; and in years
> So holy and pure, he spar'd her as a Saint.

This appeared unsigned *MP*, 14 Jan. 1803, with the title, 'Epitaph in—— Church, Wiltshire.' The alterations from the early drafts in a notebook (MS 4) used in 1788 are slight.

*30 Jan. 1802   to set down the story*   W never used the story that D so carefully writes.

*continued to live alone*   Inserted above a deleted 'alone'; *for one whole year* originally 'there was one year during which'; *a companion* originally 'a little companion'; The *mouse* originally 'The little mouse'.

*worked at the Pedlar all the morning*   Between W's 'good spirits' on 21 Dec. 1801 and his reading of 'The Pedlar' on 20 Mar. 1802, D records frequent and exhausting bouts of work. The poem was particularly close to W since, as he later told Miss Fenwick, the character of the Pedlar offered 'an idea of what I fancied my own character might have become in his circumstances' (*PW* v. 373): the Poet too loved wandering and observing human life. The Pedlar was based also on the packman W had known as a schoolboy in Hawkshead, and he was freshly based on James Patrick (27 Jan. 1802 n.). This meant alterations and additions. Further, some passages were removed and placed in the growing *Prelude*. There were several plans for the poem. In the event, it was not published until 1814, by which time the Pedlar had become the Wanderer, a character in *The Excursion*, whose first story in Book 1 was that of Margaret and the Ruined Cottage.

*31 Jan. 1802   dear Coleridge did also*   D is remembering her own walk with W from Kendal to Windy Brow in April 1794, and thinking of C's walk with him on 4 Nov. 1799, when C came to the Lake District for the first time. The 'pasture side' of Rydal, from which Nab Scar can be seen across the lake, is the south, footpath side. D's original phrasing for her love of 'that way' was 'because I first saw Rydale and Grasmere from that side of the water'.

*The sun shone*   'shone' replaces 'came'.

*cut at it with his knife*   Originally 'employed himself in making it plainer'; D then preferred the stronger 'cut at it with his knife to make it plainer', but forgot—because the word is at the end of a line—to cross out 'employed'. The stone is almost certainly the rock still by the roadside at the foot of Rydal, and with the view of the lake from it now somewhat blocked by the boathouse. Some of the rock has been cut away in road-widening, much of it is covered with moss and lichen, there is a mature oak tree growing out of it, and no initials are visible. William Knight (*DW Journals*, 1897) enigmatically remarked of the stone, 'This still exists, but is known to few.' It was in fact known in the late 19th c. as Thrang Crag, or 'Wordsworth's Seat'. There are 6 or 7 steps cut in it, and clearly there was a traditional association with W.

*Calvert*   William Calvert (1770–1829), son of Raisley (1706/7–91) steward to the Duke of Norfolk at Greystoke Castle, near Penrith, inherited the land and farm at Windy Brow, Keswick. It was there that D had her first experience of sharing a home with her brother in spring 1794, and there that W in the following autumn looked after the dying younger brother, Raisley. The latter's legacy to W in 1795—in part for the use of D—made it possible for her to think of a future independent home with W.

*mosses . . . on the chimneypiece*   There are some dozen references to gathering mosses (once, lychens). This is the first time D mentions what she did with the mosses; and see 19 Mar. 1802 where 'a few green mosses' were 'to make the chimney gay against my darling's return'. This winter decoration for the mantelpiece was often carried home in a basket or kerchief ('handkerchief'). There seems to have been no moss gathering in the summer (the mosses gathered as late as 16 and 19 May 1800 were perhaps intended for the garden, along with the 'wild plants'). When the mosses had dried and lost their green freshness, they could be burnt on the fire; they are in no way connected with the peat that was 'gathered' locally from peat mosses (e.g. 16 June 1800).

*the Encyclopaedias*   Probably the complete *Encyclopaedia Britannica*, 3rd edn. (1797); its departure must have left a lot of shelf-room, for there were 18 quarto vol. Calvert would now need them himself: he intended to pursue experiments in the laboratory of his newly built house, Greta Bank, near Windy Brow. In the event, his neighbour C's 'ardent' wish to 'initiate [himself] in Chemical science' (*CL* ii. 671) was disappointed: Calvert married Mary Mitchison, a Quaker, and Greta Bank by 1803 was a family house.

*John Bunyan any day*   John Bunyan, in many editions of *The Pilgrim's Progress* from the 3rd (1679) onwards, is pictured, in a wood-cut by Robert White, as the dreamer, sleeping with his head resting on his left hand and his elbow resting on one of the emblems from his dream, a den, and in it the lion who has to be gone past in the trial of faith. D's comparison is humorous, but see the portraits of W by Richard Carruthers (1817) and Edward Nash (1819) (W Museum).

*1 Feb. 1802  with Jenny*  Probably Jenny (Jane) Hodgson, daughter of Thomas Hodgson, labourer, baptized Aug. 1762, and recorded at her death in May 1807 as 'of near Aisdale, Grasmere, Spinster'. To reach Easedale Jenny would turn off at the Swan. D lists 'Jenny Hodgson our washerwoman' as among the newly dead when she returns to Grasmere after a winter in Coleorton 1806–7 (*MY* i. 158).

*Books came from London*  Almost a year since their brother Richard had been first asked to send 'some Books of William's with some of your and Montagu's cast−off Clothes' (*EY* p. 342). D had also requested pens and '6 quires of the largest size writing paper, for rough draughts: scribbling paper it is called at Cambridge' (*EY* p. 338).

*the Pleasures of Hope*  Published 1799, the first long poem by Thomas Campbell (1777–1844), a young Scot. Far more popular than *LB*, by 1806 it was in its 9th edn. In Mar. 1801 C had asked Godwin to return his copy 'which Wordsworth wishes to see'. The poem's opening treatment of a rainbow, 'Heaven's ethereal bow', makes clear the distance between popular taste and W's stark 'My heart leaps up' of a few weeks later.

*2 Feb. 1802  platform*  The flat area above the wall (sodded 30 May 1800) too small to be called a terrace, enough for a dozen paces.

*melted into tears*  See 18 Apr. 1802 and n. for a more precise definition of these tears.

*4 Feb. 1802  Smolletts life*  Doubtless in Anderson, x; on the strength of a handful of verses Smollett is included among the *British Poets*.

*5 Feb. 1802  Wanly Penson*  Probably the story of young Snell in the now neglected anonymous novel *Wanly Penson or The Melancholy Man: a Miscellaneous History*, 3 vols. (1792). Tom Snell's inserted story, then popular by itself, was of travel and adventures that took the character, Snell, from penal servitude in South Carolina to Greenland. The Ws' copy of this book was sold in the Rydal Mount Library sale of 1859.

*Soulby*   Probably Anthony Soulby, printer and bookseller of Penrith (1 Nov. 1800 n.). There was also an M. Soulby, bookseller. D had first written the word 'misplaced' about the leaf or two in the Chaucer, and then decided that these were 'wanting'.

*6 Feb. 1802   slept not*   Originally 'could not sleep'.

*Lessing's Fables*   When she was in Goslar 1798–9 D learned little German (though see p. 143 for her initial enthusiasm); she and W, because there was no practice of 'taking people *en pension* . . . [were] compelled to be together alone at meal-times &c, &c' (*EY*, p. 249), and lacked occasions to speak German. In Feb. 1799 W wrote to C, 'I do not consider myself as knowing *any*thing of the German language', and he could form, he said, 'no distinct idea' of the excellence of Lessing. C, in Ratzeburg and then Göttingen, a university city, already knew some German, had a better social life and was enthusiastic for Lessing; he began on a Life of Lessing. He said that he had 'imperiously excluded all waverings about other works' (*CL* i. 454), but he never wrote the Life; yet his interest, which still took shape as specific proposals as late as 1816, may well have encouraged D. She had made a first attempt with Lessing in 1798. Lessing (1729–81) was almost as chameleon-like as C himself: he was critic, poet, dramatist, scholar, writer on religion, politics, aesthetics. His *Fables*, along with Treatises on the Fable, were published in 1759. Perhaps one that D translated now, or attempted on 8 or 9 Feb., was 'Die Hunde' (see n. p. 181). D was entirely self-taught in German; two or three Fables after tea shows not inconsiderable prowess. Here, for example, is a close translation of 'Die Hunde':

'How degenerate is our race here in this country!' said a well-travelled poodle. 'In that far corner of the world, which humans call India, proper dogs are still to be found; dogs, my brothers— you may not believe me, and yet I have seen it with my own eyes —dogs which aren't even afraid of a lion and will boldly pick a fight with one.'

'But', a seasoned hunting dog asked the poodle, 'are they also then able to defeat the lion?'

'Defeat?' was the answer 'That I am not able to tell you. No matter, but just think—to attack a lion!'

'Oh', continued the hunting dog, 'If they are not able to defeat the lion, then your highly praised dogs of India are not any better than we are—but a good deal more stupid.' (Courtesy of Frederick Burwick, University of California)

*8 Feb. 1802   all the morning*   'but it was so cold that the Snow hardly melted' crossed out here.

*curling hair*   One of Willy's beautiful grandchildren was little Peggy Simpson (13 Mar. 1802). The account of the children began first with the sentence 'They had a bright wood fire'; this was deleted. It ended with their cheeks and hair making 'a beautiful sight'; this phrase was moved. The cloaks of dead men by an inn fire make a telling contrast.

*takes it all quietly*   'as a thing of course' is crossed out here.

*about France*   By 24 Feb. C was writing with considerable confidence to his wife (*CL* ii. 788) about the plan to live in France: W was to be married to MH, 'whether he shall be married at Gallow Hill, or at Grasmere', and then, 'about July we shall all set sail from Liverpool to Bordeux &c.' D and Mrs C and the children were also to go. In the event W and D went alone to France, to see Annette, not to live; W's marriage did not take place until Oct., and the Cs remained at Greta Hall.

*was starved*   First, 'grew starved', North Country dialect for 'cold'.

*cold air . . . body*   First, 'the cold air did not touch my body'.

*'a star or two beside'*   The last two sentences are inserted additions; the suddenness of the moon's appearance was impressive and D recalls that powerful moment in 'The Ancient Mariner' when the moon's sudden presence signals the turn from despair.

> The moving Moon went up the sky,
> And no where did abide:
> Softly she was going up,
> And a star or two beside—

*9 Feb. 1802   Thomas Flemings wife*   Thomas Fleming of Rydal married Dorothy Moser at Ulverston in 1795, and Dorothy's elder sister Elizabeth Moser married a John Kendall, also at Ulverston, on 3 Nov. 1800. It was this Elizabeth who drowned herself, aged 37. She had been baptized in Kendal in 1764; her younger sister Dorothy was baptized at Grasmere in 1774, and her mother, described as Elizabeth, wife of Roger Moser of Rydal, was buried in Grasmere churchyard in Mar. 1789. The funeral came past DC but burial was not immediate; the Grasmere register does not record the burial of Elizabeth, wife of John Kendall of Urswick in Furness until 16 Feb. 1802. It was probably too difficult to dig the grave: D notes every day the hard frost and snow.

*10 Feb. 1802  John Dawsons*  There are several Dawsons in the valley. The Grasmere registers around 1800 record a John Dawson, son of James of Score Crag, a John Dawson of Turnhow, a James Dawson of Wyke, and a John Dawson of Town End. This John Dawson lived at Ben Place, between Forest Side and the Swan. He was, said W later, 'a man of literary education and of experience in society much beyond what was common among the inhabitants of the Vale' (*PW* v. 467). He had been a manager of George Knott's Newlands Ironworks at Bunaw in Scotland and clerk to W's predecessor as Distributor of Stamps. He was father of 'the finest young Man in the vale', as D called young George Dawson at his death in 1807 (*MY* i. 158).

*11 Feb. 1802  past Goans*  i.e. past the Swan. Gawain Mackereth is recorded as landlord as early as 1793. In July 1802 his daughter Rebecca was buried from the Swan. He died in 1807.

*to a Spanish great Galleon*  Ben Jonson follows Phineas and Giles Fletcher in Anderson, iv. Anderson, in his Life of Jonson, quotes a paragraph from Thomas Fuller's *History of the Worthies of England* (1662), and D quotes from this paragraph, slightly misrepresenting Fuller when she records his saying that he 'had ['had' is inserted] "beheld" many, ['many' is then crossed out] wit combats between Shakespeare & Jonson'. Fuller, who was only 7 when Shakespeare died, had written less literally, 'Many were the wit-combats between him [Jonson] and Shakespeare, which two I beheld like a *Spanish great galleon*, and an *English man of war*.' Before arriving at Fuller's 'life of Johnson' (misspelt) D wrote 'Dryden' and was starting on 'Spe[nser]'.

*Innocence*  Jonson's epitaph is moving in its restraint and elegance:

> Here lies to each her parents ruth,
> Mary, the daughter of their youth:
> Yet all heav'ns gifts, being heaven's due,
> It makes the father less to rue.
> At six months' end she parted hence
> With safety of her innocence;

Whose soul heav'n's queen (whose name she bears),
In comfort of her mother's tears,
Hath plac'd among her virgin-train:
Where, while that sever'd doth remain,
This grave partakes the fleshly birth;
Which cover lightly, gentle earth.

The 'one affecting line' (in D's view) has a contemporary feel, and expresses in its plainness that early acquaintance with death that D so often notes.

*Penshurst* 'To Penshurst' is placed prominently at the start of Jonson's collection, *The Forest*. D re-reads the poem on 14 Feb.; on 13 Feb. 'William read parts of his Recluse aloud to me'; one 'part' was probably those lines about true community in a glorious dwelling place (*Home at Grasmere*, ll. 818–28), and these clearly have 'To Penshurst' behind them.

*12 Feb. 1802    He now . . . at that time* See 16 June 1800. D intensifies the pathos by adding this sentence as an insertion. For Basil see 6 June 1800 n.

*This woman's was but a common case* This sentence is an inserted addition.

*William rubbed his Table* Outdoors, W several times 'dug a little', 'raked a few stones off the garden', 'chopped wood', but this is a rare mention of his doing domestic work. In 1811 Sara Hutchinson gave him a writing desk, 'what I most wanted' (*MY* i. 510), but in 1802 it was his writing table that he polished. This was perhaps, like Sarah Green's one oaken cupboard, 'so bright with rubbing that it was plain it had been prized' (*A Narrative Concerning George and Sarah Green*, p. 55).

*14 Feb. 1802    would go to Penrith* W was going to talk, presumably about marriage and France, with MH who was staying again with Elizabeth Monkhouse. W stayed at Eusemere with the Clarksons.

*Before sunset* At first, 'At sunset'.

*quite easy about him* The day's entry continues after this with a complete, not partial, account of the Carman, the 'Road lass', and her parents. D even fills the spaces at the bottom of the two last pages of the Hamburg Journal (which meets the Grasmere Journal here). There are small alterations, and then the whole thing is crossed out. With W away D had time to rewrite the entire passage in the next notebook Journal, and incorporate further changes, e.g. the wildness of the Mountain lass is still 'in her whole figure' but previously it had been in 'all her movements' too; the 'healthy looking girl' becomes 'good-looking', while 'good-looking' is removed from the mother who now has 'a very fresh complexion'; D adds the reason for her being 'blown'—'with fagging up the hill'.

## The Third Notebook: Grasmere Journal, 14 February 1802–2 May 1802 (DC MS 19)

The third of the Journals is again a notebook of less than 4" × 6"; its boards are much worn and covered in dull brown-black paper. Both D and W had used it in Germany in 1798. There is first the scrap by W in pencil about the hurrying from snare to snare, which becomes the *Prelude* woodcock-stealing passage; then there is his substantial account of 3 conversations with Klopstock in Hamburg during late Sept. 1798 (*Prose* i. 91–5). The distinguished German poet was some 45 years older than his English visitors, W, D, and C (C for the first conversation only). The conversations were in French, and W must have recorded Klopstock's opinions of English and German literature (in English) shortly after they took place, for they are followed immediately by D's recollected diary account of the journey that she and W made from Hamburg to Goslar, 3–6 Oct. 1798. W then took the book, and from the other end, amid the snow and cold of Goslar, he wrote drafts of some of the very greatest passages about himself and about his childhood world, passages that were to become the core of *The Prelude*: among them is the introductory description of the 'mild creative breeze', the infant's relationship with the river and the summer bathing, the climbing to the raven's nest, the woodcock-snaring (again), the hooting to the owls, the boat-stealing. Then D has 4 pages of the book and makes a start, but not much more, on German grammar and on Lessing's *Fables*, beginning with the first. Klopstock in their conversation had recently pronounced Lessing to be the 'first of their dramatic authors', and on W's complaining that *Nathan* was tedious, had conceded that it had 'not enough of action in it' but that, nevertheless, Lessing was 'the most chaste of their writers'. Despite this encouragement D seems not to have progressed far with German in 1798 and W follows her brief grammatical notes with a prose attack on moralists, thinkers like Godwin and Paley who try to change men 'by a series of propositions [which] can convey no feeling' because they present 'no image to the mind'. This breaks off unfinished (*Prose* i. 103–4) and several pages have been cut out. Nothing more seems to have been done in 1798. On 6 Feb. 1802 D began again with Lessing; she tackled several Fables, made notes, and wrote out declensions. These follow the 1798 account of the arrival in Goslar. (They could belong to 1798–9, but they make good sense as belonging to the Feb. 1802 return to Lessing and the Goslar notebook.) She again did not proceed extensively with German, but now had at hand a book of 3 years before, still with many empty pages; thus, on 14 Feb., when she needed another book for the Grasmere Journal, she filled this, leaving 1 blank page, and writing on until 2 May 1802 when she met the fragment of W's essay on moralists coming from the other end.

*14 Feb. 1802   a High[land]er I suppose*   D supposes this, presumably because the man did not speak English; she recognizes the tone in which he addresses the child and the horses. Cf. the two girls who entertain D and W the next year by Loch Lomond; they are 'gabbling Erse' (*Journals* i. 280). The 'Sweet Highland Girl', subject of W's poem as well as D's entry in her Scottish Journal, spoke English like 'a foreign speech'.

*16 Feb. 1802   Hartshorn tree*   An oak-tree near Penrith associated with a legend of a hart's pursuit and death. Forty years later W told Miss Fenwick, 'The tree has now disappeared, but I well remember its imposing appearance as it stood, in a decayed state, by the side of the high road leading from Penrith to Appleby.' (*PW* iii. 535.)

   *Mrs C better*   i.e. Mrs Clarkson.

   *& we slept . . . no bad dreams*   These words have been crossed out.

   *a new cloak*   W said in 1842 that his poem 'Alice Fell' was 'Written to gratify Mr. Graham of Glasgow, brother of the Author of the Sabbath. He was a zealous coadjutor of Mr. Clarkson, and a man of ardent humanity. The incident had happened to himself, and he urged me to put it into verse, for humanity's sake.' (*PW* i. 359.) W began by telling the story to D, who wrote it here, and he composed the poem soon after, 12–13 March. Robert Grahame, a solicitor in Glasgow, visited Grasmere in 1806 and in 1808 he persuaded 9 Glaswegians to subscribe to C's *Friend*. See 8 July 1802 where D notices a child in a chaise—'Alice Fells own self'.

*17 Feb. 1802 morning* 'walked to Rydale after dinner when it cleared up a little' is crossed out here. This walk belongs to Saturday 20 Feb.

*21 Feb. 1802 1st Prologue* On the manuscript of *Peter Bell* (MS 4) at the bottom of the page containing the title, D has written 'Grasmere Sunday ½ past 5 o clock by the Gold watch, now hanging above the fire—a rainy coldish day—snow on the ground—but there is a thrush singing February 21st 1802'.

*the Tailor's* Gordon Wordsworth suggested Lenty Fleming, the tailor who lived in the cottage under Loughrigg, now enlarged and known as The Stepping Stones (*Journals* i. 117). But it is possible that W walked to one of the two tailors who lived beyond the Olliffs' while D was visiting there: George Walker of Underhelm, towards Easedale, or John Caradus of Winterseeds. See 9 Dec. 1801 where D, speaking of the Easedale area, refers to the 'green Lane behind the Tailors'. (Such a lane going towards Underhelm existed until this century, and it still is a little-frequented path.) On 25 Feb. 1802 D refers to the cottage under Loughrigg as 'Lenty Flemings', not, more impersonally, as 'the Tailor's'; Lenty Fleming's wife was an Ashburner and D would have every reason to use his name.

*22 Feb. 1802 Middleham* Bishop Middleham, 8 miles east of Bishop Auckland, where MH's youngest brother, George Hutchinson (1778–1864) was farming. Sara was keeping house for him at this point. Their brother Tom must have been visiting. Perhaps he took MH and Sara back with him; they were both at Gallow Hill by 2 March when C visited there.

*his first engraving* W wrote about Joseph Sympson's many talents soon after his death in July 1807. In 'The Tuft of Primroses' (1808), W described Joseph Sympson's last years when wife, daughter, and grandchild were dead: he asked 'What will become of him?' Would he, the poet wondered, be playing

> The harp or viol which himself had framed
> And fitted to their tasks with perfect skill.
> 'What Titles will he keep, will he remain
> Musician, Gardener, Builder, Mechanist,

> A Planter and a Rearer from the seed,
> A man of hope and forward-looking mind,
> Even to the last?'

The poem as such was unpublished in W's lifetime; rewritten for *The Excursion*, 1814. See *Tuft of Primroses*, p. 44.

It was certainly forward-looking to produce a first engraving at the age of 87; and see 13 June 1802 for Mr Sympson's 'beautiful drawing'.

*23 Feb. 1802 chearful undersong* This musical term, to be used shortly by W of the kettle, 'whispering its faint undersong' to the flapping of the flame ('Personal Talk'), is perhaps connected in D's memory with C's 1795 use of the word, like hers, in the context of birdsong,

> th'unceasing rill
> To the soft Wren or Lark's descending trill
> Murmurs sweet undersong 'mid jasmin bowers

('Lines to Joseph Cottle', ll. 22–4)

*24 Feb. 1802 Wednesday 24th* The entry first began, 'a rainy morning—I had slept badly & was unwell in the morning—I went to bed directly after Breakfast & lay till William returned from Rydale wet with letters—he brought a short one from C a very long one from Mary—.' This is crossed out, and the entry begins again, 'Wednesday 24th. A rainy Day'.

*traveller such as he* C was still in London, and when he came north, it was not immediately to Grasmere and Keswick but to Gallow Hill and the Hutchinsons where he stayed 2–13 March.

*25 Feb. 1802 Lessing's Essay* Perhaps 'Laokoon' (see *Prose* i. 178–9), an essay with some affinities with W's Preface. W must have been recently thinking about the Preface for there are variants in the next edition, *LB* 1802.

*I . . . Bowels* This sentence has been heavily crossed out.

*27 Feb. 1802 Saturday 27th* The entry originally began 'I was again obliged to go to bed in the afternoon—not [?well]—we did not walk today'. This is crossed through, presumably as belonging to the following day, and the first sentence of the entry is inserted—as is the last sentence, again about walking towards Rydal.

*28 Feb. 1802    pedlar*    D has added the information about the 'Pedlar' at the beginning and in the margins of the entry.

*1 Mar. 1802    Mrs Olliffs child ill*    On 18 March 1802 the burial is recorded of Sarah-Charlotte Daugr. of John Olive Esq. of Hollin's Grasmere.

*4 Mar. 1802    the horses for Wm*    W was going to Greta Hall—see 26 Feb. for his letters to Mrs C and to Calvert (presumably about the horse); and see 8 Mar. when D describes Friday's extraordinary moon, which she had seen over Silver Howe and W saw from Keswick 'hanging over the Newlands fells'. Clearly the Ws expected C to be in Keswick, and since he was not (see 24 Feb. n.) W came home a day earlier than expected.

*pens to make*    W no doubt always had a penknife about him for this purpose (but see 31 Jan. 1802 when he uses it to cut initials). On 25 Apr. 1802 Mr Sympson sent quills, but occasionally ready-made pens were bought (1 Feb. 1802 n.).

*apple tarts*    'He has a sweet sunshiny day' is crossed out here.

*have helped*    'a little' crossed out.

*7 Mar. 1802    the alterations*    These appeared in *LB* 1802, in print by Apr. For the new stanzas, ll. 163–8 and 175–80, see *PW* ii. 232.

*8 Mar. 1802    Newlands fells.*    Here D began, 'Tuesday a fine pleasant morning. We sate reading.' She crossed this out, returning to Monday's entry. Note the expanded description of Friday's moon.

*9 Mar. 1802    poem on Love*    Perhaps the song, 'Drink to me only with thine eyes'; or the more philosophical 'Epode', on the same page in Anderson, iv, celebrating 'chaste love', which 'in a calm, and godlike unity / Preserves community.' See 11 Feb. 1802 n. for W's interest in domestic love extending into community.

*10 Mar. 1802    Yorkshire Wolds poem    Peter Bell*; neither this nor 'The Pedlar' was published in the versions of 1802 during W's lifetime.

*11 Mar. 1802    the Singing Bird*    Published 1807 as 'The Sailor's Mother', it records an encounter with a beggar woman whose dignity of bearing and pathetic story impress the poet. D was not present and there is no Journal account. 'I met this woman', said W, 'near the Wishing-Gate, on the high-road that then led from Grasmere to Ambleside. Her appearance was exactly as here described, and such was her account, nearly to the letter' (*PW* ii. 477).

*12 Mar. 1802  in the Jig step*  Notice D has inserted phrases to improve her first account: 'I saw Jane Ashburner driving the cow from the well where she had been watering it with a stick in her hand tripping along in the Jig step . . .'. A remembered image.

*13 Mar. 1802  Poem of the Beggar woman*  'Beggars': 'She had a tall Man's height . . .'; W remembered D's account, 10 June 1800.

*Little Peggy Simpson*  Margaret Simpson of Nab Farm, Rydal, married Thomas De Quincey in Feb. 1817, and D had a less kindly view of the rose-like girl over whose 'beauty', 'good sense', 'simplicity', and 'angelic sweetness' De Quincey 'utter'd in raptures'. She saw only 'a stupid, heavy girl . . . reckoned a Dunce at Grasmere School' (*MY* ii. 372). D thought the marriage 'ruined' De Quincey, but it proved otherwise; little Peggy Simpson was to make De Quincey an excellent wife.

*grew there*  The words 'when the mother was a child before she is a woman' are crossed out here; 'years before' is inserted.

*escape from those very words*  See 10 June 1800 and n. The inhibiting effect came after W 'had half cast the Poem' during the walk before tea when they had seen a child visibly like her mother, just as—as D must then have remembered from her May 1800 encounter—the beggar boys were like their mother. If D's account, read after tea, was inhibiting, her detail that the boys were chasing a butterfly was possibly suggestive. W turned to Spenser's 'Muiopotmos: or the Fate of the Butterfly' for a startling phrase to describe the mother, 'a Weed of glorious feature', in Spenser's context about plants, in W's carrying moral overtones. W's emphasis moves to the boys, venal like their mother, yet vulnerable and beautiful as butterflies.

*14 Mar. 1802  finishing the Poem*  The children and butterfly of the previous day clearly lead to the conversation of W and D about themselves as children, the butterflies of Cockermouth, and the 'dead times' of childhood that W evokes over breakfast in his poem, 'To a Butterfly' ('Stay near me—do not take thy flight!'). (There are no butterflies in Mar.)

*the fur gown*  Perhaps W's 'green gown, lined throughout with Fox's skin' or D's 'furs that defy the cold' of the Goslar winter (*EY*, p. 245). Inside the cover of the first Grasmere Journal, among sums of what seem to be German currency, is a list, 'Furr gown  Cap Skins  Tails'. Against the gown are the figures 3—1—14, which, if these are ducats, marks, and stivers (D calls them 'sous'), would mean a price of about £1. W was wearing his gown by mid-Dec. 1798: in a letter containing copies of some of W's greatest passages about his Lake District childhood D had offered C a contrasting glimpse of her brother in the cold and foreign Goslar world, 'William's foot is on the stairs. He has been walking by moonlight in his fur gown and a black fur cap in which he looks like any grand Signior.' (*EY*, p. 242.) See 30 Apr. 1802 when D and W took the fur gown (or gowns) into the Hollins wood and lay wrapped in their cloaks. The fur tippet of 24 Nov. 1801 may also be a relic of that German winter.

*15 Mar. 1802   Maxwell*   Probably William Maxwell, Master of the *Amacree*, a Liverpool ship sailing to Africa. According to the unknown author of *Liverpool and Slavery by a Genuine "Dicky Sam"*, 1884, in 1799 this ship carried 363 slaves.

*not been in bed since*   '12 0 clock' is crossed out here.

*Longman & Rees*   W's publishers, after Thomas Norton Longman (1771–1842) and his partner Owen Rees bought Joseph Cottle's publishing business in 1800. Longman gave Cottle the copyright of *LB* (thinking it worth little) and Cottle gave it to W (who had never supposed it to be other than his own from the beginning). Printing for the second edition was still done by Cottle and Biggs in Bristol. Longman after this used London printers and brought out all W's books until 1835 when Edward Moxon took over.

*16 Mar. 1802   The Emigrant Mother*   A tale of a mother's grief at being separated from her child: 'Suggested', said W later, 'by what I have noticed in more than one French fugitive during the time of the French Revolution' (*PW* ii. 477). W's thoughts naturally turn to France during this period of deciding on a visit to Annette and on a time to marry Mary.

*like butterflies*   'or skylarks' is crossed out here.

*17 Mar. 1802   along the dark hill-side*   Helen Darbishire suggested lost lines from *Peter Bell* (*Journals* (1958), 134); but might these not be D's own lines? '*Thus* I was going on . . .'[my italics] implies, perhaps wryly, composition (out of doors, in W's manner); cf. the similar expression 'She went on—'(22 June 1802). Note that next day D 'tried to write verses but alas!'

*The sky . . . now & then*   This sentence is an insertion.

*fair . . . moonshine*   This phrase originally 'quiet & fair in the moonlight'; above 'there' in 'the Church was there' D has written 'visible in' and smudged it out.

*Poem to me in bed*   Probably still 'The Emigrant Mother', which began and ended the day's entry. The begging sailor is inserted after the concluding line.

*18 Mar. 1802   he was gone*   To Keswick again, this time to find C there, and return with him next day.

*Bright silver waves . . . went away.*   Much altered: 'were there' at first 'lived but'; 'rose up' at first 'followed'; 'they went away' at first 'the former disappeared'.

*a Cow*   Large long-horned cattle were then common (see 11 Oct. 1800 where they are pasturing even upon the hill tops).

*'That needs must be a holy place &c &c'*   Perhaps an imperfect recollection of W's 1800 poem, *Home at Grasmere*, in which the poet looks at the valley, lake, and island, as D is doing here, and feels that

> They who are dwellers in this holy place
> Must need themselves be hallowed.
>
> (ll. 366–7)

*saw this lowly Building*   D, making a choice between 'saw' and 'beheld', leaves it only just clear that 'saw' was the preferred word.

*half a poet*   Writing against her fatigue D at first wrote 'it made me more than half I was tired a poet. I was tired . . .' The word 'expecting' is an insertion.

*19 Mar. 1802   disputed about Ben Jonson*   Since 11 Feb. when D read aloud the Life and some poems of Jonson, W had several times been 'reading in Ben Jonson' and Jonson's influence can be traced in the poetry of spring 1802. C had not shared in this reading, but the causes of D's agitation were surely C's sorry domestic problems and perhaps his opium habit, as well as his literary difference with W. The two last sentences of the entry are an added insertion.

*22 Mar. 1802   Wm should go to Mary*   The Peace of Amiens was not signed until 27 Mar., but it must have been clear that Europe was now open to English visitors. W's visit to Mary, no doubt to discuss the planned expedition to France and their marriage date, takes place on his birthday, 7 Apr.

*23 Mar. 1802   the Cuckow poem*   'To the Cuckoo', 'O blithe New-Comer!I have heard, / I hear thee and rejoice', an address not to the 'bird unholy', 'the churlish bird' of 'The Cuckoo and the Nightingale', but to the 'blessed Bird' of hope that was both actually remembered from youth and brilliantly appropriated from the literary tradition of Spenser and Logan (see 3 June 1802 n.).

*24 Mar. 1802   County*   D began to write 'hou[se]' and changed it; *G Hill*, Gallow Hill, Mary's present home.

*wrote Peggy Ashburner*   Not a letter to their neighbour, but the poem 'Repentance'; this is narrated by such a wife as Peggy and is based upon Peggy Ashburner's conversation with D (see 24 Nov. 1801) about her regret at the land's being sold. D's entry establishes precisely the date of composition.

*26 Mar. 1802   the Rainbow*   'My heart leaps up'. W here makes personal perhaps the dominant image of his time; Turner and Constable arch the beautiful impermanent bow over their landscapes, and see 1 Feb. 1802 n. for Campbell's use of it. Note W's blank response in the Ode of next day, 27 Mar., 'The rainbow comes and goes.'

*27 Mar. 1802   part of an ode*   The first four stanzas of the poem called in 1815 'Ode: Intimations of Immortality from Recollections of Early Childhood'; it was some two years before the Ode was completed. See 17 Mar. 1802 for Mr. Olliff's offer of manure.

*29 Mar. 1802   Ormathwaite*   The home, until May 1804, of the Revd Joseph Wilkinson (1764–1831). It was 'immediately under the mountain of Skiddaw . . . the views wherever you turn are enchanting', wrote D in 1810 when the old house was for sale (*MY* i. 381). It had belonged to Wilkinson's wife's uncle, Dr William Brownrigg (1711–1800), celebrated enquirer into natural sciences and collector of drawings and paintings; the Wilkinsons looked after Dr Brownrigg in his last years. They left Ormathwaite in 1804 to go to Wilkinson's new living in Norfolk. The relationship with W dates probably from the Windy Brow days of 1794, and there were common connections: Wilkinson's 2 sisters married the 2 brothers of W's friend, James Losh. From Ormathwaite Wilkinson made drawings of local scenes and W must have liked these enough to consent in 1809 to write the text for a fresh series of drawings to be etched and published as *Select Views in Cumberland, Westmoreland, and Lancashire* (1810). In the event he disliked the new drawings and the text was published anonymously. It became, however, the basis of his *Guide to the Lakes* (1822). Wilkinson's early and unpublished drawings, collected and bound by him 1795–6, and now in the WL are the ones W probably first saw (and see 1 July 1802 when some drawings are sent to Grasmere); they have charm and a primitive drama; they present a world of mountains, lakes, and cottages often almost drowned in leafage, or scarcely distinguishable from the basic stone walls.

*30 Mar. 1802 30th March* Dates here are inserted later: Tuesday's correctly, Wednesday's having 1 Apr. and 30 Mar. before the correct 31 Mar. 1–4 Apr., originally 2–5 Apr., corrected by D.

*31 Mar. 1802 the Quakers' meeting* The Keswick meeting house, built in 1715, stood, and still stands (much altered as Quaker Cottage), where the River Greta bends and the old road to Carlisle meets the road out of Keswick. It was on the way to Ormathwaite from Greta Hall, and D uses it here simply as a landmark. See 19 June 1802.

*1 Apr. 1802 the How* A small hill rising from the flat land between Derwentwater and Bassenthwaite. Thomas Gray described the walk in his Journal of 1769.

*3 Apr. 1802 fine day* No mention here—perhaps D was unaware— of C's 'talking with [W] the whole night till the Dawn of the Day, urging him to conclude on marrying [MH]' (*Notebooks* iii. 3304). The next night, 4 Apr., D again apparently unaware of his tension, C wrote 'Dejection' (see 21 Apr. 1802 and n.).

*4 Apr. 1802 Mrs C* Mrs Coleridge. Greta Bank was Calvert's new house near Windy Brow.

*5 Apr. 1802 & her scholars* The school, with a new schoolhouse and an endowment of £4 per year, was in the benefaction of the Hasells of Dalemain. Dacre, with its ancient castle, by then a farmhouse, is between Greta Hall and Eusemere. W and D were in time for tea because Calvert had given W the use of a horse.

*Mrs C* Mrs Clarkson.

*6 Apr. 1802   Water side*   A house belonging to the Hasells about a mile from Eusemere on the eastern shore of Ullswater.

*7 Apr. 1802   Middleham*   George Hutchinson's farm. MH and W would there make the final decision about France and a date for their marriage.

*8 Apr. 1802   Woodside*   Catherine Clarkson, unlike D, was not a good walker: Woodside was a house just a few fields away up the stream behind Eusemere; the hill of Dunmallet on the next day was little further.

*12 Apr. 1802   to T Wilkinson's*   i.e. to Yanwath, near Penrith. The kindly Thomas Wilkinson must have walked almost 3 miles back with D who was intensely anxious to read the letter and know W and MH's decision.

*13 Apr. 1802   the Bank*   A farmhouse near Howtown about 5 miles from Eusemere, and where Swarth Fell rises most steeply out of Ullswater.

   *Mr Smith*   See 28 Sept. 1800 n.

   *shot through me*   D had hoped to meet W privately, as she explains to MH: 'Jane [the Clarksons' maidservant] met me and told me he was come. I believe I screamed, when she said so, and ran on. I then recollected myself, and told her to run on before and tell him that I was coming, in order that he might meet me; but she was stupid, and so I met him in the parlour' (*EY*, p. 350).

*15 Apr. 1802   strawberries*   These and the 'scentless violets' are an added insertion.

   *pile wort*   Mrs Clarkson was not alone in calling the 'starry yellow flower', or Lesser Celandine, 'pile wort'; (Withering, ii. 504) also offers 'Common Pilewort' as an alternative name.

   *beyond Gowbarrow park*   Walking the length of Ullswater (9 miles) on its western shore, D and W, when beyond Gowbarrow Park, were closer to Patterdale than to Pooley Bridge. Gowbarrow Park comprised the lower slopes of Gowbarrow Fell and was a deer park belonging to the Duke of Norfolk. It was noted by every Lakes writer from Gilpin in 1772 to Green in 1819. The daffodils were to be celebrated in W's poem, 'I wandered lonely as a cloud', of 2 years later. They were not, of course, the large, garden daffodils that we know today but the smaller, paler, wild daffodils, *pseudo-narcissi*.

*long belt of them*   After these words six others, 'the end we did not see', are crossed out.

*that blew upon them over the Lake*   This clause is an added insertion.

*This wind . . . over the Lake to them*   This sentence is an added insertion. Compare D's description of the walk along Ullswater in her letter to Mary, written immediately on returning home (*EY*, p. 350). Though the wind there is 'furious' and 'sometimes almost took our breath away,' it is not a creative force: no daffodils are mentioned, no partnership with the wind in dance.

*reached Luffs*   The Luffs' cottage with its 'two storm-stiffened black yew-trees on the crag above'—by which D later identified it in mist (*Journals* i. 414)—was about half a mile beyond the inn towards Brothers Water. It was not until 1808 that Luff bought the small estate, Side, across Goldrill Beck.

*Dobson's*   Also called Nell House, between the Church and Goldrill Bridge. D described their accommodation more fully to Mary as soon as they were back home, 'ham, veal cutlets, preserved plums, ale, rum and water, dry beds and decent breakfast. We paid 7/−, one shilling too much.' (*EY*, p. 351.)

*to the Library*   This same landlord must have been Bud-worth's host in 1792, for he too commented on the books. 'The landlord had been in his hay-field. We asked him to sit down, and we found him a well-informed man . . . he had some choice books in the room where we dined, and he conversed so *sensibly*, I felt even respect for him' (*A Fortnight's Ramble*, pp. 100–1). Enfield's Speaker was *The Speaker: or Miscellaneous Pieces Selected from the Best English Writers* by William Enfield (1741–97), first published to assist students at the Warrington Academy in 1778. Enfield was minister at the Octagon Chapel, Norwich. D met him briefly in Dec. 1788, 'one afternoon upon a visit at Norwich. He is, I think a very, agreeable man.' Her uncle William Cookson thought him 'a true presbyterian' but their neighbour Mrs Dix remarked 'that he would lick the feet of his benefactors' (*EY*, pp. 22–3).

*16 Apr. 1802   The Church*   D crossed out here, '& the yew tree'. This tree fell in 1883. The church is dedicated to St Patrick, whence the name, Patterdale. This Good Friday entry is carefully revised: insertions place the row of bees 'in the garden'; the fisherman in a 'meadow', originally a 'field'; the sheep came plunging through a 'river', originally a 'stream'; and D's sympathetic 'poor thing' is crossed out; D added 'stars of' to the 'like gold' of pile-wort, saw the water first 'through' as well as 'under' the boughs, described the fields as 'soft' as well as 'green', sharpened the hawthorn's green 'with black stems' and not once but twice added the hundreds of cattle to the passage.

*the two arched Bridge*   The Goldrill bridge. D and W do not cross; they walk alongside Goldrill Beck.

*the Glowworm*   The poem, 'Among all lovely things my Love had been', W's gift to D on his return from seeing Mary in Middleham the previous week; see 20 Apr. 1802 for an account of the poem's composition on horseback (Calvert's horse). It is about the finding of a glow-worm for 'Lucy' to see. 'The incident', wrote W when he copied it out to send to C that same night on reaching Grasmere, 'took place about seven years ago between Dorothy and me' (*EY*, p. 348). The gesture was delicate at Racedown in 1795, and the poem about it is particularly delicate in Apr. 1802; it clearly did reassure D that W's intended marriage would mean no diminution of his love for her.

*sights & sounds we saw and heard*   'The cock is crowing'; its extended title is specific, 'Written in March while resting on the bridge at the foot of Brother's Water', and then on the manuscript is added, 'between one and two o'clock at noon April 16 1802'. The short poem was finished before they reached Ambleside. D's account owes something to W's prior composition.

*Ambleside Church*   The old church, St Ann's; to be rebuilt in 1812, and entirely superseded in 1854 when St Mary's, much larger and with a tall spire in the Early English style, was built. After that there were no more Ambleside marriages and burials in Grasmere parish.

*the Luffs*   As to be expected (see 15 Apr.) they were in their Ambleside quarters.

*the Boddingtons*   Benjamin Boddington (1773–1855) of Keen Ground, Hawkshead, and his wife Grace (d. 1812), who in 1798 had been divorced from Samuel Boddington (1767–1843), Benjamin's own first cousin and a London West India merchant and partner of Richard Sharp. Both Boddingtons were known to the Ws; both subscribed to the fund for the Green orphans in 1808, Samuel 5 guineas, Benjamin 2 guineas (he had by then 3 children, shortly 4; and had lost 2 infant daughters, one just before the Green tragedy). Perhaps D and W did not go in to see the Luffs because, as D wrote to Mary, 'poor Luff is in the Gout' (*EY*, p. 351) and visitors were already there.

*Tom Dawsons*   How Top.

*17 Apr. 1802   on the island*   This phrase is a later insertion.

*the grey deer*   i.e the reflections of the sheep looked like the skeletal deer; there could have been no reflections of the deer on 15 Apr.: Ullswater was rough that day; cf. W's later pointing out a misreading of 'I wandered lonely as a cloud' and asking 'how it is possible for *flowers* to be *reflected* in water where there are waves' (*MY* i. 194).

*Gowbarrow park*   Here were the words, 'A letter from Coleridge not one from Sara—we walked by moonlight' and the customary line at the end of the entry. The words were crossed out and the entry was continued; 'an interlacing of ash sticks', originally 'a locking of ash twigs'; the final sentence about the robin and the scarlet Butterfly is an insertion. Presumably the butterfly was a large copper; W, in the poem about it (and in 'Beggars') describes the butterfly as 'crimson'.

*18 Apr. 1802   the Robin & the Butterfly*   'The Redbreast and the Butterfly', where W expresses his sorrow that the robin could have such aggressive instincts as to pursue the beautiful butterfly:

> Could Father Adam open his eyes
> And see this sight beneath the skies,
> He'd wish to close them again.

See 2 Feb. 1802 for the deeply moving effect of *Paradise Lost* XI. Father Adam in Milton, like W and D, was 'not unmoved' (XI. 185–92) when he saw aggression among the animals as a result of the Fall. W's 'secret reference' to Milton in his 'Redbreast and the Butterfly' was recognized by De Quincey (Masson, iii. 27)—and later acknowledged by W—but incomprehension and mockery were more general reactions when the poem was published, much revised, 1807 (as shown in the publication of, for example, *The Simpliciad—a Satirico-Didactic Poem containing*

*Hints for the Scholars of the New School*, anon. (1808); see esp. ll. 9–10, mocking Poets who 'With brother lark or brother robin fly / And flutter with half-brother butterfly' and ll. 17–20).

20 *Apr. 1802   I've watch'd you now a full half-hour*   The butterfly again (see 14 Mar. 1802) in the second poem to be entitled 'To a Butterfly'. Before, the butterfly was on the point of flying away; now it is its stillness that is impressive, for, tiny as it is, the butterfly contains a power huge as 'frozen seas' to unlock the memory and bring back the 'summer days, when we were young'. Again there is the association with D, in the 'sweet childish days' of the past, and in the invitation of the present to come to 'my Sister's flowers'. The assurance that the garden is a 'sanctuary' and that the butterfly need 'fear no wrong' is perhaps a little sweeping in view of the predatory robin of 17 Apr.

*poem of the Glow-worm*   D's interest in the composition of this poem was considerable. First, it was unusual for W to compose on horseback; his preferred mode was 'walking up and down a straight gravel-walk, or in some spot where the continuity of his verse met with no collateral interruption', or so Hazlitt tells us ('My First Acquaintance with Poets'), and we know from the Journal how very often W is walking 'backwards and forwards' on the orchard platform, in the wood beyond the orchard, or on the White Moss path. Second, the poem was a gesture for D and most of it written at the very time (see 12 Apr. 1802) when she was most anxious to be alone with her letter and conscious of the moon with its two fluctuating stars, a time, she subsequently learnt, when W was riding from Mary to her and writing 'The Glow-Worm'; the complex mutual sensitivity of brother and sister is demonstrated. The poem was composed quickly for it cannot be more than 6 miles from the start of Raby Park to beyond Staindrop. William Harry Vane, 3rd Earl of Darlington, lived at Raby Castle.

*ride*   A mistake for 'write': W could write only when the horse was walking.

21 *Apr. 1802   verses he wrote to Sara*   340 lines with the title 'A Letter to — —' and the date 'April 4 1802 Sunday Evening'; in shortened form, published as 'Dejection: an Ode' in *MP* for 4 Oct. 1802, W's wedding day (see n.) and the 7th anniversary of C's own marriage. C was by now unhappy in marriage, in love

with Sara Hutchinson, and not free to make any changes. In his poem he broods, as W had in the first 4 stanzas of the 'Ode' (27 Mar.), on loss of joy. But C can point to his own 'coarse domestic Life' as a major cause; his 'habitual Ills' defeat his imagination, he says, and his hopelessness within the poem is so powerful that the poet doubts (even as he demonstrates) his ability to write poetry. It is not surprising that D was affected and 'not being well, in miserable spirits'. She was so sympathetic that here she takes the world at C's valuation and finds the sunshine, fields, sky, and even the lambs (bounding with joy in W's Ode) sorrowful. W took up the dialogue in 'Resolution and Independence' and later in his completed 'Ode', reaching different positions about both loss and joy.

   *a thousand*   'glossy' crossed out.

   *a little muddy pond*   Echoing the 'little muddy pond / Of Water—never dry' of W's 1798 Alfoxden poem 'The Thorn'. The 'well' (still there) is a deep basin that takes its water from the nearby stream with a channel returning excess water to the stream at a lower point. When De Quincey built the high wall surrounding the garden he left gaps for the two channels. It was easier to clean in W's time.

   *Ferguson's life & a poem or two*   Probably in *Poetical Works of Robert Fergusson with the life of the author*, by David Irving (1800); appears in the Rydal Mount Library list and in the Sale Catalogue.

*22 Apr. 1802*   *'I have . . . fed by the Sun'*   A recently written short poem never published by W. Its vocabulary alludes to the stanzas of the 'Ode' and the 'Verses to Sara', but, like W's gesture of flinging stones into the river, it is affirmative: 'The things which I see / Are welcome to me'. Yet the 'deep delicious peace' of life brings 'the quiet of death' to mind. See 29 Apr. 1802 n.

   *Wilkinson*   Probably the Revd Joseph Wilkinson.

*23 Apr. 1802*   *Andrew's Broom*   References in this entry to two emblematic poems of 1800 with settings on this part of Rydal Fell. In 'The Waterfall and the Eglantine' a Briar-rose or 'happy Eglantine' grew too close to a waterfall and in winter was swept away; in 'The Oak and the Broom' Andrew, the shepherd-narrator, tells of a prudential oak doomed to be struck in a storm while a careless cheerful broom survived (Gill, pp. 211–15).

*a sweet moss carpet*   Cf. C: 'Friday, April 23rd 1802. discovered the *Double-bower* among Rydale Rocks—Ivy, Oak, Hawthorn, Mountain Ash, Common ash—Holly, Yews— / Fern & Wild Sage, Juniper, &c. Carpet of Moss—& Rocks/' (*Notebooks* i. 1164).

*24 Apr. 1802   the Barberry tree*   The fact that there was (and still is) a berberis in the garden behind DC (and see 28 May 1802) has grown in significance since July 1964 when a poem, 'The Barberry Tree' (surely W's) was published for the first time. For the text and history of this lively rhyming poem about the Barberry Tree blossoming and dancing in wind, and the poet hoping that both he and the reader might 'a store of thought lay by / For present time and long futurity', see *Poems in Two Volumes*, pp. 576–9.

*Glowworm Rock*   Still by the side of the old road just north of the junction with the new road at White Moss. 'We have been in the habit of calling it the Glow-worm Rock from the number of glow-worms we have often seen hanging on to it as described. The tuft of primrose has, I fear, been washed away by the heavy rains', said W in 1843 (*PW* ii. 523). See 30 Dec. 1802 for another tuft of primroses, and W's unfinished *Tuft of Primroses* (1808) and the late pietistic 'Primrose of the Rock' (1831).

*The clouds*   Originally 'The sky.'

*25 April 1802   a Gig with Mr Beck*   The title 'Mr' usually denotes gentlemanly estate and the gig endorses this, so Mr Beck was probably not the one Thomas Beck of the Grasmere register, nor had any connection with the Margaret Beck who was to have a bastard daughter in 1808, but was James Beck (d. 1812, aged 58) of The Grove, Hawkshead. W would pass his house on Esthwaite during his morning walks before school.

*& his Brother's book   Science revived, or The Vision of Alfred. A Poem in eight books* (1802), by the younger Rev Joseph Sympson. W later acknowledged a borrowing in his own sixth Duddon sonnet, and wrote, 'his poems are little known, but they contain passages of splendid description; and the versification of his "Vision of Alfred" is harmonious and animated . . . He was a man of ardent feeling, and his faculties of mind, particularly his memory, were extraordinary. Brief notices of his life ought to find a place in the History of Westmoreland.' (*PW* iii. 506–7.) Despite this praise of a local man and former pupil at

Hawkshead school, *The Vision of Alfred* was not reprinted in England, though, through John Wilson's good offices, it was published by John Bouvier in Philadelphia in 1810, along with biographical notes.

*26 April 1802   Peggy*   The Ws' servant at Racedown and Alfoxden, she had helped look after little Basil Montagu. She was, wrote D in Nov. 1795, 'one of the nicest girls I ever saw; she suits us exactly, and I have all my domestic concerns so arranged that everything goes on with the utmost regularity' (*EY*, p. 160). She married James Marsh, of Lyme, Dorset, a blacksmith, in 1797, and left the Ws' service when they went to Germany in summer 1798; 'it was a hard trial for her,' wrote D, 'She would have gone to the world's end with us' (*EY*, p. 225). Indeed, in their first year at Grasmere D felt that 'poor old Molly did but ill supply to me the place of our good and dear Peggy who was quite as a friend to us' (*EY*, p. 298). D sent her £1 for Christmas 1803, knowing that she had 'now a large family and is very poor' (*EY*, p. 427). In 1806 she sent Peggy £2 and Sir George Beaumont, through D, sent another £5, for Peggy by then had 'endured very much for many causes, especially the cruelty of her husband, and sickness and death of children, and her own weak health' (*MY* i. 56). Beyond this, the public house her husband had recently taken burnt down, and though the family were saved, they lost everything.

*27 Apr. 1802   the Tinker*

> Who leads a happy life
> If it's not the merry tinker

W did not publish this short-lined rhyming character sketch of a mender of pots and pans.

*verses from Coleridge*   'The Mad Moon in a Passion', joking lines mocking poets, himself and W in particular. Here are the last lines:

> So here's Botheration,
> To these Pests of the Nation
> Those fun jeering;
>> Conjuring,
>> Sky-staring;
>> Loungering,
> Vagrants, that nothing can leave in its station—

> These muttering,
>   Spluttering,
> Ventriloquo-gusty
>   Poets
> With no hats
> Or Hats that are rusty

They were never published by C.

*28 Apr. 1802   the Prioress's tale*   W's translation, see 4, 5 Dec. 1801.

*"Children gathering flowers"* 'Foresight', published 1807; verses spoken by a wise child, probably a girl with her brother, to a younger sister, explaining that all other spring flowers can be picked but not one that becomes a fruit.

*Bell Addison*   Isabella Addison (1784–1807), daughter of Henry Addison (1754–1793), a Penrith lawyer. In 1803, still single, she sent baby John W 'a blue striped Frock' (*EY*, p. 404). She married in 1806 Thomas Hutchinson's cousin John Monkhouse and died the next year. Her brother Richard Addison later became Richard W's partner.

*29 Apr. 1802   little Pony*   After this, two words, '[?Better] morning', are crossed out.

*the trench*   The word 'hollow' is crossed out before 'trench'.

*by one another*   Changed from 'by the other'.

*ones*   Hitherto read as 'our', it is more clearly 'ones' with, as often, no apostrophe, and it emphasizes the solitary, internalized nature of both the present experience (W 'with his eyes shut') and the envisaged experience of death. For W this was a happy state. This same spring he wrote of himself as

> in peace on his bed
> Happy as they who are dead
>         (Gill, p. 255)

and in the 1804 stanza eight of the 'Ode' he saw the young child as unafraid,

> To whom the grave
> Is but a lonely bed without the sense or sight
>       Of day or the warm light,
> A place of thought where we in waiting lie;

For C, however, the notion of lying awake in the grave was

'frightful' (*Biographia Literaria* xxii), and W cut the lines from the 'Ode' after 1815.

*the air coldish* 'air' at first 'wind'.

*30 Apr. 1802 Friday April 30th* D had first written 'Saturday'.

*poem of the Celandine* 'To the Lesser Celandine', a celebration of the 'little humble Celandine', a flower 'that had not previously been offered literary recognition'. W perhaps recalled D's recent observations of the pile wort, the 'starry yellow flower', the flower that 'shone like stars of gold', the 'thousand glossy shining stars' (15, 16, 21 Apr.):

> Eyes of some men travel far
> For the finding of a star;
> Up and down the heavens they go,
> Men that keep a mighty rout!
> I'm as great as they, I trow,
> Since the day I found thee out,
> Little flower!—I'll make a stir
> Like a great Astronomer.

*The Hollins* The wood, still with holly trees, above and beside DC. It stretched from the Olliffs' house (later called The Hollens) to White Moss Common. The Ws could walk easily from their orchard into the wood; there was no wall, only a rough hedge of 'Holly, Heckberry, Hazel' (to be cut down in 1811 by De Quincey—'D is so hurt & angry', wrote SH, *Letters*, 36).

*resigned to it* William Knight, Scottish Professor of Moral Philosophy and the first editor of W's poetry (1882) and of D's journals (1897), commented: ' "Resigned" is curiously used in the Lake District. A woman there once told me that Mr. Ruskin was "very much resigned to his own company".'

*1 May 1802 mossed with* D seems to have forgotten a noun; there is no space in the manuscript.

*had lost the poem* The 'lost' poem was not 'To the small Celandine' of the day before, finished that morning, but the inspiration for the second Celandine poem, 'Pleasures newly found are sweet'. W regained it by walking in the evening.

*towards Kings* Probably towards Rydal. Mr King bought the Olliffs' house, The Hollens, at about this time, but D on 1 June is still referring to the enclosures on the fell as 'Mr Olliff's Intakes'; on 3 June, however, she talks of 'Mr King's Hollins'.

*Heard the cuckow today this first of May*   Written as rhyming lines in large letters across the entry. Mr. Sympson had heard the cuckoo, presumably the first that spring, 2 days before. W wrote 'To the Cuckoo' 5 weeks earlier. 'The Rainbow' was likewise written without a rainbow late at night on 26 March, and the 'Ode' stanzas of the following day are linked imaginatively with 'this sweet May-morning'. The cuckoo is not normally heard in Grasmere before the end of Apr.

## The Fourth Notebook: Grasmere Journal, 4 May 1802–16 January 1803 (DC MS 31)

D's last Grasmere Journal is written in a small fat notebook bound in leather and with a clasp to fasten it. It begins on 3 sheets left blank among W's draft of 'Michael' and his tale of the shepherd father's rescue of his son, all written in late 1800, and then, after drafts of the new March 1802 stanzas for 'Ruth', the Journal fills the major part of the book, meeting at the other end 3 pages of W's extracts from Descartes. At both ends of the book numbers of pages have been cut or torn out. Between many pages the original interleaved thin pink blotting paper is still there.

*4 May 1802   Tuesday May 4th*   Corrected from 'Monday May 3rd.'

*the Leech gatherer*   Ultimately 'Resolution and Independence'. At this stage the poem contained more of such details of the old man's life as D had recorded on 3 Oct. 1800, and as W himself remembered, 'the account of him is taken from his own mouth' (Fenwick Note 1843, *PW* ii. 510). Indeed, W, in this version, gave the leech-gatherer much of his story to tell in his own words. See Jared R. Curtis, *Wordsworth's Experiments with Tradition*, pp. 97–113 and 186–95. See also 14 June 1802 n.

*shape & motion*   This phrase is inserted.

*Stags horn*   Stag's-Horn clubmoss. W accurately observed rustic habits when he had his Idle Shepherd-Boys in 1800 trim their rusty Hats 'with that plant which in our dale, / We call Stag-horn, or Fox's Tail' (*PW* i. 362).

*Cockermouth woman*   D's explanation for her excessive generosity, '30 years of age a child at Cockermouth when I was', is an inserted addition.

*'auld moon in her arms'* From 'the grand old Ballad of Sir Patrick Spence', undoubtedly quoted by D because C had recently cited the ballad (from Percy's *Reliques of Ancient English Poetry* (1765) ) in his Verse Letter to Sara Hutchinson (21 Apr.). His variant was, however, 'I see the Old Moon in her Lap'. D's preference for Percy's phrase could have been unconscious; she knew the *Reliques* well: in Hamburg in 1798 the Ws had bought a copy, probably the edition by Percy's nephew, 1794. (C, of course, more directly quoted Percy later in his epigraph to 'Dejection'.)

*'This is the Spot'* Eleven lines about a silent woodland place and an invitation to 'sink into a dream / Of quiet thoughts', written originally for D, 1799–1800, and about this time expanded by W and called 'Travelling'; published in part only in 'Ode to Lycoris', 1817 (*PW* iv. 423).

5 *May 1802 Thalaba Thalaba the Destroyer*, by Southey, an epic poem in 12 books (1801). Southey had had this 'Mahommedan tale' in mind since he was a schoolboy, but he wrote it quickly, completing it at Cintra, Portugal, in 1800, 'a year and six days after its commencement' (Preface to *Thalaba*, 1837). In Sept. 1803 Southey went to live at Greta Hall and his long friendship, though never intimacy, with the Ws began.

*in the twilight* After this, with the words '4th May Wednesday 1802 Brought forward' (the date uncorrected), D continues entries after W's 'Ruth' stanzas.

*a Boat without the Circle* See also next day's moon, 'a perfect Boat a silver Boat' and cf. W's *Peter Bell*, 1798:

> And now I have a little boat
> In shape just like the crescent moon

These allusions, at this time, like D's two Sir Patrick Spens echoes, are refracted through C's Verse Letter, 'yon crescent Moon . . . A boat becalm'd! dear William's Sky Canoe!' W's preoccupation with the composition of 'The Leech Gatherer', itself an 'answer' to the Verse Letter, sufficiently accounts for D's underlying and continuing awareness of C's poem.

*left him composed* The calming effect of Shakespeare's *Lover's Complaint* (Anderson, ii) on W, 'very nervous' through working on 'The Leech-gatherer' must be associated with likenesses between the two poems: the rhyme royal stanza is almost identical (though W in honour of Chatterton, 'the marvellous Boy' of his poem, has an extra long last line in each stanza); the situation is similar: the encounter by lonely water (there was no water in D's Oct. 1800 account) of troubled youth with patient age. At all events, W's energy for his poem returns, and interestingly, when he revises it in a few weeks (see 14 June 1802 n.), the influence of *A Lover's Complaint*—along with Spenser's *Ruines of Time*, printed close by in Anderson—can be detected in the vocabulary, rhythms, and dream-landscape of the new 'Resolution and Independence'.

*6 May 1802    our Bower*    The Bower, '¾ths' of it planted the day before, was the first step towards the 'seat with a summer shed on the highest platform in this our little domestic slip of mountain' (*EY*, p. 274) that D had built 'in imagination' on coming to DC in Dec. 1799. The Bower must have been below the small terrace on which W 'walked backwards and forwards' (e.g. 30 Apr. 1802). But the ambition was for the shed planned on 1 May 'for the sun was too much for us', and on finishing the Bower W and D walked to Mr Benson's at Tail End to inquire about hurdles for the shed—'no hurdles'. On 2 June they went to the old carpenter's about the hurdles, but clearly without success. The shed or Moss-Hut (it was lined with moss) had to wait until the winter of 1804–5, and was not really in use until that summer, D in the pain of John's death (Feb. 1805) going only once in 3 months to the top of the orchard. But the new door on the stairs-landing, put in during the summer of 1804, had made the garden and orchard very accessible, and the hut 'large enough for a large party to drink tea in' (*EY*, p. 521), was soon to become the place 'where we are all our time except when we are walking' (*EY*, p. 598).

*Lychnis*    Campion, cuckoo flower, ragged robin.

*verses to Hartley*    The 10-line poem, 'Do you ask what the birds say?', with its 'green leaves, and blossoms, and sunny warm weather, / And singing, and loving'. Yet, winter wind and silent birds exist even in this happy poem, and remind us that barely a fortnight before, C had written the first version of 'Dejection'. Published *MP*, 16 Oct. 1802, with the title, 'The Language of Birds: Lines spoken, extempore, to a little child, in early spring'.

*& Sara H.*    Probably the verses beginning, 'If thou wert here,

these tears were tears of light!', published *MP*, 19 Oct. 1802, with the title, 'The Day-Dream: From an Emigrant to his Absent Wife'.

*We read the Review &c.*   The *Monthly Review* for Mar. 1802. Several items would catch the Ws' attention: a review of a translation of the Vicomte de Ségur's *History . . . and Political Picture of Europe, 1786–1796*, containing a summary account of the Revolution in France (of interest for both the content and the author: W had translated a poem by de Ségur; his version, 'a most exquisite Imitation of some beautiful French Verses', said Francis Wrangham, was published in the *Morning Chronicle*, 21 Aug. 1795, under the title, 'The Birth of Love'); a review of William Godwin's reply to the attacks of Dr Parr, Mackintosh, and Malthus (W had been a frequent visitor to, and even disciple of, Godwin in 1795); a review of John Stoddart's *Remarks on the Local Scenery and Manners of Scotland* (see 22 Oct. 1800 n.; D and W were to cover some of the same ground as Stoddart, taking his *Remarks* with them, in their own tour of Scotland in 1803); a review of a Life of Buonaparte, up to the beginning of 1801 (W was shortly to write two sonnets on Buonaparte; see 21 May 1802); an account of an experiment on Galvanic Combinations performed by their friend Humphry Davy at the Royal Institution; a poem from which D quotes (see following note); and an admiring account of the character of Toussaint L'Ouverture, the black ex-slave governor of St Domingo, whose imprisonment by Napoleon in June 1802 W was to lament, and yet hail as a blow for freedom in his sonnet of August, 'Toussaint, the most unhappy Man of Men!'.

*8 May 1802   read in the Review*   The *Monthly Review* (see above); the poem, 'Solitude', is one of two specimens from *Leander and Hero translated from . . . Ovid . . . with other Poems* (1800). The unnamed author envisages Cowley on an American plantation, dead to the 'polished walks of social life', an exile, like Odysseus 'on Calypso's magic coast', who

> Wept, as sharp anguish came on memory's wing,
> For names, sounds, paths, delights and duties lost!

D wrote 'paths' before 'sounds', and then corrected the line. This is a rare quotation from a poet other than W.

*the orchard steps*   Tradition has it that W did more than add a last step, that he, with John Fisher, built the entire run of steps to the top of the orchard. It is not unlikely. William Knight, who knew W's grandson, Gordon W, attributed them to W in 1897 (with John Fisher's help). The second set of steps coming down from the shed on the north side of the garden was put in by the Trustees to make it easier for visitors in considerable numbers to move up and down the garden without damaging plants.

9 *May 1802   Castle of Indolence*   Written 1748, in the manner of Spenser; W's 'Within our happy Castle there dwelt one etc.', is in the manner of both Spenser and Thomson. In Spenserian verse, and like Thomson, who offers portraits of the Castle guests (*Castle of Indolence* i. stanzas 57–60 particularly), W offers portraits of himself and C as mock yet serious figures of fluid sensibility, poets, and friends.

12 *May 1802   that large geranium*   The wild geranium, Wood, or more probably, Meadow Cranesbill; its blue/purple colour not unlike that of the male Common Blue or Holly Blue butterfly. D's 'I often see some small ones' suggests that more Holly Blues were about; these are on the wing slightly earlier than the Common Blue, from the third week in April to mid-May, and their larval foodplants are the holly and ivy native to Lake District woods. D's alternative description, 'Emperor's eye colour' is a reference probably to the butterfly soon to be popularly known as the Purple Emperor. This name was already one variant, but there were several others, and the word 'eye' was not uncommonly included in vernacular butterfly naming. D's allusion reveals a long-standing interest in butterflies (and see 14 Mar. 1802); the Purple Emperor could have been recollected from D's first Forncett summer 1789, or from Racedown or Alfoxden days; these butterflies have never been recorded in the north.

*Geordy Green's house*   George Green in 1802 lived at Kittycrag in Easedale (not the present Kitty Crag but the cottage near it, known now as Jackdaw Cottage). Since Green's marriage, as a widower, to Sarah Wilson in 1792, 5 children had been born at Kittycrag (one, Jane, in 1796 at Cragtop in Easedale). By Feb. 1803 he was at Blintern Gill when his son William was baptized, and here the family remained until the death of George and Sarah Green in snow in Mar. 1808. D, at W's request, wrote an account of this disaster, vivid in its 'minute detail', and moving as a 'record of human sympathies' (W's Preface). Friends read her narrative, subscribed to the fund for the children, but D's account remained unpublished in full until this century (*George and Sarah Green—A Narrative*, by Dorothy W, ed. E. de Selincourt (Oxford, 1936) ).

*14 May 1802  Brothers wood*  Associated by the Ws with the poem, 'The Brothers' (1800): 'This poem was composed in a grove at the north-eastern end of Grasmere Lake, which grove was in a great measure destroyed by turning the high-road along the side of the water. The few trees that are left were spared at my intercession.' (*PW* ii. 467.) The new road was made in 1831.

*difficult sauntering Road*  A memory, indeed an echo, of the occasion behind 'Point Rash Judgement' when D, W, and C had 'Sauntered on this retired and difficult way' in this same Brothers Wood (see 10 Oct. 1800 n.).

*blue Hyacinth*  The bluebell (*Hyacinthus non-scriptus*); Withering's name is English Hyacinth. The word 'bluebell' is not recorded for this flower until 1794; earlier uses of 'bluebell' appear to refer to the harebell (*Campanula rotundiflora*); this is still Scottish usage.

*Gowans*  Normally the dialect word for daisies but clearly this is not the meaning for W in his 'poem on Going for Mary' (see 29 May 1802):

> Thou like the morning in thy saffron coat,
> Bright Gowan! and marsh-marygold, farewell!

Withering gives many common flower names, but omits 'gowan', perhaps because of its restricted northern use. In Scotland a gowan can mean not only a daisy, but a dandelion, globe-flower, buttercup, marigold, or any yellow wild flower.

*a star without a flower*  Probably butterwort or bog violet (*Pinguicula vulgaris*). Its flower does not last long, but its insectivorous leaves, low to the ground, and in the shape of a star, are seen from spring onwards. Withering (see 16 May 1800 n.) begins a note on the butterwort, 'If the fresh gathered leaves are put into the filtre or strainer through which warm milk from the reindeer is poured . . .'; a substance the consistency of yoghurt would seem to be the result. Few people could have conducted this experiment.

*black Rocks—*  Two words, illegible, with '&' between are crossed out here.

*15 May 1802    cheerless morning*   D's second beginning for 15 May is a summary; compare her first fresh, forgotten one, written while W was sleeping. And see below, 3 June, where D writes at length while W sleeps; she finds new matter for days already recorded, crosses out, describes the present, recollects anew, and finally, as here, returns later and starts again.

*18 May 1802    Froude*   The Revd Robert Hurrell Froude (1771–1859), from 1799 Rector of Dartington, Devonshire; from 1820 Archdeacon of Totnes. He was at Oriel College, Oxford, at the same time as John Spedding and was shortly to marry Margaret Spedding. Of his 4 sons, 3 were distinguished: Richard Hurrell (1803–36) theologian, William (1810–79) engineer and naval architect, and James Anthony (1818–94) historian.

   *Wilkinsons*   Of Ormathwaite.

*19 May 1802    then got supper*   'went' is crossed out before 'got supper'.

*20 May 1802    not to go to Keswick*   But C had not entirely abandoned the idea of having the Ws in Keswick, even as lodgers in Greta Hall. 'I said I could not see any good whatever to arise from this,' wrote D firmly on 14 June (*EY*, p. 363).

*21 May 1802    Milton's sonnets to him*   In 1822 W recalled, 'my Sister happened to read to me the sonnets of Milton, which I could at that time repeat; but somehow or other I was singularly struck with the style of harmony, and the gravity, and republican austerity of those compositions. In the course of the same afternoon I produced 3 sonnets.' (*LY* i. 125–6.) Only one of these sonnets has been identified, 'I griev'd for Buonaparte'. It was published, unsigned, *MP*, 16 Sept. 1802.

*23 May 1802    William was very nervous*   This is crossed out.

   *S & M Points*   See 1 Aug. 1800 n.

*24 May 1802    Miss Taylor & Miss Stanley called*   Elizabeth Stanley (b. 1781) niece of Sir Michael le Fleming of Rydal Hall; probably staying there. Her mother Dorothy Fleming (died 1786) had married George Edward Stanley (1748–1806) of Ponsonby Hall, W. Cumberland. Elizabeth Stanley married in 1805 John Cumberland Hughes and her descendants inherited the Rydal estate. Miss Stanley could have been a friend of 2 (or 3) local Miss Taylors. One was the daughter of Peter Taylor (died 1789), a Whitehaven plantation owner whose affairs in S.

Carolina were sorted out by Sir Michael le Fleming; her mother built Belfield in the 1790s at Bowness near one of the famous Thomas West 'stations' on ·Windermere. Then there were 2 Miss Taylors, daughters of that other widowed Mrs Taylor who built The Cottage, now Iveing Cottage, Ambleside (see 18 May 1800 n.): Mary, who married in 1824 Henry Thomas Lutwidge, and Sarah. Possibly all these Miss Taylors were known to the Ws: in 1808, when they were involved in raising money for the Green orphans, a guinea was subscribed by the 'Miss Taylors' and a guinea each by Mrs Taylor and Miss Taylor of Belfield.

*I was ill . . . Mrs Simpson* This sentence has been crossed out; so has the last sentence of 27 May, about W's sleep, and the third sentence of 28 May, about D's poor spirits.

27 *May 1802   Rd C*... *& Cook* i.e. Richard and Christopher W and Richard Cooke, lawyer and friend of Richard W and Basil Montagu; he became involved in Montagu's old debt to W, helping Montagu out. He stayed with the Ws for a few days in Apr. 1800 and when he came to Ambleside for a month in 1803 with his wife, he visited.

*he slept downstairs* See 24 May 1800 n.

28 *May 1802   Dial-like yellow flower* D used her Withering (now in WL, see 16 May 1800 n.): the flower was *Lysimachia nemorum*. Its blossom is described by Withering as 'wheel shaped' (cf. D's 'Dial-like'). In a pencil note dated May 30th 1802 on the fly-leaf of Withering, i, D copies the Latin and the two English names: 'Yellow Pimpernell of the Woods. Pimpernell Loose-strife'. Withering supplies the information that the flower likes 'moist shady places' and is in bloom in May and June (ii. 237–8). We do not know how much D used Withering in the first spring and summer of having it—1801—since her Journal is lost for that period. But pressed between pages are several leaves clearly brought back for identification, and a few notes, such as that D found the Marsh Trefoil growing among 'Low rocks . . . Head of Rydale Mere' on one 11th May, where Withering places it in 'Ponds and pits' in June and July.

29 *May 1802   on Going for Mary* 'Farewell, thou little Nook of mountain ground', a formal farewell to the garden, and a promise to return with 'her who will be ours' and who will 'love

the blessed life which we lead here'; thus also a reassurance to D; published 1815, with the heading 'Composed in the Year 1802'; after 1827, entitled 'A Farewell'. The Ws did not leave for Gallow Hill and then France until 9 July when D wrote her own impassioned farewell (see entry begun 7 [8] July 1802). On 29 May she wrote out W's poem, wrote to Mary, and on the inner third of a page in the Journal, otherwise torn out, she tried out three names:

Dorothy Wordsworth
William Wordsworth
Mary Wordsworth
May 29th 6 o'clock
Evening

Sitting at small table
by window—Grasmere 1802

*31 May 1802    John Wilson of Glasgow*    John Wilson (1785–1854), an undergraduate at Glasgow, was 17 and had been reading *LB* (1802). His letter drew from W a careful reply (5–7 June) discussing the poet's task and readers' entrenched attitudes to those 'in low conditions of society', in the extreme case, idiots. The letter was drafted (*EY*, pp. 352–358), then copied. After this defence of 'The Idiot Boy', the Ws got to know John Wilson well, particularly after 1810 when he came to live at his cottage, Elleray, Windermere. He built a house there and stayed for periods throughout his life. He became well known as 'Christopher North', was a founding contributor of *Blackwood's Magazine* from 1817, and from 1820 Professor of Moral Philosophy at Edinburgh.

*2 June 1802    unwell*    The words 'William was very unwell' have been crossed out.

*dry as powder*    The usual line concluding an entry is drawn here. D, however, inserted the note on wind portending Rain, and began a recollection of Tuesday: 'I ought to have said that on Tuesday June 1st in the ev([?saw] 13 primroses here & there in the Hollins).' This is crossed out and D returns to Wednesday to record the silent communion at the window, 'After we came in . . . Broth for our suppers'. Another concluding line is drawn. This added passage is heavily crossed out. When D begins again a recollection of Tuesday she does not mention the primroses.

*Little John Dawson . . . shoulder*. This sentence is an added insertion.

*3 June 1802  them injured* D inserted the explanation for the brown oaks in June, 'with the late frosts'; the frosts were also responsible for the injured ash trees, see entries 15-18 May.

*passages in his poems* John Logan (1748-88) whose Life and writings the Ws read in Anderson, xi. Much of his information for the Life Anderson took from Logan's friend Dr Robertson, and he writes sympathetically of 'the pensive melancholy which he [Logan] felt in common with men of genius and feeling'. He discusses Logan's 'ardent sensibility', his spirits, 'always much elated, or much depressed'. Logan in his increasing bouts of melancholy 'eagerly snatched that temporary relief which the bottle supplied', and thus hastened his early death. Logan was an admired poet and popular divine and preacher. D's view of him as 'poor Logan' places him in the company of the poets of 'The Leech-gatherer' (much in the Ws' consciousness) who suffered swings of mood from joy to depression and met untimely deaths: Chatterton, Burns, by implication possibly C, and even W himself, and now, John Logan. Logan cannot have been new to D or W; John, about to take a new set of Anderson on a voyage, had written to D about Logan in May 1801 wanting advice on 'good poems.' The first of Logan's poems in Anderson is 'Ode to the Cuckoo' (the second is 'The Braes of Yarrow'). W clearly knew Logan's 'Cuckoo'; it anticipates his own 'Cuckow poem' on which he had been recently at work, see 23, 26 March, 14 May. It may well have been the actual cuckoo heard in the morning that stimulated the Ws to reread Logan in the afternoon. The 'affecting line' is from Logan's 'Ode: written in a visit to the country in autumn':

> What voice [can] console the incessant sigh,
> And everlasting longings for the lost?

*John Dawson* Above the line, faintly written, are the words 'who crossed us'; see end 2 June.

*Goan's dying Infant* Aggy Fisher of course was Gawain Mackereth's sister. The parish register records a burial on 6 June: Rebecca daughter of Gawen Mackereth of Lane end Grasmere. Molly Fisher went to the funeral.

*4 grown-up Children in one year* The parish register seems not to record 4 children of 1 family in a single year, but it does record 3 buried 22 years before:

1780

April    4th    Sarah Daugr of John Hird of Fellfoot Little Langdale.

        12th    Anne Daugr of Ditto Ditto of Ditto

        13th    Mary Daugr of Ditto Ditto of Ditto.

Mary was almost 4, Sarah, 6; Anne's baptism seems not to be recorded at Grasmere, nor does her parents' marriage.

*trip*    Written over 'pass'.

*Thursday June 3rd*    D enters the date a second time and now writes retrospectively. She mentions reading Milton, but not Logan.

*4 June 1802*    *William had slept . . . into the orchard*    This sentence has been heavily crossed out.

*our favourite path*    Gordon W, the poet's grandson, knew which path D referred to. It lies on the fellside of the wall behind John's Grove. Before a descent begins the path turns left and over White Moss Common. This is neither big nor high nor steep but it commands in one view the two entire lakes and valleys of Grasmere and Rydal. See 2 June 1802 for D's celebration of White Moss. The path joins the top road (the White Moss path or 'coffin path').

*Mother Hubbard's tale*    Spenser's 'Prosopopoia: or Mother Hubberd's Tale' (Anderson, ii) is a tale of two rogues, a Fox and an Ape; their cheating adventures give Spenser scope to satirize soldiering, country folk, Church, and Court. Finally, one animal cheats the other, and the Ape loses his tail and half his ear. The poem offers a dark picture of town society; D, like W, was always thankful to live removed both from real poverty and from such needs to court the great as Spenser had had in the 1590s: see 12 Feb. 1802.

*5 June 1802*    *flower*    First 'blossom', then 'bloom'.

*walked late . . . upon our path.*    This sentence is crossed out, presumably because D recalled that the walk belonged to Friday.

*6 June 1802*    *Ellen*    Mrs Clarkson's housekeeper and companion. She lived at Eusemere and looked after the house while the

Clarksons were away. When the Ws 'ate our dinner' at the foot of Kirkstone (see 16 Apr. 1802) it was 'upon some pies which Ellen made us' (*EY*, p. 351), and it was Ellen who gave D and Sara 'tea by the kitchen fire . . . nice Bread and everything comfortable' (*EY*, p. 474) when they walked over from Park House in May 1804.

*7 June 1802    C Indolence poem*    See 9 May 1802 and n.

    *Rydale Falls*    See 18 June 1800 n. on the Lower Falls. The Upper Falls were almost equally celebrated.

*8 June 1802    nice looking statesmen's houses*    W writes in the *Guide* that some of these houses of '*estatesmen*', 'houses of a middle rank between the pastoral cottage and the old hall residence . . . are generally graced with a little court or garden in front where may yet be seen specimens of those fantastic and quaint figures which our ancestors were fond of shaping out in yew-tree, holly, or box-wood' (*Prose* ii. 206).

    *to the Station*    D and Ellen rode down the western shore of Windermere along Claife Heights, leaving the road for the lake-shore track at High Wray, and riding down through John Christian Curwen's new plantations, 'shrubberies', as D contemptuously termed them (see 23 Oct. 1801 n.). The Station was Thomas West's first station above Windermere. In his *Guide* of 1778 West famously designated places to stand to obtain the best views. W came to this one as a schoolboy in the 1780s; by the time D and Ellen came the hillside was no longer covered with West's 'ancient yews and hollies', and it 'suffered much from Larch plantations'; the station had become an octagonal pleasure-house with castellated curtain walls. These were 'obtrusive embellishments' in planting and architecture deplored by W (*Prose* ii. 263).

    *we went to the Island*    Bella Island, later Belle Isle, called after Isabella Curwen, heiress of Workington Hall, for whom the island, previously Long Island, was bought in 1781. It had been the previous owner, Thomas English, who had begun, and been bankrupted by, 'that great house' that so offended D. The house was, as it still is, a round classical villa, with portico, columns, pilasters and even a dome; John Plaw, its designer (1775), intended the house within its setting to be a demonstration of 'Taste accompanying Rural Simplicity'.

*as if they were half starved*   Thomas White, the Curwens' landscape architect, in the wake of Capability Brown, destroyed the walled garden, planted clumps, a single tree here and there, and a belt of trees around the new stone-embanked shores and park-like paths. The 'artificial appearance' displeased W (*Prose* ii. 209).

*not pained*   D clearly meant either 'not pleased' or 'pained'.

*'veins of gold'*   From W's 1800 poem, 'To Joanna':

—'Twas that delightful season when the broom
Full flowered, and visible on every steep,
Along the copses runs in veins of gold.

It was perhaps D's laughter at the conspiratorial warning of the passenger to his companion that put her in mind of W's poem about laughter in the mountains.

*'The sun has long been set' &c*—   Published 1807 and reprinted from 1835 'at the request of my Sister, in whose presence the lines were thrown off' (*PW* iv. 396). It contrasts the 'innocent blisses' of rural sounds under star and moonlight with the 'parading' and 'masquerading' (quoting Burns' 'The Twa Dogs') that goes on in London.

*12 June 1802   Robert*   Old Mr Sympson's grandson, Robert Jameson (1796–1854), brother of Tommy (see 31 May 1800 and n.); protégé of Basil Montagu; from 1825 husband of Anna Murphy, the writer Mrs Jameson; in 1829 a judge in Dominica, and from 1833 holding high legal office in Upper Canada.

*13 June 1802   altering the poem to Mary*   See 29 May 1802 where the poem was described as 'finished'. W sent MH these alterations next day, 14 June: a new stanza ('Dear Spot . . . etc.'), the less local 'magnificent temple' in place of 'Fairfield's mighty Temple', the changing of the inappropriately Spenserian phrase 'Primrose vest' (*EY*, pp. 365–6).

*no little Birds*   D does not normally describe negatively; she is alluding to 'The Sun has long been set':

The Stars are out by twos and threes,
The little Birds are piping yet
Among the bushes and trees;
There's a Cuckoo

*Evening is fairly set in*   D first wrote 'after dark'.

*& lengthened out*  Compare the owlets of 'The Idiot Boy' (1798), 'They lengthen out the tremulous sob' (l. 300).

*14 June 1802  about the Leech-gatherer*  This joint letter (*EY*, pp. 361–68) was begun by D from her sick-bed at 4 in the afternoon and finished by her, well again, at 8 at night. W wrote a section to Sara, 'explaining in prose my feeling in writing that Poem', and replying to her charge that the leech-gatherer's relation of his own unfortunate history (see 3 Oct. 1800) was tedious. W defends the tediousness as in character but, in fact, takes note of Sara's comment, makes changes, and in the final 'Resolution and Independence', finished 4 July, the mythic rather than the historic aspect of the old man is emphasized. D adds her own reprimand to Sara for not reacting to the 'tediousness' in the right spirit. The spirit with which 'our Haircutter' responded as W read him the poem while having his hair cut in the afternoon is not recorded (*EY*, p. 364).

*15 June 1802  till dinner time*  Here D has crossed out, 'old Mr Simpson came in & drank tea with us'; this belongs to the following day.

*a few lines about the night-hawk*  These lines possibly became the beginning of 'The Waggoner' in its first version (1806),

> At last this loitering day of June
> This long, long day is going out
> The Night-hawk is singing his frog-like tune
> Twirling his watchman's rattle about

(See *Benjamin*, pp. 7–9)

Later W refers to the Night-hawk, i.e. the nightjar, as 'the buzzing dor-hawk'.

*one from Wade*  Josiah Wade, a prosperous linen-draper and accountant of 5 Wine Street, Bristol; he did, as C phrased it, 'ever behave to me with steady & uniform affection' (29 July 1802, *CL* ii. 829). He had frequently helped financially, and W, who knew him 'a most excellent and liberal Man, and one who highly values Coleridge' (*EY*, p. 339) was now thinking of him as perhaps the means for sending C abroad for his health: C's friends feared that he would die young.

*16 June 1802  'tall and erect'*  From 'Nutting', written in Germany 1798–9, published *LB* 1800:

the hazels rose
Tall and erect, with milk-white clusters hung.
(ll. 17–18)

*about having a cat*   At first 'about keeping a cat', changed presumably because of the 'Birds keeping us company' of the next sentence. For MH's anxiety about mice, see 14 Dec. 1801. We sense D's fear for the birds and yet her desire not to offend. But see her letter of 13 Nov. 1803 indicating a calm though tempered acceptance of a cat: 'we have got a little cat . . . We are almost over-run with Rats . . . I should now think that the house could scarcely have been right without one, if it were not for the Birds in the orchard' (*EY*, p. 421). D's minor revisions: 'a Bird had perched', originally 'a young Bird . . .'; 'unacquainted with man & with na[ture]'—the last two words deleted and expanded to 'unaccustomed . . . winds'; 'the Bird seemed bemazed', originally 'the little Bird . . .'; 'not strong enough', originally 'strong', then 'stout', then 'strong'; 'They twitter . . . hanging', expanded from 'They hang'.

*at my room window*   i.e. In the front room next to the sitting-room upstairs. This had been W's and John's (it had two beds) but see 27 May 1802 and n.; on 14 June D wrote to MH and Sara, 'You must know that we have changed rooms, my regular sleeping bed is William's. I make John's my sick bed' (*EY*, p. 361).

*fairy Queen to William*   This sentence and the report of a letter from C are crossed out.

*17 June 1802   Ode he is writing*   The 'Ode: Intimations of Immortality' (see 27 Mar. 1802 when the first four stanzas were composed). We do not know what 'little' W added at this time; he completed the 'Ode' in early 1804.

*18 June 1802   to pay all debts*   Sir James Lowther (1736–1802), the recently dead 'bad' Earl of Lonsdale, owed some £4,500 salary and expenses to the Ws' father, his former attorney and law-agent. John W died in 1783 and there had been an unsuccessful law-suit on behalf of the children. In 1802 James Lowther was succeeded by his cousin Sir William Lowther (1757–1844) of Swillington, Yorkshire, created Earl of Lonsdale, 1807. He immediately had an advertisement placed in The *Cumberland Pacquet* desiring 'all Persons with any demands on the late Earl' to send in their claims. Richard W, with anxious advice from W, acted for the Ws: 'We are to receive', wrote D in July 1803, 'eight thousand five hundred pounds. The whole of the money is to be paid in a year.' (*EY*, p. 397.) This sum included interest. The new Lord Lowther moreover became a patron of the arts and a friend of W: *The Excursion* (1814) was dedicated to him.

*19 June 1802  Poor old Willy*  The Grasmere parish register has a burial for 30 May 1802, 'William Udale of Coathow Loughrigg a pauper'. D first began the next sentence positively: 'we often pass . . .'; her original 'seeing his figure' became 'having his figure brought back to our minds.'

*Botanists may be often deceived*  'often' inserted.

*Churchills Rosciad*  Churchill's first poem, 1761 (Anderson, x), about theatre and theatre-people. Anderson called Churchill 'the British Juvenal'. W in 1806 had been 'long since' resolved 'to steer clear of personal satire' (*MY* i. 89), and had abandoned his Imitation of Juvenal; see J. P. Collier, *Notes on C's Conservation* (1811), for C's admiration of Churchill.

*. . . my sweet Brother*  The entry originally finished at 'composed myself to sleep'. The note, 'Charles Lloyd called', and the quotation—not hitherto noticed as a quotation, and so far unidentified—were added.

*20 June 1802  my heart . . . like a vision to me*  Originally 'our hearts' and 'to us'.

*how coldly Mr Simpson received it*  Mr Sympson's response perhaps stemmed from his own bitter experience with titled people. His story lies behind W's pastor in *The Excursion* VII. 31–310. He perhaps feared that the Ws would become friends with the titled (as indeed they did).

*21 June 1802  above the Blacksmiths*  See 5 June 1800 n. W was going over Grisedale Pass to Eusemere. It was Thomas Clarkson who had seen the Lowther advertisement, walked with it to Luff, who rode over from Patterdale with the news, and W was now on his way back to Clarkson's to draw up a memorial of the account with the help of Clarkson and his uncle by marriage Thomas Myers.

*daughter came to tea*  'William Towers husbandman and Betty Grave spinster', both of Grasmere parish were married on 10

Feb. 1793. They lived at Townhead. A daughter Elizabeth was baptized on 29 June 1794 and buried on 26 July. Jane was baptized on 2 Oct. 1795, and William on 24 June 1798. These are the 2 children who came to the Sympsons to tea.

*take the water out* Here, in the middle of this anecdote (evidence of the high price of tea) D turns over two pages. Her account below of Aggy Fisher's conversation with Mary Watson completely fills the overlooked page.

*22 June 1802    lying* Originally 'sitting'.

*Tamar* Gordon W identified Tamar as daughter of Robert Dockray of Underhow, baptized 27 Dec. 1759 (*Journals* i. 162); a relative therefore of Jenny. Another Tamar, wife of George Dodgson, slategetter, lived across the lake at High Close.

*for Betsy* Elizabeth Hutchinson (1776–1842), MH's younger, mentally defective sister. The house was that of Mr and Mrs Elstob, at Greatham, south of Middleham, and of Mrs Elstob Sara H wrote in 1813, 'Every time I see [her] I am more pleased . . . She governs . . . without seeming to do so. and Betsy feels as she were her own Mistress entirely.' (*Letters*, 67.) Betsy occasionally visited Sara and the Ws at Rydal Mount.

*about her son* John, baptized from Moss-side, Grasmere, 9 Nov. 1778, died 1827, and apparently a disappointment to his parents. C tells us in 1803 that John Fisher's 'Son, his only one, [was] in the Army' (*CL* ii. 973). He is the 'poor dissolute Son' who 'constrained forgiveness, and relenting vows, / And tears, in pride suppressed, in shame concealed' of *The Excursion* VI. 713–15; he is a Luke figure who came back to live at Sykeside some time after his mother's death in 1804. Like his father he became a cobbler and in 1817 married Mary Dawson who had been in the service of the Ws at DC (after Molly stopped in 1804) and of the Lloyds at Old Brathay, then of De Quincey, and finally of the Ws again, as cook in 1814 at Rydal Mount. W in his late years would call at Sykeside to talk over old times with Mary Dawson.

*when the Child died* Rebecca Mackereth; see 3 and 6 June 1802.

*drowned last summer* William Watson, aged 23, was drowned in Grasmere 'on a fine summer's Sunday afternoon' in Aug. 1801. D gives a vivid account of Mary Watson's agony, walking 'up and down upon the shore', at the end of her narrative of the Greens' disaster, 1808. Mary Watson, when her son died, was 73 years old. She continued to live in her cottage at Beckhouses until her death in Sept. 1813, and D records her violent end in pencil in a late final note on her Green manuscript: another son with whom she lived, 'a poor Maniac', had murdered her.

*over in a trick of passion* An inserted additional phrase, providing telling contrast with the painfully slow riding of the sick man.

*to take him off suddenly* Mary Watson's daughter Agnes married Leonard Holme of Ambleside, 21 Nov. 1795, and had 2 daughters, Mary, baptized Oct. 1796, and Margaret, May 1799. Aggie's theory that a providential death might solve the family's problem was soon to be tried: the register records the burial of Leonard Holme, of Ambleside, house-carpenter, on 30 July 1802.

*LB*   The new edition, *LB* 1802

*23 June 1802   ½ past 3 o clock*   Corrected from '3 o'clo'; 'before 4' corrected from 'at 4 o''—D's intense precision about her early rising.

*Leslie*   John Leslie (1766–1832), knighted 1832. Leslie, mathematician and natural philosopher, must have met C through Tom Wedgwood with whom Leslie had travelled in 1796. Like C, Leslie had an annuity from Wedgwood. He later became a Professor at Edinburgh.

*24 June 1802   fresh*   The word 'rested' is crossed out here.

*25 June 1802   these Swallows*   Originally 'they'; 'watched them early' changed from 'watched these Birds early'; 'in the day' replaces 'through the day'; 'both morning & night' is an inserted phrase.

*a low song to one another*   A page has been torn out here. The missing entries of 26, 27, 28 June must have recorded W's visit to Keswick and the second start on the swallows' nest. See 5 [6] July for its completion. This time the nest stayed up and when the swallows returned in May 1803 D recorded that it needed 'no repairs whatever' (*EY*, p. 393).

*30 June 1802   I then said What . . . care of myself*   This is an added insertion.

*Marquis of Granby*   John Manners, Marquis of Granby

(1721–70), eldest son of 3rd Duke of Rutland (1696–1779). The old man's admiration is not surprising: George II had great affection for him, and so had his soldiers, in the Highlands after Culloden in 1746, and in Germany during the Seven Years War when he was a brilliant Colonel, 1758–63. Even the austere Prince Ferdinand of Prussia liked the hard-drinking English lord. He was painted 12 times by Reynolds, and after a very few years of civil life died in debt.

*A weight . . . blessing*   This comment and further words which appear to read 'I befriend myself' are inserted additions, perhaps transcriptions of the old man's words.

*5 July 1802   Dove Nest*   John Benson (d. 1808, and described as 'of Dove Nest'), W's landlord, had been for some years owner of Dove Nest, near Lowwood, Windermere. This house was usually let, but probably he was there himself in 1802; the Ws would need to see him, perhaps about rent, perhaps about their proposed lengthy absence, perhaps about their friends, the Clarksons and Charles and Mary Lamb, staying for short periods in the house during the summer.

*7 July 1802   the trees*   Originally 'fruit trees'.

*Molly Ritson*   D was busy settling affairs before leaving Grasmere; on 24 June she had been grinding paint; the next day Miss Sympson coloured walls and D white-washed the ceiling. They were making the house fresh to welcome Mary. Molly Ritson's family appears to have been connected with house-painting. She was of Soulby, near Pooley Bridge, Ullswater, and had a son John, a bleacher at Eamont Bridge, whose wife Elizabeth is surely the Betty Ritson to whom D refers in a letter to Mrs Clarkson of June 1803; D asks Mrs Clarkson to 'get for us two pounds of green verditer the same as Betty Ritson got for us, also the proper quantity of Ivory Black for making the black' (*EY*, p. 393). Mrs Clarkson would know the Ritsons because they were Quakers, and the Clarksons, though never joining the Society of Friends, were involved with the Quaker movement, passionate in its opposition to the slave trade.

*in bed when they shine*   The words from 'Walked on . . .' are an added insertion. They echo (or possibly anticipate) W's

Now that the Children are in their Beds
The little Glow-worm nothing dreads

This is another of the 'images of the evening' of 15 June 1802 (see n.).

*8 July 1802   Farewell*. ——— D's handwriting becomes larger and looser as the moment to leave approaches and she continues to write. She still manages to insert the extra word 'white' to describe the sky-like brightness of the lake.

[*9 July 1802*]   *Nelly Mackareth*   The register records her baptism on 1 Mar. 1789: 'Ellin dau. of George Mackereth of Knotthouses Gras.' She went ahead on horseback with the luggage while the Ws walked.

[*11 July 1802*]   *the family greatness*   Hutton John, home of the Hudlestons, may have appeared a 'decaying Mansion' to D, partly because it was a 16th-c. building, and partly because the current owner, Andrew Hudleston (1734–1821), was a barrister in London and spent little time on his estate.

    *a stony bedded stream*   'little' is crossed out in front of 'stony', presumably in response to the replacement of 'There' (i.e. Dacre) with the expanded and precise phrase 'A little above Dacre'.

[*14 July 1802*]   *Bird's Nest*   Brougham Hall. The manor of Brougham, through the marriage of John Bird of Penrith to a Brougham in the 15th c., came wholly into the possession of a James Bird in 1676. He built Brougham Hall, known as Bird's Nest. The estate was bought back by a John Brougham in 1726 and came, via brothers and cousins, to Henry Brougham, the great Whig opponent of the Lonsdales (and of W) in the 1818 Westmorland elections. The Hall was demolished in 1934. (Not to be confused with the ruins of Brougham Castle.)

    *more snugly*   Replaces 'so snugly', presumably because of the nearby 'so close'; 'cold' crossed out before 'very rainy'; 'Lough' at first spelt 'Luff'; 'more bright than earthly trees', originally 'more soft . . .'.

[*15 July 1802*]   *Thirsk to Breakfast*   Gordon W noted: 'Thirsk, 13 m. from Leeming Lane. The inn was The Three Tuns, in the market-place, still the principal inn. The little stream of water on Sutton Bank is now given a spout and called Wordsworth's Well. The road climbs 600 feet in less than a mile, and the summit is 964 feet above the sea.' (*Journals* i. 170) *when we had climbed part of the hill*  D had begun less accurately, to say that they finished their sandwich 'at the T[op]. . .'.

*with wild flowers*  Rievaulx, the 12th-c. Cistercian Abbey, was by 1802 properly picturesque, the low parts of the ruins having turned into green hillocks covered with wild flowers; 'about the Ruins' at first 'among the Ruins'; 'upon the abbey' at first 'upon the Ruins'.

*Mr Duncombe's terrace*  Charles Slingsby Duncombe (d. 1803). His son in 1826 was created Baron Feversham of Duncombe Park. The house was originally designed by Vanbrugh in 1718, the park was the largest deer park in Yorkshire, the terrace was broad, grassy, ½ a mile long, curving, with great trees on one side and the view over Rievaulx on the other. There were (and are) temples at either end.

*a very nice Inn*  For many years now the Old Manor House, and no longer an inn. See D's further description, p. 127.

[*16 July 1802*]  *a double horse*  Normally, one horse, two persons taking it in turns to walk, and to ride ahead and rest; though see W's account of the first part of the journey to Grasmere, Dec. 1799, 'D. on a double horse behind that good creature George' (*EY*, p. 277).

*Church & Churchyard*  At Brompton where W and MH were to be married on 4 Oct. 1802.

[*26 July 1802*]  *two little villages*  'hamlets' deleted.

*Boats moving about*  Originally 'Boats sailing'.

[*28 July 1802*]  *The Farmer's Boy*  By Robert Bloomfield, 1800. The little girl was one among the 26,000 people who bought *The Farmer's Boy* within 3 years of publication; it is a straightforward account in couplets of the pathos and pleasure of a working life on a farm. D's story of the girl and *The Farmer's Boy* is remembered later and inserted at the end of the paragraph.

[*31 July 1802*]  *the 31st of July*  This date is inserted.

*St pauls . . . a multitude*  At first, 'St pauls, the River with a multitude . . .'.

*overhung*  At first 'capped'.

*nature's own grand Spectacles*  Two lines are heavily crossed out here: they appear to read 'made by herself & for herself thrown over that huge City'. Compare W's 'Sonnet Composed upon Westminster Bridge' where there is a similar comparison with natural splendour, and an image of the morning's beauty worn by the city (?thrown 'like a garment' over it?). We cannot certainly know which came first, sonnet or journal account; W's dating is imprecise by a month—Aug. or Sept., while D's account is thoroughly retrospective in tone (witness her muddle about most dates). Her writing-up (from remembered conversation? from notes? with the sonnet in mind?) was not immediate; quite possibly it had to wait until the week of 23 Oct. (see entry).

*30 years ago* D is fairly accurate. In 1769, 33 years before, the poet Gray came to the Lake District, and was perhaps the first outsider to the region to react fully and excitedly. His Journal was published posthumously with his *Collected Poems* in 1775, and with its suggestions of 'Elysium' and 'paradise' it made the 'Cumberland mountain wilds' attractive to travellers. Dr John Brown's Letter to Lord Lyttleton, describing the 'beauty, horror and immensity' of the vale of Keswick, had been published earlier in 1766, but it was Gray's popularity as a poet that made his Journal known, and its open-eyed adventurousness made the tourist impact.

*new ones . . . everywhere* At first 'new large ones . . . everywhere about it'; 'among so many upstarts' at first 'with so many upstarts about it'; 'we drank tea' at first 'we went off'.

*honorable Mr Knox* The honorable Mr Knox was probably the young Thomas Knox (1786–1858) who, on the death of his father in 1818, became 2nd Earl of Ranfurly.

[*1 Aug. 1802*]   *chez*   Replaces 'at the'.

[*Aug. 1802*] *opposite two Ladies*   There is a separate copy of this Calais section made probably for friends such as Mrs Clarkson. It has small variants: cuts out the dirt in the yard—though keeping the smells, refers to Annette and Caroline by initials, makes no mention of D's cold and W's bathing, but expands here: 'Two ladies lived in the house opposite to us, and we, in our idle moods, often amused ourselves with observing their still more idle way of spending their time—they seemed neither to have work nor books; but were mostly at the window.'

*Evening star . . . of the sky*   At first '. . . of the west'; see W's sonnet 'Fair Star of Evening Splendor of the West'.

*for ever melting away*    The last words before half the page is torn off; there had been further writing, for one or two inkmarks remain, and this had probably been a discarded version of what follows, for 'upon the sands' continues the sentence on the other side of the same half page.

*ever half so beautiful*    Three lines are crossed out here: 'nothing ever half so like a—it was not like as if it had been made by any human ha . . .'.

*overspread with lightning*    At first the sky was 'overspread with a fire'; the word 'distant' is inserted; 'roared & broke' was at first 'broke'; 'as they broke . . . towards us' is crossed out; 'they were interfused with' was at first 'they were all alive with'.

*calm hot nights*    The later copy of the Calais section confirms the reading 'nights', not 'night'.

*the little Boats row*    At first 'the little Boats sail'; 'with wings of fire' at first 'with two wings of fire [? along] the sea'; '& the sailboats' at first '& the little sailboats'.

*Caroline was delighted*    Omitted in the later copy. See W's sonnet 'It is a beauteous Evening, calm and free'.

[*29 Aug. 1802*]    *the 29th of August*    D in fact crossed out 'August' and substituted, incorrectly, 'September'.

[*30 Aug. 1802*]    *& tender thought*    See particularly W's sonnet 'Dear fellow Traveller! here we are once more'.

*an English Lake*    At first 'a Lake'; '30th August', at first '30th of July', then '30th Sept', finally 'August'—the date required was 31 Aug.

[*22 Sept. 1802*]    *22nd of September*    'The Wordsworths are at Montague's rooms, near neighbours to us. They dined with us yesterday, & I was their guide to Bartlemy Fair!' wrote Charles Lamb to C on 8 Sept. 1802. The Ws were 3 weeks in London, not only going to Bartholomew Fair (*The Prelude* VII) with Lamb, and dining several times with Charles and Mary Lamb (who had spent a day or two at DC during the Ws' own absence in France), but visiting Uncle William Cookson and his family at Windsor, and seeing, in D's words, 'all our Brothers, particularly John' (*EY*, p. 378); John reached London after his long voyage on 11 Sept. This was the last time the Ws were to see him; he did not go north after his next voyage in 1804.

[*24 Sept. 1802*]    *24th September*    D wrote the month twice, 'September

24th September'; 'the garden looked gay' was first '. . . fresh & gay'; the sentence 'I looked at everything . . . the time of our stay' (previously misread) has been crossed out. D's illness at Gallow Hill immediately after the two-day journey from London and her continuing 'poorly' during most of the week of their stay had had its origin in London. They had been 'detained', wrote D on Saturday 29 September to Jane Marshall, by 'unexpected events'—the arrivals of Christopher and John, and '(. . . the only unfortunate one) by my being exceedingly unwell, in a violent cold caught by riding from Windsor in a long-bodied coach with 12 passengers. This cold detained us in Town till last Wednesday. I am now perfectly well, except that I do not feel myself strong, and am very thin, but my kind Friends help me to take such good care of myself that I hope soon to become as strong as anybody.' (*EY*, p. 377)

That 'half dread' of the 'concentration of all tender feelings' (see xv) and some real physical weakness combined to keep D from Church on Monday morning, W's wedding day.

[*1 Oct. 1802*]  *Friday Evening 1st October*  MH's brothers arrive for the wedding, with the exception of Henry who was away at sea. There were no guests of the older generation. MH's bachelor uncle Henry 'had no high opinion of Young Men without some Profession, or Calling' (Memoir by MW, Nov. 1851, WL, quoted in *MW Letters*, xxv); he designated W 'a Vagabond' and did not reply to MH's letter telling him of her intention to marry. Cousins of her father acted similarly: the Scurfields, a bachelor brother and 'three Maiden Sisters' living in a 'dignified Mansion, within a high-walled Court in Pilgrim Street, Newcastle' had sent a Silver Coffee Pot to another Hutchinson marriage, but they neither came nor sent anything to MH and W. They did however give W the basis for 'many jocund sallies of wit' upon MW's '*blasted expectations*'; 'and we have done very well without a *Silver Coffee Pot* to this day. Whether it was in consequence of our friends' thinking us an improvident Pair, I do not know—but it is a fact that we did not receive a single *Wedding Present*' (ibid). If not strictly a wedding present, MW did receive a personal present from John W: he wrote to D on 22 Oct. 1802, 'I am glad & rejoyced to hear that my *Sister* Mary liked the choice of *my* New Gown may she live long wear it & I see it—' (*LJW*, p. 127).

[*2 Oct. 1802*]    *to Hackness*    A local beauty spot on the Yorkshire River Derwent, and seat of Sir Richard Johnstone.

[*4 Oct. 1802*]    *my Brother William was married to Mary Hutchinson* D makes this formal statement even within a private journal. Formal announcements were made in the *York Herald*, 9 Oct. and the *York Courant*, 11 Oct. 1802. The *Morning Post*, on the wedding morning, printed C's 'Verses to Sara', now called 'Dejection: an Ode, written April 4 1802'; the name 'Sara' was taken out and replaced by 'Edmund', a name for W since Alfoxden days, and some lines were omitted so that the emphasis on C's personal pain was reduced. Thus the prayer for Joy at the end of the poem was a prayer for W (and M). This was C's wedding gift. *MP* carried yet another reference to W's wedding the following week: it was revealed on 9 Oct. that W. Wordsworth Esq. after the marriage 'proceeded immediately, with his wife and his sister, for his charming cottage in the little Paradise-vale of Grasmere. His neighbour, Mr Coleridge, resides in the vale of Keswick' and there followed in some detail a description of the view from C's house. This 'most ridiculous paragraph' D thought later (*EY*, p. 615) was the editor Stuart's way of 'obliging his Friends'—though possibly Charles Lamb was the culprit.

*I gave him the wedding ring . . . blessed me fervently* D's formal tone has dissolved. These two sentences are heavily scored through. That D wore the ring the night before denotes her full acceptance of MH and the marriage, and that W slipped it for a moment back on to her finger was surely a pledge that the marriage would not exclude her. D could have taken care of the ring, even worn it, on the way back from France. The actual ring is in the W Museum, Grasmere; traditionally known as MW's ring, it was examined by the Goldsmiths' Company in 1975. It is 18 carat gold marked with an erased horse's head on the outside (in Continental fashion). In the early 1800s this was a Brussels mark—Belgium then was part of Napoleonic France. Most probably W bought the ring in Calais in Aug. 1802. The sentences crossed out have been heavily covered with ink, not in order to correct or emend, but to make the words impossible to read. In fact, under a bright light, they can be read with the naked eye; only the final word 'fervently' is not a secure reading. They reveal an intensity which had always been D's, and to which W responded (see Introduction, pp. xii–xv). The ink that has been used is iron-based, and thus D herself, either soon afterwards or in later life, could have been the one to cross out the sentences, realizing as she must have, that the drama of tenderness of that morning was perhaps played over-consciously and in any case was not for other eyes—not even perhaps for W's. The account was not of course written on the wedding day, but after the return to Grasmere, when D still had the wish to make a full record of the tensions of that day of change. W himself, it is interesting to recall, though, finally, in 1841, giving consent to his daughter Dora's marriage, at the last minute 'could not go to Church' (*LY* iv. 198).

*the two men*    John and Thomas Hutchinson; 'coming to tell us' at first 'that came to tell us'.

*till I met my beloved William & fell*    The word 'fell' is crossed out before 'met'.

*welcome my dear Mary*    Sara made the wedding breakfast, Joanna was bridesmaid, John and Tom Hutchinson were witnesses, and D passed through an intensity of feeling. Totally welcome to D as this marriage was it brought change and children, and life at DC was to move towards a different rhythm of creativity. 'Mary was much agitated' had begun 'Mary was greatly . . .'; 'parted from her Brothers', '& Sisters' added in an insertion.

*had only lived 4 years*    De Selincourt (*Journals* i. 177) quotes Gordon W's transcription from the tombstone at Kirby Moorside and his comment: ' "In memory of John and Susanna Cullon's children—Elizabeth died 1795, aged 18 months, Mary d. 1796 aged 2 years, James d. 1796 aged 4 years, David d. 1797 aged 1 year, John d. 1798 aged 5 months, Thomas d. 1804 aged 7 weeks, Mary d. 1810 aged 9 months". It will be seen that the Cullons were as unfortunate after D.W.'s visit to the churchyard as before it.—G.G.W.'

*lifting itself above the common buildings &*    Four words precede this: 'and preminent above the', the last three crossed out.

*the gay Duke of Buckingham*    George Villiers (1628–87), 2nd Duke of Buckingham, Dryden's 'Zimri', inherited Helmsley

Castle. All his estates were forfeited during the Civil War and Protectorate, not once but twice (the first time he was forgiven his royalist activities on account of youth). Helmsley was given to Lord Fairfax; Buckingham prudently married Fairfax's daughter in 1657 and retrieved the estate, but it had to be sold after his death to pay debts. It was bought in 1692 by a London goldsmith, Sir Charles Duncombe (see n. p. 245).

*its low, double gavel-ended front*    At first 'low gavel-ended roof'—D's accurate emendation confirms the identification of the inn (see n. p. 245); 'old trees, chiefly ashes' began by being 'old Ashes'; 'yet' is crossed out after 'inhabited'.

*Duncombe House*    This 'large' Building was at first 'huge'; 'up a long hill'—'steep' is crossed out; 'walked down this valley' at first 'walked through this valley'.

*a minster with its tower . . . with a dome*    This is a lengthy inserted addition; reminiscent of W's 'Minster with its Tower,' his 'Grecian Temple, Minaret and Bower' perceived in the clouds of the western sky; see the sonnet 'Ere we had reach'd the wish'd-for place, night fell'. This was composed, he told Miss Fenwick, 'after a journey over the Hambleton Hills on a day memorable to me—the day of my marriage.' Compare the July walk when there had been no clear view in either earth or sky, see p. 121.

*bottomless Tarn*    Lake Gormire, one of Yorkshire's few natural lakes; perhaps because of its singularity it has attracted legends. It is only 21 feet deep, and, as D notes, is in a hollow at the side of the hill. This is one of the glacial channels that cut across the Hambleton Hills.

*Mr John Bell's Birthday*    John Bell of Thirsk Hall was born 3 Oct. 1764 and married in Oct. 1800. D is right about the birthday celebration—held on Monday 4 Oct. rather than Sunday—but the family tree records no heir born in 1802. The eldest son, Ralph, born in 1804, died young; the second son, John, died without issue and the line continued through the daughter Frances.

*Leming Lane*    From Leeming Lane the Ws do not retrace their route of July, but go to Leyburn and then take a post chaise through Wensleydale: this was the beautiful way that W and D had walked in Dec. 1799 when they had gone from MH's home at Sockburn to make their own home at DC.

[*5 Oct. 1802*]    *with a beautiful church*    Bedale; its church having both 9th-c. Danish stone carving and a tower strengthened almost to fortification in the Middle Ages.

*the green slopes of Middleham*    At first 'the green hills of Middleham & Middleham Castle'. The castle with its massive Norman keep was made magnificent by Richard Neville (Warwick, the 'Kingmaker'); it had Edward IV as a guest. Richard III owned it, and lived there for a while; his only son died there, aged 10, in 1493. It then declined and has simply now, beneath its great walls, the green slopes and windings of the River Ure as D saw them.

*left to ourselves*    D is recalling the journey of 1799; George Hutchinson had come with them 8 miles beyond Richmond, almost to Leyburn (see n. p. 245), but then W and D had walked to Grasmere 'as a home in which we were to rest.' Grasmere fulfilled their need, and the feeling behind D's writing here must arise from the sense that the Grasmere home will now be modified and tested.

*concealed retreats*    The word 'before' crossed out after 'which'; the word 'added' crossed out in front of 'made'; the word 'here' inserted after 'Summer time'.

*village on the side of a hill*    West Witton.

*Poor Mary!*    Mary Queen of Scots. The sonnet, 'Hard was thy Durance Queen compared with ours', was written, W told Miss Fenwick later, 'to beguile the time . . . but it was not thought worthy of being preserved' and it has not survived. The Ws waited in front of Bolton Hall for the Post-Boy to bring the horse. The Scrope family had built this house and abandoned Bolton Castle in 1678. It was in the Castle that Mary Queen of Scots was imprisoned in the autumn of 1568.

*to see the waterfalls*    The Ure at Aysgarth comes down a series of limestone terraces. From the Elizabethan bridge they would all see the Upper Falls, while W walking later along the river bank would come to the tiers of cataracts at the Lower Falls. D's description has the winter walk of 1799 in mind, and perhaps even W's letter to C of that Dec.: the Falls, he wrote, were 'such a performance as you might have expected from some giant gardiner employed by one of Queen Elizabeth's Courtiers, if this same giant gardiner had consulted with Spenser and they two had finish'd the work together' (*EY*, p. 277). Where D puts 'less interesting than in winter', 'winter' is written over 'summer'; 'did not in winter remind' was at first 'does not remind'; 'as if there had been' is inserted before the Shakespearean 'agency. . . "Mortal Instruments" '.

[*6 Oct. 1802*]    *Hawes*    This time W and D did not turn aside on leaving Haws to show M the long drop of Hardraw Force that had so excited them in 1799. Now, they were riding, and had paid as far as Sedbergh. Indeed, in stages, they rode all the way back to Grasmere.

*our road to Grasmere*    i.e. in Dec. 1799 when they went to live at DC.

*dear Sara had lived*    When she had lived with the Patricks; see 27 Jan. 1802 n.

*at Pennington's*    At 8 Stricklandgate, Kendal. William Pennington, with his wife Agnes Wilson, was a bookseller and printer; he became closely involved with editions of Thomas West's *Guide to the Lakes*, 1778 onwards, especially after West's death in 1779. He was responsible for the influential frontispiece for the second edition, 1780, an engraving of Grasmere by John Feary. He became an Alderman of Kendal, and was a close friend of the painter Daniel Gardner.

*our pilgrimage together*    This time, D's first walking journey with W, Apr. 1794, when D and W walked from Kendal to William Calvert's house at Windy Brow, Keswick.

*Richard Bateman*    It was Robert (not Richard) Bateman (born *c.* 1678) for whom 'a gathering' was made at the church door and who set off, 'a poor Adventurer to London', and who ultimately, a rich merchant in Leghorn, sent back marble from Italy and money to rebuild his native chapel. W had told part of his story in 'Michael' in 1800. Bateman died suddenly on his way home and never saw his handsome church. The Sanctuary has still a patterned marble floor, but the paintings are gone.

*Windermere*    The lake, not the town, which came into existence largely as a result of the railway of 1847.

*Portugal Laurels*    A splendid specimen still flourishes beside the house near the 'newspaper room'.

*11 Oct. 1802*    *to hunt waterfalls*    From the last line of 'Louisa', written early 1802; a portrait of a girl whose response to nature's more wintry weather is energetic and delighted. The girl could be a composite of D and Joanna and MH.

*15 Oct. 1802  to L[or]d Wm Gordon's*  i.e. to Water End; see 15 Aug. 1800 n.

*23 Oct. 1802  the golden woods of Autumn*  D has had time to bring her Journal up to date, and she gives attention now to the present scene: after 'Autumn', the words 'tranquil & silent & stately' are crossed out; 'in their decaying' was first 'in their decay'.

*31 Oct. 1802  John Monkhouse*  John Monkhouse (1782–1866), Mary Hutchinson's cousin on her mother's side. After the death of his wife Bell Addison (see 28 April 1802 n.) he farmed at Stowe in Radnorshire, 12 miles from Mary's brother Tom at Hindwell. He did not remarry. 'Fortunately,' said D, 'he is very fond of reading.' (*MY* ii. 162.) The Ws often visited.

*distant Birch trees*  'distant' is inserted.

*1 Nov. 1802  Mr Simpson's'*  after 'Mr Simpson's' the words 'Mr B S came in at tea-time' are crossed out; 'Mr B Simpson' is written and crossed out a second time.

*Wrangham*  Francis Wrangham (1769–1842), at this stage rector of Hunmanby in East Yorkshire, later archdeacon of Cleveland. In the summer of 1795 he was known to both W and C before they met each other. W could just have known Wrangham at Cambridge, but Wrangham was a year older and a brilliant third wrangler. W probably met him in London in 1794 through Basil Montagu, and together they began to translate Juvenal's eighth satire.

*7 Nov. 1802  Ariosto*  Only ten stanzas from Canto I of *Orlando Furioso* survive (*PW* iv. 367–9). W continued for some years after this to make short verse translations from Metastasio, Michaelangelo, and Tasso. He learned Italian at Cambridge—though his relatives thought he should have concentrated on the regular mathematical and classical course. His teacher, by private arrangement, was the well-loved old Italian scholar Agostino Isola, who had been reappointed as official Italian master in 1768 through the good offices of the poet Thomas Gray.

After a gap of 6 weeks, on the eve of her 31st birthday, D briefly took up her Journal again.

*24 Dec. 1802    Charlotte Smith's sonnets*    Charlotte Smith (1749–1806), born Charlotte Turner; persuaded into a loveless marriage at 16, she had to turn to her pen for the support of her 12 children (8 surviving) and her husband Benjamin. She published *Elegiac Sonnets* (1784) at her own expense. W, then an undergraduate, subscribed to the 5th edition in 1789. On his way to France in Dec. 1791 he called on Charlotte Smith in Brighton and she gave him letters of introduction to Helen Maria Williams (who was not in Paris when W arrived). W admired both poets, and in 1830 he particularly wanted Alexander Dyce, compiling a Selection, to include Charlotte Smith's 'I love thee, mournful, sober-suited night'; this is no. xxxix of the *Elegiac Sonnets* whose leaves W was turning over beside D.

*with Wedgwood*    Thomas Wedgwood (1771–1805), son of the great potter Josiah, at whose death in 1795, Thomas, along with his brothers and sisters, inherited considerable wealth. With this, in 1798, he established the Bristol Pneumatic Institute under Dr Beddoes; he provided an annuity for John Leslie; another (with his brother Josiah) of £150 for C so that the poet need not become a Unitarian minister; in 1803 and 1804, when the threat of invasion was strong, he equipped the Loyal Wedgwood Volunteers at Patterdale under the command of Captain Luff. His own researches, with encouragement from Humphry Davy, have led to his being known as the first photographer. But in 1802 he was in search of health; one plan was that C might accompany him to France and Italy, or even Tenerife. C attempted to allay Mrs C's anxieties about this Christmas visit to Greta Hall by suggesting that Wedgwood stay as 'Mr Jackson's visitor' in the rooms still known as Peach's (*CL* ii. 898 and 20 Nov. 1800 n.). The extra difficulty was the new baby whom D mentions in this entry. This was Sara C who lived to edit her father's work; she died in 1852. Wedgwood stayed only a few days and on 30 Dec. visited Luff in Patterdale.

*11 Jan. 1803    before me*    i.e. with D behind him on the horse.

*poem to C    The Prelude.*

*from Taylor on Wm's marriage*    Most probably John Taylor (1757–1832), like his father and grandfather, an oculist, and with his brother, from 1789, oculist to George III, and later to George IV. He was dramatic critic and for a time editor of the *MP* and later editor and co-owner of *The Sun*. He must have heard of W from Daniel Stuart, but was gratified to discover that 'a poet of such original merit, and residing at so distant a place' had heard of him (*Records of My Life* (1832) ii. 287). W sent him *LB* in early 1801 with a letter desiring to know what impression the poems 'had made upon a man living in the bustle of active life'. Mr Taylor clearly wrote back testifying to the 'impressive simplicity and original genius' of the work. His sister Anne Taylor also wrote enthusiastically and asked for biographical details. W summarized the facts of school, his parents' early death, and university, and said 'my life has been unusually barren of events, and my opinions have grown slowly and, I may say, insensibly' (*EY*, p. 327). John Taylor remarked that there was 'a little farther correspondence between us' (*Records* ii. 288). This may have included a letter 'on Wms marriage.'

*Canaries*   C had been hoping that Tom Wedgwood would fix upon a period abroad for his own—and C's—health, but Wedgwood finally decided on Crescelly in Wales. After Crescelly Wedgwood did go abroad, but C remained in England until April 1804 when he sailed for Malta, *en route* for Sicily, a surprise guest for John Stoddart and his wife in Valletta. In the event, C remained in Malta and obtained the temporary post of Public Secretary under the Governor, Sir Alexander Ball.

*Italian poems for Stuart*   MW was probably copying both Italian originals and W's translations. There was one Italian sonnet by Milton, translated as 'A plain youth, Lady! and a simple lover' (*PW* iii. 577 and *MP*, 5 Oct. 1803), and 6 poems from Metastasio (5 in *PW* iii. 369–70): 'Laura, farewell my Laura!' (*MP*, 17 Oct. 1803), 'To the grove, the meadow, the well' (*MP*, 22 Oct. 1803), 'The Swallow that hath lost' (*MP*, 2 Nov. 1803), 'Gentle Zephyr' (*MP*, 15 Nov. 1803) and 'Oh! bless'd all bliss above' (*MP*, 12 Dec. 1803); and a 6th short poem, 'I will be that fond Mother' that was not published in the newspaper. The Metastasio poems were out of W's old Cambridge copy of *Pieces Selected from the Italian Poets* by Agostino Isola, 1784. Stuart printed the Italian as well as the English; W did not sign the verses. He had recently sent Stuart several political sonnets, (see 18 Dec. 1801 n., 27 Jan. 1802 n.) and here was more poetry; but unlike 'Is it a reed that's shaken by the wind' and 'I griev'd for Buonaparte' (*MP*, 13 and 29 Jan.

1803), this was not political, and had to wait until late autumn before Stuart found a place for the verses.

   *a nice Calais Book*    D's resolve to continue her Journal and to use a notebook for it that they had bought in Calais seems not to have been kept. (No other section of the Journal had been accorded a new notebook!) The Journal comes to an end with all but one letter of the word 'Monday' written and a small drawing of a chair standing above the quotations from Descartes that come from the other end of the book!

*16 Jan. 1803    They were so grateful*    The words 'for the Sixpence' are crossed out here.

# SELECT BIBLIOGRAPHY

Includes all works listed under *Abbreviations* and the following:

BARTON, Anne, 'The Road from Penshurst: Wordsworth, Ben Jonson and Coleridge in 1802', *EIC* 37 (1987), 209–33.

BEATY, Frederick L. (ed.), *The Lloyd–Manning Letters* (Bloomington, 1957).

BICKNELL, Peter, and WOOF, Robert, *The Discovery of the Lake District 1750–1810* (Grasmere, 1982).

BOUMPHREY, R. S., HUDLESTON, C. Roy, and HUGHES, J., *An Armorial for Westmorland and Lonsdale*, Lake District Museum Trust and Cumberland and Westmoreland Antiquarian and Archaeological Society, ES xxi (1975).

BURKE, John, *Peerage and Baronetage: A Dictionary of the British Empire*, 5th edn. (London, 1838).

CLARKE, James, *Survey of the Lakes*, 2nd edn. (London, 1789).

CURTIS, Jared R., *Wordsworth's Experiments with Tradition: The Lyric Poems of 1802* (Ithaca, NY, and London, 1971).

CURWEN, John F., *Kirbie–Kendall* (Kendal, 1900).

GITTINGS, Robert, and MANTON, Jo, *Dorothy Wordsworth* (Oxford, 1985).

HOWE, H. W., *Greta Hall: Home of Coleridge and Southey*, rev. by Robert Woof (Norfolk, 1977).

HUDLESTON, C. Roy, BOUMPHREY, R. S., and HUGHES, J., *Cumberland Families and Heraldry*, Cumberland and Westmoreland Antiquarian and Archaeological Society, ES xxiii (1978).

HUTCHINSON, Sara, *Letters*, ed. Kathleen Coburn (London, 1954).

HUTCHINSON, William, *The History of the County of Cumberland*, 2 vols. (Carlisle, 1794).

MACALPINE, Rachel (ed.), *Grasmere: A Short History, compiled by members of the Women's Institute*, (Kendal, 1979).

McCRACKEN, David, *Wordsworth and the Lake District: A Guide to the Poems and their Places* (Oxford, 1984).

MOORMAN, Mary, *William Wordsworth: A Biography; The Early Years: 1770–1803* (Oxford, 1957)

260 BIBLIOGRAPHY

—— *William Wordsworth: A Biography*; *The Later Years: 1803–1850* (Oxford, 1965).

NICOLSON, Joseph, and BURN, Richard, *The History and Antiquities of the Counties of Westmorland and Cumberland*, 2 vols. (London, 1777).

REED, Mark, *Wordsworth: The Chronology of the Early Years 1770–1799* (Cambridge, Mass., 1967);

—— *Wordsworth: The Chronology of the Middle Years 1800–1815* (Cambridge, Mass., 1975).

SELINCOURT, Ernest de, *Dorothy Wordsworth: A Biography* (Oxford, 1933).

THOMPSON, T. W., *Wordsworth's Hawkshead*, ed. Robert Woof (Oxford, 1970).

WOOF, Pamela, *Dorothy Wordsworth, Writer* (Grasmere, 1988).

—— 'Dorothy Wordsworth's Grasmere Journals: Readings in a Familiar Text', *The Wordsworth Circle*, 20/1 (1989), 37–42.

—— 'Dorothy Wordsworth and Mary Lamb, Writers',*The Charles Lamb Bulletin*, n.s. 66 and 67 (1989), 41–53 and 82–93.

WOOF, Robert, 'Wordsworth's Poetry and Stuart's Newspapers: 1797–1803', *Studies in Bibliography* 15 (1962), 149–89.

—— 'John Stoddart, 'Michael' and *Lyrical Ballads*', *Ariel*, 1/2 (1970), 7–22.

WORDSWORTH, Dorothy, *Journals*, ed. William Knight, 2 vols. (London & New York, 1897).

—— *Journals*, ed. Helen Darbishire (Oxford, 1958).

—— *A Narrative Concerning George and Sarah Green*, ed. E. de Selincourt (Oxford, 1936).

WORDSWORTH, Mary, *The Letters 1800–1855*, ed. Mary E. Burton (Oxford, 1958).

WORDSWORTH, William, *The Prelude, 1799, 1805, 1850*, eds. Jonathan Wordsworth, M.H. Abrams and Stephen Gill (New York, 1979).

# INDEX

For works and authors read by D, MH, and W see 'Reading' in entries for Dorothy Wordsworth, Mary Hutchinson, and William Wordsworth. Figures in italics refer to Notes.

OXFORD

# MORE OXFORD PAPERBACKS

This book is just one of nearly 1000 Oxford Paperbacks currently in print. If you would like details of other Oxford Paperbacks, including titles in the World's Classics, Oxford Reference, Oxford Books, OPUS, Past Masters, Oxford Authors, and Oxford Shakespeare series, please write to:

**UK and Europe:** Oxford Paperbacks Publicity Manager, Arts and Reference Publicity Department, Oxford University Press, Walton Street, Oxford OX2 6DP.

Customers in UK and Europe will find Oxford Paperbacks available in all good bookshops. But in case of difficulty please send orders to the Cash-with-Order Department, Oxford University Press Distribution Services, Saxon Way West, Corby, Northants NN18 9ES. Tel: 0536 741519; Fax: 0536 746337. Please send a cheque for the total cost of the books, plus £1.75 postage and packing for orders under £20; £2.75 for orders over £20. Customers outside the UK should add 10% of the cost of the books for postage and packing.

**USA:** Oxford Paperbacks Marketing Manager, Oxford University Press, Inc., 200 Madison Avenue, New York, N.Y. 10016.

**Canada:** Trade Department, Oxford University Press, 70 Wynford Drive, Don Mills, Ontario M3C 1J9.

**Australia:** Trade Marketing Manager, Oxford University Press, G.P.O. Box 2784Y, Melbourne 3001, Victoria.

**South Africa:** Oxford University Press, P.O. Box 1141, Cape Town 8000.

# POETRY FROM OXFORD PAPERBACKS

Oxford's outstanding range of English poetry offers, in a single volume of convenient size, the complete poetical works of some of the most important figures in English Literature.

## WORDSWORTH

### Poetical Works

This edition of Wordsworth's poetry contains every piece of verse known to have been published by the poet himself, or of which he authorized the posthumous publication. The text, which Thomas Hutchinson based largely upon the 1849–50 standard edition, the last issued during the poet's lifetime, was revised for the Oxford Standard Authors series by Ernest de Selincourt.

The volume preserves the poet's famous subjective arrangement of the Minor Poems under such headings as 'Poems Referring to the Period of Childhood', 'Poems Dedicated to National Independence and Liberty', and 'Sonnets Upon the Punishment of Death'. *The Prelude* is given in the text of 1850, published shortly after Wordsworth's death, and *The Excursion* as it appears in the 1849–50 edition. Two poems of 1793 are included, 'An Evening Walk' and 'Descriptive Sketches', and a group of other pieces not appearing in the standard edition. The text reproduces Wordsworth's characteristic use of capital letters and in most cases his punctuation, though spelling has been regularized. The poet's own Notes to the 1849–50 edition, as well as to some earlier editions, are reprinted, along with his Prefaces.

The edition also contains a chronological table of Wordsworth's life, explanatory notes on the text, and chronological data for the individual poems.

Also in Oxford Paperbacks:

*The Prelude*   William Wordsworth
*Poetical Works*   John Keats
*The Golden Treasury*   Francis Turner Palgrave

## OXFORD POETS

Oxford has one of the finest lists of contemporary poetry. It includes work by important women writers from Britain, Europe, and the Commonwealth, including Anne Stevenson, Penelope Shuttle, Carole Satyamurti, and Gwen Harwood.

### FLEUR ADCOCK
#### *Time Zones*

In this lively new collection, Fleur Adcock's subjects range from domestic matters—recalling the birth of her son some years back; remembering her father, the news of whose death in New Zealand reaches her, the expatriate, in England; working in her own London garden—to matters of contemporary concern, such as the Romanian bid for freedom in 1989, and support for Green causes, including the anti-nuclear stand.

'She is an eminently readable poet, whose quiet accuracy sometimes makes me laugh out loud.' Wendy Cope, *Guardian*

Also available:

*Selected Poems*   Fleur Adcock
*Orient Express*   Grete Tartler
*Letters from Darkness*   Daniela Crasnaru
*Broken Moon*
*Changing the Subject*   Carole Satyamurti

## OXFORD BOOKS

Beginning in 1900 with the famous *Oxford Book of English Verse*, the Oxford Books series now boasts over sixty superb anthologies of poetry, prose, and songs.

'These anthologies—along with digests and reference books—are exactly what the general reader needs.'
Auberon Waugh, *Independent*

## THE NEW OXFORD BOOK OF
## IRISH VERSE

### *Edited, with Translations, by Thomas Kinsella*

Verse in Irish, especially from the early and medieval periods, has long been felt to be the preserve of linguists and specialists, while Anglo-Irish poetry is usually seen as an adjunct to the English tradition. This original anthology approaches the Irish poetic tradition as a unity and presents a relationship between two major bodies of poetry that reflects a shared and painful history.

'the first coherent attempt to present the entire range of Irish poetry in both languages to an English-speaking readership'
*Irish Times*

'a very satisfying and moving introduction to Irish poetry'
*Listener*

Also in Oxford Paperbacks:

*The Oxford Book of Travel Verse*
edited by Kevin Crossley-Holland
*The Oxford Book of Contemporary Verse*
edited by D. J. Enright
*The Oxford Book of Late Medieval Verse and Prose*
edited by Douglas Gray

# PAST MASTERS

### General Editor: Keith Thomas

*Past Masters* is a series of concise and authoritative introductions to the life and works of men and women whose ideas still influence the way we think today.

'Put end to end, this series will constitute a noble encyclopaedia of the history of ideas.' Mary Warnock

## SHAKESPEARE

### Germaine Greer

'At the core of a coherent social structure as he viewed it lay marriage, which for Shakespeare is no mere comic convention but a crucial and complex ideal. He rejected the stereotype of the passive, sexless, unresponsive female and its inevitable concommitant, the misogynist conviction that all women were whores at heart. Instead he created a series of female characters who were both passionate and pure, who gave their hearts spontaneously into the keeping of the men they loved and remained true to the bargain in the face of tremendous odds.'

Germaine Greer's short book on Shakespeare brings a completely new eye to a subject about whom more has been written than on any other English figure. She is especially concerned with discovering why Shakespeare 'was and is a popular artist', who remains a central figure in English cultural life four centuries after his death.

'eminently trenchant and sensible . . . a genuine exploration in its own right' John Bayley, *Listener*

'the clearest and simplest explanation of Shakespeare's thought I have yet read' Auberon Waugh, *Daily Mail*

Also available in Past Masters:

*Paine*   Mark Philp
*Dante*   George Holmes
*The Buddha*   Michael Carrithers
*Confucius*   Raymond Dawson

# CLASSIC ENGLISH SHORT STORIES

The four volumes of *Classic English Short Stories* have been compiled to reflect the excellence and variety of short fiction written in English during the twentieth century. Each volume covers a different period and represents the most distinguished writers of their day.

## THE DRAGON'S HEAD

This collection contains stories written in the years between the turn of the century and the outbreak of the Second World War—'a restless and impatient age'. The authors include John Galsworthy, 'Saki', Naomi Mitchison, H. G. Wells, Dorothy L. Sayers, and Somerset Maugham.

## THE KILLING BOTTLE

This collection brings together 12 very different authors whose short stories, written in the 1940s and 1950s, helped establish or extend their reputations as writers of stories, novels, or poetry. The 12 include Evelyn Waugh, Elizabeth Bowen, Graham Greene, V. S. Pritchett, Dylan Thomas, and Frank O'Connor.

## CHARMED LIVES

This collection contains stories written in the 1950s and 1960s, many of which demonstrate the impressive and accomplished skills of Commonwealth writers who began to achieve world-wide reputations during that period, including Ruth Prawer Jhabvala, Nadine Gordimer, H. E. Bates, Bill Naughton, L. P. Hartley, and Peter Ustinov.

## THE GREEN MAN REVISITED

This collection includes works written in the 1960s and 1970s by authors living all around the world, including Chinua Achebe, Kingsley Amis, Susan Hill, Olivia Manning, V. S. Naipaul, William Trevor, John Updike, and Patrick White.

# THE WORLD'S CLASSICS

'An excellent series all of which can be recommended.'
*Sunday Times*

Oxford Paperbacks offers the best new translations of the classic works of world literature, from the epic poetry and political and literary theory of the ancient world to the drama and fiction of the nineteenth and twentieth centuries.

## THE KALEVALA

*Translated and Edited by Keith Bosley*
*Foreword by Albert B. Lord*

> Words shall not be hid
> nor spells buried;
> might shall not sink underground
> though the mighty go.

*The Kalevala* is the great Finnish epic which, like the *Iliad* and *Odyssey*, grew out of a rich oral tradition with prehistoric roots. During the first millenium of our era, speakers of Uralic languages (outside the Indo-European group) who had settled in the Baltic region developed an oral poetry that was to last into the nineteenth century. This poetry provided the basis of the *Kalevala*, assembled by a Finnish scholar Elias Lönnrot and published in its final form in 1849. It played a central role in the process towards Finnish independence and inspired some of the greatest music of Sibelius.

The poet Keith Bosley is the prize-winning translator of the anthology *Finnish Folk Poetry: Epic*. This translation of the *Kalevala* is the first truly to combine liveliness with accuracy in a way that reflects the richness of the original.

Also available in the World's Classics:

*The Iliad*   Homer
*The Koran*
*The Chronicle of the Abbey of Bury St Edmunds*
Jocelin of Brakelond
*The Paston Letters*

## ILLUSTRATED HISTORIES IN
## OXFORD PAPERBACKS

Lavishly illustrated with over 200 full colour and black and white photographs, and written by leading academics, Oxford Paperbacks' illuminating histories provide superb introductions to a wide range of political, cultural, and social topics.

## THE OXFORD ILLUSTRATED HISTORY
## OF ENGLISH LITERATURE

### *Edited by Pat Rogers*

Britain possesses a literary heritage which is almost unrivalled in the Western world. In this volume, the richness, diversity, and continuity of that tradition are explored by a group of Britain's foremost literary scholars.

Chapter by chapter the authors trace the history of English literature, from its first stirrings in Anglo-Saxon poetry to the present day. At its heart towers the figure of Shakespeare, who is accorded a special chapter to himself. Other major figures such as Chaucer, Milton, Donne, Wordsworth, Dickens, Eliot, and Auden are treated in depth, and the story is brought up to date with discussion of living authors such as Seamus Heaney and Edward Bond.

'[a] lovely volume . . . put in your thumb and pull out plums' Michael Foot

'scholarly and enthusiastic people have written inspiring essays that induce an eagerness in their readers to return to the writers they admire' *Economist*

Other illustrated histories in Oxford Paperbacks:

The Oxford Illustrated History of Britain
The Oxford Illustrated History of Medieval Europe